Baronets and Buffalo

Baronets and Buffalo

**The British Sportsman
In the American West,
1833-1881**

John I. Merritt

Maps by the author

MOUNTAIN PRESS PUBLISHING COMPANY
MISSOULA, MONTANA
1985

Copyright © 1985
Mountain Press Publishing Co.

Library of Congress Cataloging-in-Publication Data

Merritt, John I.
  Baronets and buffalo.

  Bibliography: p.
  Includes index.
  1. Hunting—West (U.S.)—History. 2. Fishing—
West (U.S.)—History. 3. Hunters—Great Britain—
Biography. 4. British—West (U.S.)—History.
I. Title. II. Title: The British sportsman in the
American West, 1833-1881.
SK45.M47   1985   799'.0978   85-13677
ISBN 0-87842-189-0
ISBN 0-87842-190-4 (pbk.)

To Nancy,
who introduced me to the West

Although liable to an accusation of barbarism, I must confess that the very happiest moments of my life have been spent in the wilderness of the Far West.

—George Frederick Ruxton

Preface

Baronets and Buffalo is a narrative history of the American West as seen through the eyes and exploits of British sportsmen who ventured beyond the Missouri between 1833 and 1881. These gentlemen adventurers were drawn to this extraordinary country by what they had read and heard about it: the limitless herds of buffalo and other game, the chance to wander for months or years through one of the great wildernesses on earth, and—not least—the danger of Indians, which provided, as one of them put it, "that dash of excitement which is always needed to make any life really perfect."

As Europeans whose own true wilderness had disappeared a millennium before, they were in a special position to appreciate this vast and still relatively unexploited territory. The earliest sportsmen to penetrate the West followed the paths of fur trappers who had opened the country in the 1820s. The American wilderness had cast its spell—at least vicariously—on Europeans long before then, however. The Romantic poets in particular had found in it a kind of lost Eden where, safe from the degrading influences of civilization, man might still perfect himself. Lord Byron, drawing on a ghost-written autobiography of Daniel Boone, made the great trail blazer an international celebrity by invoking him in his narrative poem *Don Juan*. And Samuel Taylor Coleridge borrowed heavily from William Bartram's *Travels*—a natural history of the Carolinas and Florida in the 1770s—for the imagery in "Kubla Khan" and "The Rime of the Ancient Mariner." Similar echoes from Bartram resounded in the works of other romantic writers like Wordsworth, Southey, and Chateaubriand.

American attitudes toward wilderness were beginning to

change by the time James Fenimore Cooper appeared on the literary scene with his sagas of the noble Hawkeye and Chingachgook. American literary tastes followed European models, and by the 1823 publication of *The Pioneers*, the first in Cooper's Leatherstocking Tales, Americans had begun to embrace the romantic conventions already well established abroad.

Cooper's influence was especially strong on the imaginations of young men, whether cultivated easterners or Europeans, instilling in them a passionate desire to experience the wilderness at first hand. The Philadelphian John Kirk Townsend, traveling on the plains in 1834, came to idolize the caravan's chief hunter as "an exact counterpart of *Hawk-eye* in his younger days," while the Englishman George Frederick Ruxton, who in 1846 would travel the length of Mexico and up the Rio Grande into the Colorado Rockies, professed that Cooper's "admirable romances" had early inspired him to a life of adventure. Strongly implicit in this romantic view was an awareness of time passing. Ruxton and many of the other British sportsmen who hunted and traveled in the West were acutely conscious that this wilderness could not long endure and that they bore, therefore, a responsibility for recording it for posterity.

There is no way of knowing how many British sportsmen set out across the plains from Independence, Omaha, and other jumping-off points in the nineteenth century, but their number was surely in the hundreds. Of these, little more than a dozen left book-length accounts. As chroniclers of the hunt they were part of a venerable line that harkened back to Edward, Duke of York, whose *Master of Game* in 1405 was the first sporting book to appear in English. The sporting tradition codified by Edward nearly a half millenium before had, by the fourth decade of the nineteenth century, taken on a global dimension. The spread of empire and new wealth created by the Industrial Revolution spawned a new type of hunter who could look beyond the hedgerows and fox runs of his native countryside to the awesome vistas of Africa, India, and the American West. English gunsmiths like Manton and Purdy, meanwhile, met the needs of this new breed with weapons of superb craftsmanship and matchless accuracy.

By the 1850s the British sportsman had fixed his stereotype firmly in the folklore of the frontier: blue-eyed and ruddy faced, dining on tinned meats and sipping five o'clock tea poured by a liveried servant, under a ruffling linen tent pitched on the plains. A few indeed lived up to the image of sumptuous wealth: Sir St. George Gore, an Irish baronet led by Jim Bridger, slept in a brass bed and included in his caravan packs of pure-bred hounds, dog-tenders, secretaries, stewards, and a professional "fly-dresser" for tying trout lures. Gore's three-year safari through Colorado, Wyoming, and Montana left thousands of slaughtered animals in its wake and so outraged American officials as to threaten an international incident.

Doubtless there were others like Gore who, in kind if not degree, exemplified the more extravagant character of Victorian society. A very few exhibited an imperious disdain for the country and its people. But the best of them were full of good humor and a high sense of adventure, rejoicing in the wild free life and drinking from a common jug with their guides. A marvelous sense of excitement infuses the writing of men like Ruxton and Charles A. Messiter, making their accounts of frontier life among the most vivid in the chronicles of the West.

*　　*　　*

In researching and writing this book I owe much to many people. They include my in-laws, Ned and Betty Russell of St. Louis, who with my wife, Nancy, introduced me to the West. For inspiration, by either example or direct encouragement, I am indebted to such writer friends as Landon Jones, John McPhee, George Reiger, Ann Waldron, William Howarth, and Dan White. My thanks, too, to Dave Flaccus, who saw potential in this idea when other publishers did not. Finally, I would like to thank the Rare Books staff of Princeton's Firestone Library for their always cheerful assistance.

List of Illustrations

List of Maps

Table of Contents

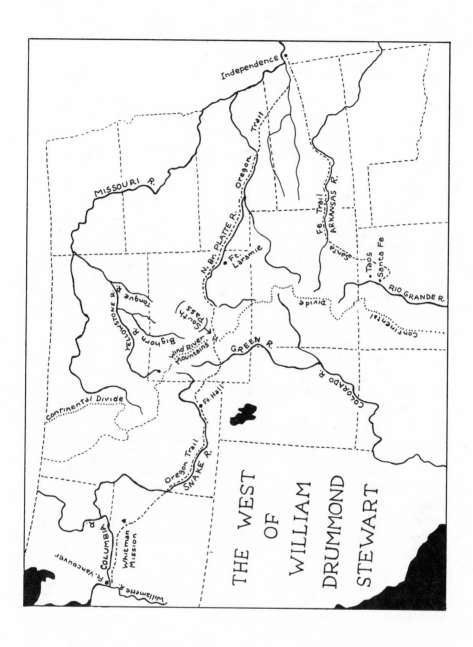

THE WEST OF WILLIAM DRUMMOND STEWART

1

Wellington's Soldier

What was his name? All the boys called him Cap'en, and he got his fixings from old Choteau; but what he wanted out thar in the mountains, I never just rightly know'd.

—George Frederick Ruxton,
Life in the Far West

A WIND RUNS across the prairie grass, and buffalo graze beneath the shining mountains as far as the eye can see. In the eyes of Captain William Drummond Stewart, second son of a Scottish baronet and a veteran of Waterloo, it is the wildest place on earth, in a time beyond time, where a thousand years of history can drift from memory as easily as a buffalo corpse down an alkali river. In the company of wild Indians and half-wild mountain men he has ceased to think of his hated elder brother and the stone heap of Murthly Castle. At night, when sleep closes in as he lies beneath the prairie sky, his mind plays on a vision of freedom: the sprint of an antelope, the rolling gait of a grizzly feeding on rosebuds, the cry of a falcon whistling down the wind.

"Sleep in those days," he would write, "was too sound to dream, and the startling cry of the gray dawn came upon men who leaped from the earth as if into a new life."

It is late June in the year 1833. Stewart's party of forty men and 120 mules are in sight of the Wind River Mountains, their summits still gleaming in winter snow. In another week they will cross South Pass, a low saddle in the Continental Divide, and descend into the valley of the Green River for the annual trappers' rendezvous. They have been living fat off the land since coming into buffalo country a month before. The small scattered herds they had seen grazing beneath the cedar-covered Laramie Hills, beyond the forks of the Platte, have swelled by now into a vast brown sea of bison.

The exhilaration of the bison run is like nothing else Stewart has experienced in his thirty-seven years. Not even the melee of battle can compare to it in the intensity of life lived to the brink.

On a typical morning's hunt he finds that he can approach downwind of a herd to within a hundred yards before it stirs into motion, beginning a deceptively slow canter across the rolling plain. He is riding a mule, a practical if unglamorous substitute for his fine roan, left behind in camp, which he regards as too valuable for such pursuits. Marveling at the great beasts in flight, he keeps pace with them for several minutes before spurring his mount and closing with the herd. To escape the suffocating dust he attempts to cut upwind through a narrow rank of bison. But the column closes up, wedging him deeper into the hurtling mass—no time to worry about prairie dog holes or other obstacles now. Head craning and ears back, the mule charges on while the rider whips its gasping flanks, hollering like a madman, his voice lost in the pounding din.

With mule and hunter locked in its midst, the herd stampedes up rises and down draws. It plunges through a shallow pond and climbs a steep incline, slowing momentarily as the hunter, his eyes on the rump of a fat cow, closes within a few yards of the frantic beast. Rising in his stirrups, he jams the Manton rifle to his shoulder and sends a ball cracking behind the ribs, a perfect kidney shot. The cow falters as the hunter flies past in pursuit of another kill, oblivious to the wounded animal's bellowing above the thundering herd.

At last he reins in his exhausted mount and looks back at the ground they have covered. His woolen shirt is soaked with sweat and silence rings in his ears. The mule snorts and wheezes for breath, its lathered sides working like bellows. The prairie is littered with dead and dying buffalo, and already the other hunters are beginning the job of butchering—peeling back the shaggy coat and slicing the favored hump ribs from the enormous backs. They take only the best parts and leave most of the carcasses for the wolves and vultures, returning to camp with pack mules heavy with meat and with the dripping tongues of their prey hanging from their saddles like trophies.

So it goes for Captain Stewart and his companions, on the high plains beneath the Mountains of the Winds, in "the evening of the roving life of the Far West." While understanding him is beyond the ken of their experience, the mountain men whom Stewart accompanies respect this strange, Byronic foreigner with his romantic notions about their wild and often desperate life. He pays his way like a gentleman traveler but stands watch at night like the lowest contract man, and he boasts the best shooting eye among them. More than respect, they like him—in part because this half-pay British officer obviously likes and admires them, members of "that glorious race, the Free Trappers," and envies the extraordinary freedom they enjoy.

*   *   *

It was constraints on freedom in his own life that brought Stewart west in the first place. That, and a restlessness typical of the second sons of gentry in a society whose laws of inheritance were grounded on the rock of primogeniture.

Stewart was born on the day after Christmas, 1795, at the family estate of Murthly, on a hill above the River Tay in Scotland's Macbeth country. As a boy he cavorted on a pair of ancient oaks on the Murthly estate, all that remained of Birnham Wood, where the Thane of Cawdor came to his grandeloquent end at the hands of Macduff. His father was Sir George Stewart, Seventeenth Lord of Grandtully and Fifth Baronet of Murthly, but these noble titles and the vast landholdings they entailed were destined not for William but for his elder brother, George's firstborn, John.

Like many in his circumstance, William was groomed for the military, a profession that would channel his energies into honorable activity while keeping him away from the family estate, which he might otherwise covet too much. His father purchased him a commission at age seventeen in the Sixth

Dragoon Guards. By age nineteen he was a seasoned veteran, having fought under Wellington through the bitter Peninsula Campaign in Spain. A year later, as lieutenant of cavalry, he would be decorated for bravery at Waterloo, leading charge after bloody charge against ranks of imperial lancers in the final battle of the Napoleonic Wars. Twenty years later he would display a similar bravery in skirmishes with Blackfeet, while around the campfire his accounts of campaigning with the Iron Duke would hold their own with the most adventuresome of trapper tales.

Napoleon's defeat and subsequent exile on St. Helena left the young professonal soldier chafing. Peace was an anticlimax, but he continued in the army for five dull years of barracks life at Dundalk, on the east coast of Ireland. Promoted to captain in 1820, he retired the following year on half pay and for the next decade led the aimless life of a gentleman sportsman, hunting in Russia, Turkey, and other parts of the continent. He occasionally visited Murthly, despite a growing estrangement with his elder brother, who inherited all titles and properties on their father's death in 1827. William was left with three thousand pounds, an adequate if far from extravagant sum for those times. To his great bitterness, the inheritance was not granted outright but placed in a trusteeship managed by his brother.

The family regarded John as the steady one, while the restless and probably dissolute William was not altogether to be trusted. This lack of confidence would be borne out three years later when he got with child a maidservant from a neighboring estate. To his credit, Stewart married the beautiful if baseborn Christina and established her and the infant—a son named George—in comfortable domesticity in Edinburgh. He visited them rarely and, after a last bitter quarrel with his brother, said goodby to all his family for six long years, quitting his homeland for what adventure he might find in America.

*   *   *

The spring of 1833 found Captain Stewart in St. Louis, preparing for an expedition across the Great American Desert to the Rocky Mountains. He had arrived there the previous fall, having journeyed by horseback from New York City via Niagara Falls and the Ohio Valley, and during the winter he had managed to ingratiate himself with everyone who was anyone in the bustling river town. His friends included the Red-headed Chief, General William Clark, superintendent of Indian affairs and the man who with Meriwether Lewis had opened the western country to Americans a quarter-century before; General William H. Ashley, the pioneering fur-trade entrepreneur; and William Sublette and Robert Campbell, outfitters for the Rocky Mountain Fur Company, who for five hundred dollars agreed to take Stewart on their annual trek to supply the trappers beyond the Continental Divide.

Stewart was in the vanguard of greenhorns who over the next decade would traverse the western prairie to the Rockies and beyond, following the route of the Platte River across what is now Nebraska, to the Sweetwater and over South Pass into the Green River Valley. The route, blazed by Ashley's fur brigades in the 1820s, would later be known as the Oregon Trail, the path of settlers bound for the Pacific Northwest.

In retrospect he would look on 1833 as the last great year of the mountain fur trade, before this extraordinary country was invaded by Yankee peddlers and missionaries and—most distressing of all—by white women. In *Edward Warren*, one of two romantic novels Stewart would write based on his western experiences, he noted the Indians' astonishment at their first sight of the pale-faced squaws "hung on the side of their horses." When the plains were sufficiently tame for ladies to cross them riding side saddle, Stewart lamented, the fate of the Red Man was sealed.

It was in *Edward Warren* that he would describe himself (through his autobiographical antagonist) as the "one man, in all that region of the hunter, who was not there for gain, but for the love of sport." Stewart became the first in a long line of British sportsmen who would visit the West over the next fifty years. In his later expeditions he would don some of the trappings of extravagant wealth that, in the popular imagination at least, would be seen as typical of his breed. But in 1833 his tastes—dictated in part by his wallet—were simple. His modest outfit, purchased in St. Louis, consisted of a woolen overcoat with hood, a broad-brimmed white hat (forerunner to the Stetson), a leather belt and leggings, pants, and a half-dozen heavy shirts. Brought from Scotland were some fancier clothes reserved for the rendezvous, a spyglass, a pocket compass, a brace of pistols, and a fowling piece and rifle made by Joseph Manton, the celebrated London gunsmith.

The world Stewart entered that spring of 1833 was a sport hunter's Eden, comparable in its awesome scope to the yet unexplored East African savanna. In evolutionary time it was the last instant in the long spring of North America's Pleistocene fauna. The landscape that opened before his eyes, and the animals that filled it, were essentially unchanged since the end of the Ice Age ten thousand years before. The naturalist Ernest Thompson Seton estimated that as many as sixty to seventy million buffalo may have roamed the plains between Texas and Saskatchewan. In addition there were uncountable numbers of antelope, elk, mule deer, mountain sheep, and their predators—wolves, pumas, and grizzlies. The chief predator on the scene, and in Stewart's eyes its romantic apogee, was the mounted Indian. The horse culture of the plains tribes had spread from Mexico a century before, transforming in a generation these mainly agricultural peoples into the nomadic bands of legend.

During the previous decade an even newer element had introduced itself into this primeval landscape: the fur trapper or mountain man. By Stewart's time the fur trade had evolved into the rendezvous system. Trappers, having wintered in the mountains, would gather at a predetermined time and place each year to exchange their pelts for trade goods brought overland by pack train. The trapper might be a wage-earning contract man for one of the several fur companies vying for control of the trade in the central and northern Rockies, or an independent "free trapper" who sold his plews for the best price he could obtain. The rendezvous was a riotous bacchanal of drinking, gambling, brawling, wenching, shooting, and horse racing. Confined to his tent with illness, a companion of Stewart at the rendezvous of 1834 would bemoan "the hiccoughing jargon of drunken traders, the *sacré* and *foutre* of Frenchmen run wild, and the swearing and screaming of our own men who are scarcely less savage than the rest." These people, he wrote, "with their obstreperous mirth, their whooping and howling and quarrelling, added to the mounted Indians who are constantly dashing into and through our camp yelling like fiends, the barking and baying of savage wolf-dogs and the incessant cracking of rifles and carbines, render our camp a perfect bedlam." Liquor and trade articles sold at wildly inflated prices, and by the time the revelry ended most of the participants were broke or in debt to their suppliers. With pounding hangovers they would stagger back into the mountains for another season of following the beaver and guarding their scalps against marauding Blackfeet or Crow. Rendezvous, the historian Bernard DeVoto has written, was all in one "the mountain man's Christmas, county fair, harvest festival, and crowned-slave carnival of Saturn."

The rendezvous was the only real social event in the trapper's lonely life. He prepared for it accordingly, cutting his hair, perhaps even shaving, and donning a new pair of buckskins made, if he were fortunate enough to have one, by his Indian wife. Recognizing the formality of the occasion, Stewart outdid himself in sartorial elegance, exchanging his rank trail clothes for a splendid Savile Row outfit packed away since leaving St. Louis. The engagés of the Rocky Mountain Fur Company could only gawk in astonishment when the Scotsman paraded into camp in a white leather hunting jacket festooned with pockets, plaid hunting trousers, and Panama hat.

As an educated Briton who came of age in an era of romanticism, Stewart brought to the rendezvous a unique perspective. He was aware, as no one else in his company would have been, of time passing, of this montane frolic as a glorious but fleeting climax in the brief history of the mountain trade. Men not yet out of their twenties had already achieved a half-legendary status in that history, and most of them were present at Horse Creek: the irrepressible Joe Meek, Tom "Broken Hand" Fitzpatrick, Joe Walker, and the great Jim Bridger. A few men of more civilized mien could be found at the rendezvous as well, interlopers trying to carve out for themselves a piece of the lucrative beaver trade: the Bald Chief, Captain Benjamin Bonneville, late of the U.S. Army and a possible secret agent gathering intelligence on British and Spanish strength in the West; and Nathaniel Wyeth, a Boston ice merchant whose courage and grim determination to make his fortune in furs could never quite overcome an appalling lack of experience and the bad luck that plagued his enterprise.

Stewart became party to a memorable if tragic incident at the rendezvous when a rabid wolf sneaked into camp at night and ravaged several men, including a likable lad "of blithe and sunny smile" named George Holmes. The wolf bit Holmes on the ear and face as he lay sleeping. Stewart felt a certain responsibility for the poor man's fate. They had been sharing the same birch and willow bower, but Stewart expected an Indian girl to come calling that night so asked Holmes to sleep elsewhere. His cheerful companion, Stewart recalled in *Edward Warren*, "changed from that hour. Instead of alertness and joy, melancholy and despondency grew upon him day by day, and though I stood beside him in another night, when we were but a small party in the hands of the Crow Indians and when neither of us thought to see another sun, I felt I was linked in a death struggle with one who, whatever he might do to help a friend, considered his own fate as sealed." Holmes traveled with Stewart's party north into Crow country after the rendezvous broke up. Before long he developed a phobia for crossing streams. Ineluctably, the rabies virus took hold. Delirious and naked, he wandered off from camp one night and died alone in the wilderness.

*   *   *

Stewart departed the rendezvous at Horse Creek at the end of July, accompanying a brigade of mountain men led by Tom Fitzpatrick, heading north for a fall hunt in Crow country. Bonneville joined them for part of the trip. The party also included Nat Wyeth, homeward bound via the Yellowstone and Missouri to Cambridge, Massachusetts for the winter, and Dr. Benjamin Harrison, son of the hero of Tippecanoe and a reformed boozer traveling in the West for reasons of health.

Riding with Stewart was a young halfbreed he had met at the rendezvous named Antoine Clement, a Canadian by birth, the son of a Cree woman and a *voyageur* of the Hudson's Bay Company. With his lithe body, "light brown hair worn long and the almond-shaped hazel eyes of his mother's race," Clement fulfilled Stewart's ideal of the perfect child of nature; a handsome, buckskinned youth very much like him appears as a kind of leitmotif throughout *Edward Warren*. The Scotsman fancied Clement greatly and took him on as a paid companion, factotum and sometime manservant. They would be together off and on for the next ten years. The Quixote of the Plains had found his Sancho Panza.

The documentation is scanty here, but another notable halfbreed may have been riding with the party as it crossed South Pass and followed the Popo Agie north to the Wind and Bighorn rivers. If Baptiste Charbonneau really was present, as Bernard DeVoto suggests, Stewart must have found him an enchanting and almost unbelievable character. As the infant immortalized as "Pompey," the son of Sacajawea, he had accompanied Lewis and Clark on their great journey of discovery to the Pacific. Adopted by Clark on the expedition's return and educated in St. Louis, he later spent six years in Germany as a

William Drummond Stewart and Antoine Clement, sketched in the field by Stewart's artist, Alfred Jacob Miller.

9

royal guest at the court of Prince Paul of Wurtenberg. He spoke at least four languages and could read Latin and Greek. Charbonneau eventually returned to the Far West and was active in the fur trade at the time of our narrative, and it is likely that Stewart knew him.

It was mid-summer now, and the country they rode through was hot and dessicated. The wildflowers that had covered these hills a month earlier had withered, and under the relentless summer sun the green bunchgrass had turned a universal sere. Most of the game had migrated to higher elevations, but there were still a few buffalo and antelope to keep the hunters busy, as well as the ubiquitous grizzly bear.

Of all the game that Stewart encountered, none could compare to the silvertip in ferocity and fearlessness. A full-grown male grizzly might weigh a thousand pounds and stand eight feet tall when raised on his hind legs, sniffing the wind for man scent. His unpredictability and aggressiveness were the stuff of legend among prairie travelers from the days of Lewis and Clark. In a footnote in *Edward Warren*, Stewart describes a greenhorn's near fatal encounter with "Old Ephraim," one of several terms of ironic endearment given the grizzly by the mountain men. He writes in the third person and sets the scene in the Laramie Range, but the greenhorn is probably Stewart himself, and the incident is the sort that might well have occurred on their trek toward the Bighorn. Having sighted a grizzly,

> The cry was no sooner raised than every disposable hand was off: one hunter, better mounted than the rest, made for the opposite side of the stream and did not pull up until at its head, where there was a bushy thicket; there he awaited the bear, while the whole course below rung with the challenges of the eager troop. It was not long before the bear was heard by the solitary hunter (who was a greenhorn), he then got a sight of him through the bushes, put up his rifle, which snapped; it was a Manton which never missed fire; there was not even a cap on it, it had been washed the night before and never reloaded. The bear heard the snap but saw nothing and hesitating to face an unseen foe turned back; the hunter jumped down to load; the pursuers were coming on and the ball was home when the horse broke away from the slight hold and bounded off; the bear was again tearing

up through the bushes.

The hunter adjusted the percussion cap, raised his rifle and fired. Ephraim was a stride away when the bullet hit, piercing the monster's cheek and ripping through his gut. The bear roared in pain, tumbling backward down the slope and tearing at the brush. The rest of the party arrived to finish off the wounded animal in a hail of bullets. A cook in the group claimed the kill, as he was the only one loaded with slugs; amid the cheers of the rest, he took the bear's feet as a trophy while the hunter looked on, acquiescing in the bloody rite. "He [the cook] never was told the bear was in his death agony before he fired," noted Stewart.

Fitzpatrick's brigade continued north, crossing the Little Bighorn and turning east toward the Tongue River. They were deep in the country of the Crows, traditionally friendly Indians who would surprise them now with an overt act of hostility in which Stewart would play a central, if reluctantly passive, role.

On September 5 they camped in the vicinity of a Crow village. Fitzpatrick went to pay his respects to the chief, leaving his men, horses and supplies under Stewart's command. With Broken Hand and the chief parlaying some miles distant, a band of larcenous Crow braves rode into camp and stripped it clean. Stewart and the other men, outnumbered four to one, could only grit their teeth and look on helplessly. The Crows took horses, furs, trade goods, firearms, and Stewart's watch. Fitzpatrick would later praise his lieutenant for making the best of a bad situation. The Crows got the draw on them immediately, and Stewart's restraint in the face of overwhelming numbers surely prevented a massacre of the twenty-five men in his charge. It must have taken an extraordinary effort for the choleric Scotsman to hold his temper while the cocksure braves rifled the camp, adding insult to injury with their strutting and arrogant display. Stewart would have expected none of this from the reputedly friendly Crows, and anyway he had been instructed by Fitzpatrick to make any Indian visitors welcome. They could not have known that their erstwhile friends had been bribed by Fitzpatrick's rivals in the fur business to make life miserable for the Rocky Mountain Fur Company. Stewart would later take literary revenge on the Crows,

Attack by Crow Indians, *Miller's reconstruction of the 1833 incident. Stewart and Clement are at center stage.*

depicting them in his novels *Edward Warren* and *Altowan* as skulking cowards, while lauding their enemies the Blackfeet as paragons of noble savagery.

An enraged Fitzpatrick took his grievance over this wholesale robbery to the chief, and by skillful negotiation he was able to recover some of the horses, firearms and provisions. He wasted no time in departing the Crow country, returning across the Divide to meet Jim Bridger for reprovisioning.

Stewart's wanderings cannot be traced for the winter of 1833-34, although during the fall he probably transferred to Bridger's brigade. Together they may have passed the snow months in the southern Rockies, perhaps in Taos. He does not come into focus again until the spring, when he appears as the centerpiece of another incident that would enrich the trappers' repertoire of campfire tales.

Stewart at the time was riding north with Bridger and his men. The party included one Markhead, an estimable trapper whose instincts for sniffing out beaver and surviving in the wilderness compensated for what seems to have been a marginal intelligence. Among the contract men was a halfbreed named Marshall, a shirker and troublemaker who routinely tested Bridger's patience. Following some last, exasperating infraction, Old Gabe fired him, repossessing his outfit and horse and ordering him to walk on foot behind the rest of the brigade.

In what seems like an uncharacteristic gesture, Stewart took pity on the outcast and hired him to assist in camp chores. Marshall repaid the Scotsman's generosity by riding off one night with his favorite rifle and two of his mounts, including his best running horse, Otholoho, who had beaten the swiftest Indian ponies at the rendezvous. Stewart discovered his loss the next morning and raged that he would give five hundred dollars for the thief's scalp. To his ultimate chagrin, Markhead took him at his word. Riding ahead as part of a two-man search party, he found Marshall riding buffalo on Otholoho and dropped him with a single shot. "In the evening," Stewart recalled in *Edward Warren*, "between us and the sun, loiterers of the camp saw two men leading two horses making their way towards camp, and on a rifle was displayed the scalp of the horse-thief. This was a little more than I looked for and I tore the bloody trophy from the gun and flung it away." But Stewart would not renege on his word, and after cooling down he dutifully paid the bounty.

The rendezvous of 1834 brought several new types into the mountains. Wyeth's party included a pair of naturalists, the eminent botanist Thomas Nuttall of Harvard and a young Philadelphia ornithologist, John Kirk Townsend. Nuttall and Townsend would travel all the way to Fort Vancouver with Wyeth, distinguishing themslves as the first naturalists to cross the Rocky Mountains, while the treasure trove of animal skins and botanical pressings they shipped back would greatly enrich knowledge of the continent's fauna and flora. John James Audubon would rely heavily on Townsend's bird specimens to complete his monumental *Birds of America.*

Wyeth's party also included the missionary Jason Lee, sent by the Methodists to minister to the Flathead Indians in the region of the Bitterroot Valley, in what is now western Montana. "I go as Paul went to Jerusalem," Lee pronounced of his mission, although he would ultimately abort it and turn his considerable energies instead to spreading the gospel in the richer pastures of Oregon. The nominally Catholic Stewart mistrusted missionaries, preferring Indians in their wild if unchristianized state. We have no record of what he thought of Jason Lee, although they seem to have gotten along well enough. In Bernard DeVoto's characterization, Lee was "hearty, adaptable, courageous, ingenious, ready"—words that could describe Stewart equally as well—with little or none of the self-righteousness that marked many of his fellows in the business of saving savage souls. Stewart lent Lee his copy of Byron's "Sardanapolus," whose author the missionary found to be an infidel or at least "a total stranger to all vital experimental religion."

Stewart joined Lee, Nuttall and Townsend, and the other members of Wyeth's party when it left the rendezvous after July 4 celebrations. They were following what would become the Oregon Trail north into the vast lava plain of the Snake River, thence west to the Columbia to winter at Fort Vancouver, the headquarters for Hudson's Bay Company operations in the Northwest. Encounters with grizzlies were almost daily occurrences, and along the way they picked up several mascots: a baby antelope named Zip Coon, several buffalo calves with a propensity for butting, and a snappish grizzly cub that proved to be untamable. On a tributary to the Snake, Wyeth established the trading post he named Fort Hall, after one of his Boston investors, and beneath its poplars Lee preached to Stewart and the rest what is recorded as the first sermon heard in Oregon. Later that day a halfbreed French Canadian was killed in a horse race, presenting the missionary with the opportunity to ply his trade again. "The service was performed by the Canadians in the Catholic form, by Mr. Lee in the Protestant form and by the Indians in their form, as he had Indian family," Wyeth noted in his journal. "He at least was well buried."

Stewart passed most of the winter of 1834-35 at Fort Vancouver on the lower Columbia, enjoying the post's relative comforts and the hospitality of its benevolent dictator, the six-foot-seven-inch White-Headed Eagle, Dr. John McLoughlin. We find him the following summer at the rendezvous at New Fork. Fitzparick's pack train had brought with it this time two more missionaries, the Reverend Samuel Parker and Dr. Marcus Whitman, come to establish a mission to the Nez Perces and to determine the fate of Jason Lee, who had not been heard from since his departure for the mountains more than a year before. From Stewart they were shocked to learn that Lee had betrayed his mission to the Flatheads and had settled instead in the Willamette Valley.

Whitman was a medical missionary and like Lee a robust character who gained the respect of the godless trappers, "a most excellent man and a bold operator," as Stewart remembered him in *Edward Warren*. Before a gallery of Indians and trappers he performed some impromptu surgery on Jim Bridger, removing from his lower back a three-inch, barbed iron arrowhead received in the Battle of Pierre's Hole three years earlier. Whitman was amazed that Old Gabe could function so, but Bridger made light of any infirmity the arrowhead might have caused: "In the mountains, Doctor, meat don't spoil." Bridger presented the arrowhead to his old friend Stewart, who carried it for the rest of his life as a memento of the particular brand of toughness bred in the Rockies.

Frontispiece from Murray's Travels in North America.

2

Kilts and Buckskins

There is probably not another tribe on the continent that has been more abused and incensed by the system of trade and money-making than the Pawnees. Mr. Murray . . . made his way boldly into the heart of their country, without guide or interpreter, and I consider at great hazard to his life.

—George Catlin, *Letters and Notes on the Manners, Customs, and Conditions of North American Indians*

As STEWART made his way to the rendezvous at New Fork that summer of 1835, a fellow Scotsman of equally aristocratic lineage was proceeding up the Missouri for a summer of adventure on the prairie. Charles Augustus Murray, second son of the Fifth Earl of Dunmore and late of Eton and Oxford and the salons of London society, was twenty-eight years old and had been traveling in the United States for the last fourteen months. He possessed, a friend recalled, "a charm of manner and conversation which endeared him to all his acquaintance," including such prominent Americans encountered on his peregrinations as Henry Clay and James Fenimore Cooper.

Like Stewart, the manor-born Murray was unburdened by familial responsibilities and seemed quite content to follow a gentlemanly life of leisure. Summers were passed in shooting and fishing on the ancestral estate at Glen Finart in the Scottish Highlands, winters in the perpetual round of dinner parties and balls that constituted the London social season. After he left for America in 1834, a society letter noted, the ladies would "sigh and soften their voices" whenever his name was mentioned. "To them he is a creature of romance, though to their mothers the most dangerous of all detrimentals."

The mothers had legitimate cause for worry, it seemed, for the dashing Scot had a reputation for wildness that he was quick to establish in American society. At a dinner party in Washington following his arrival in the United States, he begged the hostess's pardon and proceeded, on a wager, to smash his fist through the parlor door.

In contrast to Stewart, Murray possessed a sunny disposition and a sense of humor that brighten his *Travels in North America*, the engaging account of his United States visit, published in 1839 and dedicated to the young Queen Victoria. Shyness never inhibited him, and wherever his travels took him he went out of his way to meet the famous men of his day, especially literary men. Once, on a tour of the continent, the charming young Scot cajoled his way into an audience before the great Goethe, and at home in Edinburgh he enjoyed the friendship of Sir Walter Scott.

Murray especially admired the American novelist Fenimore Cooper. Following his arrival in New York at the start of his American visit, he found himself on a Hudson River steamer with the celebrated author of The Leatherstocking Tales and lost no time ingratiating himself with the squire of Cooperstown. It was actually their second meeting, as they had been introduced on Cooper's tour of Britain several years before, and their paths would cross again in the closing months of Murray's three-year sojourn in America. Like any adventurous young man of his generation, Murray was an enthusiast of Cooper's romantic tales, epitomized by *The Last of the Mohicans*, set on the New York frontier during the French and Indian War. In the seventy-five years since the time of Cooper's narratives the frontier had shifted a thousand miles, to Fort Leavenworth at the bend of the Missouri, where Murray was now heading with the notion of living, like Natty Bumppo, among the Red Men. Cooper's idealistic and nostalgic view of Indians would have some small influence on Murray, although in the main his impressions were clear-eyed enough— sympathetic but without sentiment, and always presented with great good humor. But then, Murray's accounts of Indian life were based on first-hand experience; Cooper's were not.

Standing on the deck of the steamboat *Hancock*, the young Scotsman watched the Missouri slipping by, marveling at its speed and at the size and quantity of flotsam it carried—whole forests, it seemed, being swept on its roiling current toward the sea. Everything about the country impressed him: the densely wooded banks with their monarch sycamores and cottonwoods, the fearsome lightning and torrential thunderstorms, and the extremes of temperature that left the passengers soaked in sweat one moment and wrapped in blankets, shivering before a fire, in the next. "Who can wonder," he asked, "at the fevers, agues, and bilious diseases prevalent in such a climate?" In fact, many of the passengers were suffering from cholera, and during the nine-day passage from St. Louis they buried one and and put ashore several more near death.

Murray himself had nearly died of cholera while journeying down the Ohio several months before, but he was in fine fettle and hearty spirits now as he disembarked at the village of Liberty, just east of present-day Kansas City, and set about outfitting himself for prairie travel. He purchased five ponies and a mule—two mounts for his personal use, one for his valet, and three for packing the sundry goods and articles needed for prairie travel: lead shot and powder, cooking utensils, canteens, blankets, bacon, sugar, flour, and trinkets for trading with the Indians. His wardrobe included a broad-brimmed hat, a pair of stout corduroy breeches protected by buckskin leggings, and a black velveteen shooting jacket with enormous pockets. (He also on occasion wore a kilt.) He carried a Purdey double-barrelled rifle—as fine a gun as England made—as well as a brace of pistols, a hunting knife, and a short cut-and-thrust sword "as is sometimes used in Germany in a boar-hunt, and nearly resembling the old Roman sword." Crowning this martial figure was Murray's handsome visage, graced by flowing handlebar mustaches and tanned "nearly of an Indian colour" by the relentless prairie sun.

A ride of some thirty miles, across undulant glades of tallgrass prairie bobbing with wildflowers, brought him to Fort Leavenworth overlooking the Missouri. Approaching the garrison, they passed through several villages of Indian tribes recently removed from eastern states as part of the government's massive (and shameless) resettlement program initiated under Andrew Jackson. Murray found the Kickapoos, emigrants from Illinois defeated in Black Hawk's War, particularly degenerate—"a weak, and daily decreasing tribe," their natural nobility "much changed by constant communication with the whites."

The indigenous Pawnees, however, were another matter. Several days following Murray's arrival at Fort Leavenworth, a large contingent of this traditional plains tribe showed up at the garrison. The young Scot was dining in the officers' mess on July 4 when a dozen chiefs paraded in. These "genuine children of the wilderness" impressed him with their dignified decorum, which broke down somewhat after a round of Madeira when they joined in the Independence Day celebration, howling and yelping their way through a ceremonial chorus "sufficient to deafen a delicate ear."

Determined to carry through on his plans to live among the Pawnees—"a strange and wild experiment," he cheerfully conceded—Murray hired a trail hand and a halfbreed interpreter "who spoke very bad French, very good Pawnee, and no English" and set off with the Pawnee contingent to rejoin the main party farther out on the plains. Riding northwest, they passed through rolling, flower-dotted prairie punctuated here and there with copses so "carefully grouped as to remind me of Windsor and other noble English parks." Like most travelers on the eastern plains, he found the area surprisingly scarce of game and had to content himself with bagging a fawn and a half-dozen Carolina paroquets. The latter were pretty green-and-yellow birds that, while common enough at the time, like the bounteous passenger pigeons were already slipping toward extinction. Murray cooked the birds for supper and found them "fat, and by no means unpalatable." The fawn furnished them but a single dinner, thanks to the ravenous appetite—and impeccable Indian manners—of a Pawnee guest: "Ribs, head, shoulders, etc. disappeared one after the other. He quietly ate everything placed before or near him, without the slightest symptom of diminished power; and I was not *then* aware of the incredible capacity of Indians, or of their notion that it is impolite to decline proferred food under any circumstances."

Murray was shocked by the gusto with which the Pawnees attacked their food—"tearing the meat from the bone with their strong teeth, and masticating slices, each of which would be a day's dinner to a Yorkshire ploughman." But he soon lost all traces of fastidiousness, becoming especially fond in his own right of raw buffalo liver sliced from the freshly killed carcass and devoured while still warm—"as tender as any morsel I ever tasted."

On one occasion he found himself in a ceremonial feast in which the guests raced each other in gulping down a cloying mess of boiled maize. "I have read in travel-volumes, and I have *seen* instances, of the extraordinary speed with which the mixed company at crowded American hotel or steam-boat dinners can clear a well-loaded table; but here they would have been distanced, and beaten by all comparison." He gamely attacked his three-quart serving but found that "the solid, sticky, indigestible mass resisted my utmost efforts," while the nauseating gruel flowed easily "down the Indian-rubber throats of my competitors." Fortunately, a huge warrior came to his aid and helped him finish off his bowl. "Alas! even with this powerful auxiliary, I was last *but one* in the sweepstakes."

Murray subsisted well enough on his Pawnee diet, however unappetizing. He tried the potato-like roots of *Psoralea*, a common prairie legume, and found them "nutritious and not unpalatable," at least if sufficiently spiced by hunger. But he never did acquire the Pawnee taste for dog—especially when the *table d'hôte* included "Peevish," his own trusting pet, whom his hosts lured away and killed for the stew pot one night while he slept. (It is a little hard to understand this unfortunate incident when we consider the ubiquity of camp dogs: Murray estimated that the village population of "mongrels and curs" averaged seven per tipi, for a village total of some four thousand.

The scarcity of game may have contributed to the meagerness of the Pawnee menu, and the Pawnees themselves were not always adept at hunting what was available. Murray found them "very much inferior to our highland deer-stalkers in taking advantage of wind and position of ground, although far superior to them in following a foot track." For their part, the Pawnees marveled at Murray's marksmanship and the breathtaking accuracy of his Purdey rifle, which he once used to bring down a running antelope at more than two hundred yards. "Much more to my astonishment than to theirs," he reports, the ball went through the hind-quarters of the animal. "Shouts of admiration and surprise were raised by the savages, who ran to secure the little prize; but I pretended that it was a mere matter of course, said nothing, laid down my rifle, and continued my meal."

The incident shows Murray's intuitive grasp of Indian psychology. "In all my intercourse with the Pawnees," he wrote, "I made it a rule to humour their prejudices, and to accommodate myself to their usages, however absurd. Moreover, I endeavoured to make them believe that I could surpass them in anything which I chose to attempt." Among all of Murray's skills, none impressed the Pawnees more than his ability to read—pronounced "great medicine" by all who witnessed it. His traveling library consisted of the Bible, Sophocles, the first half of the Odyssey, and Milton. "Frequently my brother, the son of Sa-ni-tsarish, would come and look over my shoulder, and glance his eyes from my face to the book, with a mingled expression of curiosity and surprise. I tried to explain to him that it 'talked to me, and told me of many things past, and many far away.' Then he would take it up, and turn it round and round, looking steadfastly at the page; but he said he could hear nothing and see nothing."

In this and other incidents, Murray humored his Indian hosts and scrupulously avoided embarrassing them in any way. Once, trading for horses, he spread out his packet of goods "like an Israelite in Monmouth street" and invited the Pawnees to do business. When an elderly chief—a "very large corpulent man"—coveted a flannel undercoat, a memorable burlesque ensued:

> He said he would like to try on the jacket; and as he threw the buffalo robe off his huge shoulders, I could scarcely keep my gravity, when I compared their dimensions with the garment into which we were about to attempt their introduction. At last, by dint of great industry and care, we contrived to get him into it. In the body it was a foot too short, and fitted him so close that every thread was stretched to the uttermost; the sleeves reached

a very little way below his elbows. However, he looked upon his arms and person with great complacency, and elicited many smiles from the squaws at the drollery of his attire; but as the weather was very hot, he soon began to find himself too warm and confined, and he wished to take it off again. He moved his arms—he pulled the sleeves—he twisted and turned himself in every direction, but in vain. The woolen jacket was an admirable illustration of the Inferno of Dante and Virgil, and of matrimony, as described by many poets.

For some time I enjoyed this scene with malicious and demure gravity, and then I showed him that he must try and pull it off over his head. A lad who stood by then drew it, till it enveloped his nose, eyes, mouth, and ears; his arms were raised above his head, and for some minutes he remained in that melancholy plight, blinded, choked, and smothered. He rolled about, sneezing, sputtering, and struggling, until all around were convulsed in laughter; and our squaws shrieked in their ungovernable mirth in a manner that I had never before witnessed.

Murray eventually freed the chief of his flannel straight-jacket. The Pawnee "made a kind of comic-grave address" and did his best to salvage what remained of his dignity. "I was so pleased with his good humour, that I gave it to him, and told him to warm his squaw in the ice-month."

By early August, Murray was planning his return to civilization. While he had lived with the Pawnees for only a month, he had packed so much experience into his stay that it must have seemed much longer. (As it does to the reader of Murray's *Travels*, which, while covering three years in America, devotes about forty pecent of its text to his relatively brief sojourn on the prairie.) Murray's party included, besides his valet, an American hired hand and a German gentleman named Vernunft, whom he had met in Kentucky at the estate of Henry Clay. On the morning of August 8 they bid goodby to their Pawnee hosts and set out across the rolling country, led by a pair of Indian guides enlisted to take them the distance to Fort Leavenworth. Murray anticipated a march of some seven hundred miles and estimated it would take them about three weeks.

Almost immediately they were beset by problems. Murray had worried about Vernunft's ability to handle the volatile

Indian pony he was riding, and his worst fears were realized when the horse threw and partially trampled the young German, forcing a return to the Pawnee village for a brief convalescence. After getting underway again, Murray wandered off on a hunt and lost his bearings, and it was only with luck and the help of some Pawnee hunters that he found his party again. They were also beset by biting flies and mosquitoes (which had never bothered them among the Pawnees—presumably, surmised Murray, because the terrible stench of an Indian encampment served as a natural repellant), and by towering prairie storms that left them drenched and shivering. Worse, after a week on the trail their Pawnee guides, fearing confrontation with a larger band of Sioux or some other unfriendly tribe, balked at proceeding farther.

In the middle of the plains and with hundreds of miles still to go, Murray gathered his little group for a decision. The only alternatives were returning to the Pawnees for the winter or continuing on alone. Fearing they had already overstayed their welcome and having bartered all their trade goods, they seriously questioned how the Pawnees might receive them. And while the adaptable and somewhat atavistic Murray could certainly have survived a winter among his savage brothers, the others were desperately homesick for civilization. So they dimissed their guides and elected Murray, who rose admirably to the occasion, to lead them the rest of the way to Fort Leavenworth.

"The very feeling of the responsibility of my charge gave me excitement," he would recall, "so, with my telescope, compass, and rifle ready for use, I rode on a hundred yards ahead, and began my career as guide."

And a remarkably successful career it turned out to be. With his quick intelligence, Murray had learned more than he knew during his two months on the prairie, and he applied it now with a skill that must have surprised him. He read the land and accurately interpreted sign—gleaning from the remains of an abandoned campsite, for example, the size, composition, and tribal identity of the Indian party that had rested there. He faced down a party of Pawnee horse thieves, found water in country seemingly barren of it, and ferried his group safely across the swollen Kansas River. With his trusty Purdey he kept the group supplied with meat and on one occasion revived sagging morale by exercising his "culinary invention" to create a luxurious dessert of wild plums stewed in sugar and brandy. It rained almost every day, and by their arrival in early September at Fort Leavenworth they were wet, ragged, filthy and covered with vermin, yet in pretty good spirits overall. "I regret very much that there was no artist present, who could give a faithful sketch of us in our various costumes as we sat huddled round our dim and smoky fire, each endeavoring to extract a small blaze to warm some favoured part of his person."

*　　*　　*

After recouping at Fort Leavenworth, Murray resumed his travels through the United States and returned to England at the end of 1836. For the next nine years he lived the rarified existence of a courtier, serving as Master of the Queen's Household and regaling the young Victoria, we may imagine, with all manner of fantastic tales of his life among the Pawnees. In 1844 he published *The Prairie-Bird*, a popular romantic novel based on his western adventures.

Murray's friends the Pawnees fared less well. The year following his return to Britain, the tribal branch with which he had associated was decimated by smallpox carried in scalps brought back from a raiding party against their traditional enemy, the Oglala Sioux. The Great Scourge weakened all the northern plains tribes but the Pawnee especially, and after 1837 they ceased to be reckoned as a major force in the trans-Missouri frontier.

3

'H'ar of the Grissly'

Crossed a ridge of land today; called the divide, which separates the waters that flow into the Atlantic from those that flow into the Pacific, and camped for the night on the head waters of the Colorado.
—Entry of July 4, 1836 in the diary of
Eliza Spalding, who with Narcissa Whitman was
the first woman to cross the Rockies.

WHILE MURRAY rested at Fort Leavenworth, recovering from his trek across the plains, his fellow countryman Captain Stewart was several hundred miles to the northwest, proceeding east along the familiar Platte route to St. Louis, in the company of Tom Fitzpatrick. Stewart had passed three summers and two winters in the Far West, ranging from Taos to the Yellowstone to the fog-drenched Pacific cliffs of Oregon. He had shot buffalo, elk, antelope, mountain sheep, and grizzly and had survived a dozen skirmishes with Indians. The manor-born aristocrat enjoyed full standing in the fraternity of mountain men and was a familiar enough figure to be granted his own symbol in the sign language of the plains: a crooked finger held to the face, in honor of his aquiline nose.

Stewart looked forward now to reacquainting himself with the comforts of civilization. After a short stay in St. Louis he took passage on a river steamer to New Orleans, the better to indulge his sybaritic tastes, while turning some highly profitable deals on the cotton exchange that would allow him to live in the grander style to which he aspired. By spring he was back in St. Louis—via Havana, Charleston, Philadelphia, and Cincinnati—and readying for his fourth summer in the West.

Stewart's new outfit reflected his recently upturned fortunes. Over the winter he had made the acquaintance of a gentleman named Sillem, a German adventurer of kindred spirit who jumped at the chance to accompany his Scottish friend to the rendezvous at Horse Creek. They made the usual arrangements to travel overland with Fitzpatrick, who embarked that year from the little settlement of Bellevue at the mouth of the Platte. Their imposing impedimenta, tended by three servants, included a string of blooded horses, two hunting dogs, and a pair of wagons filled to the freeboard with canned delicacies, vintage wines, and brandy. Stewart would show the mountains how a gentleman lived. While such trappings of aristocracy may have awed the simple trappers, to at least one member of the caravan Stewart and his epicurean style represented sheer abomination. William H. Gray, the "secular agent" to another party of missionaries led by the redoubtable Marcus Whitman, seems to have been weaned on lemons. Gray was overbearingly self-righteous, a Presbyterian and Anglophobe without a hint of charity, who has left us with a vivid if jaundiced description of our aristocratic sportsman:

> He was about five feet nine inches high. His face had become thin from the free use of New Orleans brandy, rendering his nose rather prominent, showing indications of internal heat in bright red spots, and inclining a little to the rum blossom, that would make its appearance from the sting of a mosquito or sand-fly, which to his lordship was quite annoying. Though his lordship was somewhat advanced in age, and according to his own account had traveled extensively in the oriental countries, he did not show in his conversation extensive mental improvement; his general conversation and appearance was that of a man with strong prejudices and equally strong appetites, which he had freely indulged, with only pecuniary restraint.

Stewart, according to Gray, "had been spending his winters in New Orleans with the Southern bloods" and was now traveling in the West for pleasure in the company of Sillem (whom he improperly identifies as English). Between the two of them they had three servants, two dogs, and four extra fine horses, to run and hunt the buffalo. Occasionally, they would give chase to that swiftest of mountain animals, the antelope, which, in most instances would, especially where the grass was short, leave them in the distance, when Sir William [Gray is premature in granting Stewart a title] and his companion would come charging back to the train, swearing the antelope could outrun a streak of lightning, and offering to bet a thousand pounds that if he had one of his English 'orses he could catch 'em.

It is reasonable to assume that Gray also resented Stewart's courtly manners toward Dr. Whitman's fetching new wife. The presence in Fitzpatrick's train of Narcissa Whitman and another missionary spouse, Eliza Spalding, was nothing short of extraordinary. They were the first white women to make the overland crossing, and to the hundred or so trappers at Horse Creek they must have seemed a mirage. For the Indians present at the rendezvous—some fourteen hundred Snakes, Bannocks, Flatheads, and Nez Perces—national pride dictated an appropriate greeting. Naked except for breechclouts and feathers and with burnished bodies adorned in warpaint, two hundred braves cantered across the valley and saluted the missionary wives in a whooping roundalay. "The two ladies were gazed upon with wonder and astonishment by the rude savages," one first-hand observer recalled, "they being the first white women ever seen by these Indians and the first that had ever penetrated into these wild and rocky regions."

(A Sioux chief, DeVoto wrote, "is supposed to have once said that his people were not alarmed till they saw plows in the emigrant wagons and his remark has served innumerable chroniclers who may forget that the Sioux had no way of knowing what a plow was. A truer symbol for the chief would be these two women surrounded by Indians and men in buckskin, in Oregon, west of the Continental Divide.")

Narcissa Whitman was everyone's favorite, including Stewart's, and for a brief moment she kindled in him a longing for the life of quiet domesticity that he had deliberately rejected five years earlier. She had strawberry blond curls and a pleasing figure that showed beneath her calico dress, and the fervor of her religious feeling took nothing away from her vivacious charm. Some found her flirtatious. On the passage out she hosted a regular afternoon tea, the guests sipping from tin saucers as they sat cross-legged on an India-rubber sheet. She had married Whitman the previous fall and at the time of the rendezvous was several weeks pregnant. The misson she would help her husband to establish in the Walla Walla Valley would become an important way station on the Oregon Trail. Their ministrations to sick and weary travelers, exhausted at the end of eighteen hundred bone-rattling miles of trail, would earn them the undying gratitude of thousands of emigrants. Sadly, the spirit of both Whitmans, admired by Stewart and so many others, would be snuffed out by Cayuse Indians in a bloody native uprising in 1847.

* * *

While the missionaries proceeded on to Oregon, Stewart made his usual post-rendezvous hunt in the Wind River Mountains. Later, he met up with Jim Bridger and returned to Fort Laramie and St. Louis, where some momentous news awaited him. A letter from home reported that his older brother John was mortally ill. The prodigal realized that he might be returning to Murthly sooner than expected, not as the scorned second son but as Sir William Drummond Stewart, Sixth Baronet of Grandtully. Stewart recognized that his days of galloping freedom were drawing to a close and that he would be fortunate to have, at best, one more season in the West. That winter in New Orleans, there was doubtless a certain urgency in his mind when he engaged a young Baltimore artist to travel with him to preserve, at least on canvas, the life of abandon he had relished these last five summers.

The artist, Alfred Jacob Miller, was twenty-six years old and had recently moved to New Orleans from his native Baltimore. He had studied the great masters in Rome and Paris, where he was known with some exaggeration as "the American Raphael." Like Stewart, he held the romantic perceptions common to his time, and he would leave us with a captivating vision of mountain life as a kind of arcadian frolic of Indians and trappers. He took immediately to Stewart's halfbreed squire, Antoine Clement, while noting that this "wild child of the prairie" seemed lost in New Orleans' cosmopolitan environment.

It was not long, however, before Antoine and Stewart, with the artist in tow, were readying for a return to their beloved mountains. Before departing for the West they paid a visit to Bill Sublette's horse farm outside St. Louis, where "Cut Face" (as Sublette was known) kept a paddock of buffalo and several grizzly bears chained to stakes. Miller learned more about the country he would soon be entering from other veterans, for Fitzpatrick's caravan that year included Black Harris, Jim Bridger's rival as a teller of tales ("Lies tumbled out of his mouth like boudins out of a bufler's stomach," the mountain men said of him); and ancient Etienne Provost, an original Ashley man and at fifty-five a Methuselah of the trade, with "a corpus round as a porpoise," according to the artist. The mountain men captivated Miller with their fantastic stories of Indian fights and the wonders of the Yellowstone country with its geysers and "putrified" forests, and he drew them dancing to a Jew's harp in Saturnalian circles around the campfire.

"At other times," Miller reported, "our leader Stewart would entertain them with his adventures in foreign lands, the curious cities and monuments of antiquity he had visited. It was edifying to see the patience with which he answered their simple questions as if they were matters of course and full importance, all the while maintaining a gravity that was almost amusing. It is not to be wondered at that he became immensely popular among them. No doubt all of the men would have followed him into any danger regardless of consequences. One of them told us that he (the Captain) had a 'h'ar (hair) of the Grissly in him,' meaning bulldog courage."

The young artist served his trail apprenticeship under a task master. Stewart, the old army hand, insisted that Miller take his turn at the routine camp chores. He allowed him the single privilege of paying a substitute for night guard—in compensation, perhaps, for making him stay awake during the afternoon siesta to sketch the caravan at rest on the prairie. On another occasion, Stewart upbraided Miller for failing to record several scenes that caught his eye. "I would be glad to paint more sketches," the artist retorted, "if I had six pairs of hands."

Miller painted Jim Bridger in a cuirass and helmet brought to him by Stewart.

Stewart served as an unofficial second-in-command to Fitzpatrick, and according to Miller he understood "the management of unruly spirits" and would brook no breach of discipline, dressing down miscreants like a drill sergeant. He drove Miller hard and at one point taught him an object lesson in survival. The greenhorn was absorbed in sketching Independence Rock when Stewart stole up behind him and locked his head in a full-nelson. Miller assumed his assailant to be an Indian and gave himself up as a goner. "In five minutes, however, the hands were removed. It was our Commander. He said, 'Let this be a warning to you or else on some fine day you wi'l be among the missing. You must have your eyes and wits about you.'" The lesson stuck.

The one man in camp as headstrong as Stewart was Antoine Clement, and later in the expedition Miller would witness a falling out between them over the halfbreed's refusal to obey one of the captain's orders. The two were escorting the artist on a sketching trip and twenty miles from camp—"well mounted, armed with Manton rifles, neither knowing what fear was"— when the storm crackling between them threatened to explode into gunfire. Miller looked on helplessly, fearing the worst, when a sighting of buffalo saved the day. "The ruling passion overtopped everything," he reported, and the two nimrods were off at a gallop, their quarrel forgotten.

Despite their difference in background, Miller and Antoine took well to each other. The artist painted a romantic portrait of the halfbreed as a Rousseauian figure in buckskins, while Antoine looked out for Miller during his apprenticeship on the trail. During the trip out, Antoine assisted him in getting close enough to a buffalo to sketch it. Antoine went about this task in "his own peculiar fashion," according to Miller, by grazing the beast with a rifle ball. The superficial wound stunned the buffalo, so that rather than taking flight it stood stock still. As Miller was creeping up to it, however, his subject came suddenly to life and charged, sending "pencil and paper flying" and the artist in headlong retreat. Later he witnessed Antoine in an act of prairie bravado, grabbing fast to the tail of another wounded buffalo while "the astounded brute turned first one way and then another, swinging Antoine about as if he was a feather, and lifting him completely from the ground." The tenacious Antoine held on till the beast dropped dead.

Miller especially looked forward to meeting and painting the plains Indians, those "wild sons of the West" who played so prominent a role in the campfire stories that were nightly fare on the prairie crossing. In their fierceness and naked savagery they did not disappoint him. Early in the journey a visit by a band of Kansas Indians gave him the chance to pose its leader, White Plume, in his cherished silver peace medal presented him by President Adams a decade earlier, and at Fort Laramie he did a splendid portrait of the tyrannical Oglala chief, Bull Bear. The Sioux, wrote Miller, "reminded us strongly of antique figures in Bronze & presented a wide & ample field for the sculptor. Nothing in Greek art can surpass the reality here." Later, at the rendezvous on Green River, he exhilarated at the procession of Snake Indians parading in welcome, led by Stewart's friend, Little Chief, riding a white horse and resplendent in his war bonnet and necklace of grizzly claws.

Miller's patron also figured prominently in his paintings. Wih his Roman nose, ramrod bearing, and tailored buckskins, riding a white horse with an English saddle trimmed with buffalo fur, Stewart commands center stage in the artist's sweeping canvases and intimate vignettes of mountain life. We see him leading a band of hunters at the start of a buffalo chase, or greeting a party of mounted Indians, their rifles blazing in salute, or making his way through a Snake encampment on the tipi-dotted plain of the Green.

For compositional purposes Miller took occasional liberties with his subjects, and he could not always resist romanticizing situations like the marriage tableau in "The Trapper's Bride," one of his most sentimentalized and popular works. But in the main his paintings are authentic renderings of an extraordinary time and place—our sole visual record of the mountain fur trade. Although lacking in the almost clinical detail of paintings by his contemporaries Charles Bodmer and George Catlin, they are infused with a kind of wide-eyed wonder and idyllic charm. In part because of his retiring nature and indifference to self-promotion, Miller during his lifetime never achieved the recognition afforded Bodmer and Catlin. But his "flair for conveying movement and for capturing . . . The poetic essentials of Indian life," according to one art historian, was unsurpassed.

Bodmer and Catlin, while great Indian artists, were limited in their travels to the plains; Miller alone penetrated the Rockies to capture on sketch pad and canvas the spectacle of the trappers' rendezvous. One of the many memorable scenes he recorded shows Jim Bridger mounted on an Indian pony and parading about like Ivanohoe in a suit of medieval armor, courtesy of his friend Captain Stewart. Later, Joe Meek borrowed Jim's cuirass and helmet and rushed through camp, Stewart recalled, "looking for another Richmond" and shouting, to great guffaws from all assembled, "A horse, a horse, a kingdom for a horse!" Like Bridger, Meek was illiterate. but one could imagine him learning his lines from Stewart, reading aloud from Shakespeare by the campfire light.

Miller reveled in the Saturnalian spectacle of the rendezvous and sketched other famous mountain men, including the great Joe Walker, Bonneville's former partisan, whose wanderings four years earlier across the Great Basin and Sierra Nevada led to the discovery of Yosemite Valley. He captured Walker's gritty toughness in his drawing of the "bourgeois," or brigade leader, on a wiry Indian mount, his Hawkins rifle straddling the saddle and his squaw riding behind him at a respectful distance. The artist looked on his subject with a certain awe, having heard that Walker had once unknowingly eaten the remains of his own men, served up to him by vengeful Indians whom he had defeated in battle. Miller wanted to ask him about the incident but decided it would be in bad taste. Later, Walker presented him with a dozen pairs of moccasins embroidered with porcupine quills by his wife.

Joslyn Art Museum, Omaha, Nebraska

Joe Walker and his squaw, as captured by Miller at the 1837 rendezvous.

Stewart departed the rendezvous for a hunt in his old stomping grounds of the Wind River Mountains, packing along his fancy tinned meats, his cheeses and fine wines, and two ten-gallon casks filled with brandy and port. The party idylled for several weeks amid the splendor of alpine lakes, stalking bighorn sheep and hauling cutthroat trout from the sparkling streams. (Stewart lost his flies but found the fish so gullible that he could catch them on bare hooks fashioned from pins.) Miller took advantage of the spectacular scenery, which reminded him of Switzerland, and painted a series of lake pictures infused with mystic pearly light.

From the Winds they traveled to the Grand Tetons and the lower Yellowstone. At some point during their peregrinations, Stewart fell sick from a mysterious illness. When visited by an itinerant Jesuit missionary from a nearby Indian village, the lapsed Catholic vowed if he recovered to return to the faith of his ancestors and restore the chapels at Murthly and Grandtully to their former glory. This must have had some effect, for in a few days Stewart was up and about, and on his return to St. Louis he made good immediately on one of the promises by receiving baptism.

The illness of John Stewart, meanwhile, lingered on. As long as his elder brother lived, there was no point in returning to Scotland, so after wintering in New Orleans he journeyed west again for a sixth consecutive summer in the mountains, Stewart was fording the South Platte on the day his brother died, nearly half a world away, in Paris, but he would not learn of his extraordinary change in fortune until his return to civilization that fall.

4

Goodbye to All That

On the south bank of the Tay, on the slope of Birnam Hill where Macduff's men plucked the branches of the augury, shaggy brown-black cattle with humps and evil eyes cropped the Scottish grass. Antoine and Sir William could come down from the pile of Murthly and stand pondering the buffalo. If the halfbreed in kilts felt his trigger-finger twitch, it was as vain as the twitch in the baronet's daydream, for the Tay was not the Siskadee, there was no main herd on the far side of the hill, and the cottagers spoke of these beasts as bison.
—Bernard DeVoto,
Across the Wide Missouri

ST. LOUIS HAD been buzzing for weeks in preparation for the steamboat *Weston's* departure, and now that she was on her way at last, several thousand people gathered on the levee to give her a proper sendoff. As the boat slipped from the dock and churned upriver, the well-wishers cheered and waved their handkerchiefs, while the jubilant young men on deck answered with wild whoops and shouts. The spirited passengers included scions of prominent St. Louis families as well as young bloods from New Orleans, Baltimore, Savannah, and other parts of the Republic. There were also journalists, soldiers, scientists, a painter, and various hangers-on, to the total of at least sixty adventurers, bound, as a local newspaper announced, "for the Indian Country, Rocky Mountains, and other parts inhabited by *Ingens* and other 'wild varmints.' "

The scene had the air of a holiday excursion—a grand lark, a "hunting frolic," as it was billed, of a few weeks' duration, rather than six months' wandering in dangerous country where grizzly bears and hostile Indians posed a daily threat. The members of the expedition had apparently been chosen with little or no consideration of their ability to endure the hardships and discipline of the trail. Among the wastrels and idlers assembled were a young man on the lam for forgery and "a drunken lout" named Matthew, as a journalist on board reported, who "pours whiskey into his throat through a funnel."

In addition to these ne'er-do-wells and revelers, however, the party included a few sober-sided young gentlemen. Among them were two cousins, not yet out of their teens, who were about to experience first-hand a country that must have seemed theirs by birthright. Jefferson Clark and William Clark Kennerly were native St. Louisans and the son and nephew, respectively, of William Clark, the man who with Meriwether Lewis had first explored the Far West nearly forty years earlier.

It was May 1843. Clark had been dead for six years, and we can only surmise what he might have thought of the motley assemblage bound for glory aboard the *Weston*. The serious effort being made in behalf of science would doubtless have pleased him, for among the party were botanists from Germany and Scotland, an ornithologist, and a London mineralogist. To care for various exigencies of the trail there were also, fortunately, at least one physician, several Army officers from Jefferson Barracks who presumably knew something about fighting Indians, and a handful of experienced wilderness travelers led by tough old Bill Sublette. Of this odd assortment, wrote Cut Face in his diary, some were "of the armey Some professional Gentlemen Some on the trip for pleasure Some for Health &c &c So we had doctors Lawyers botanists Bugg Ketchers Hunters & Men of nearly all professions."

The man responsible for collecting and outfitting this expedition—the West's first grand-scale dude excursion—was an old friend of Sublette, Sir Willam Drummond Stewart. The master of Murthly and Grandtully, homesick more than he knew for his adopted country, had set aside his ancestral responsibilties and returned to America for a final Rocky

Mountain romp.

Stewart had been gone for four years—some two years longer than he had anticipated in May 1839, when he had left the United States for Scotland to take charge of the family estates inherited on the death of his elder brother. As mementos of his six years in the Far West, the new baronet took home with him his old hunting companion, Antoine Clement, as well as two Indians, a mated pair of buffalo, a young grizzly, and seedlings of various western trees (among them, one assumes, Douglas fir, lodgepole pine, cottonwood, and aspen). Planted on the slopes of Birnam Hill, the American trees would share a view of the River Tay with the two ancient English oaks remaining from Macbeth's time.

The buffalo included in Sir William's entourage adapted well to domesticity and Scottish heather, and for company they had the bison herd of Sir William's neighbor, Lord Breadalbane, propagated from other bison that Stewart had shipped from St. Louis several years earlier. In February 1840, the young Queen Victoria honeymooned in Scotland and on a visit to Breadalbane's estate remarked on "those strange hump-backed creatures from America." Stewart, however, missed his chance to greet the twenty-year-old monarch and her equally young consort, Albert. Longing for a whiff of exotica to relieve the cares of stewardship, he had taken off for a brief visit to Istanbul.

In September of that year, Alfred Jacob Miller arrived to execute a series of grandiose canvases for his patron. By the following spring the drab stone walls of Murthly were brightened by scenes of the buffalo hunt, the trappers' rendez-vous, and the Turneresque splendor of Wind River lakes and gorges. Miller worked from the watercolor sketches he had done on the trail. Stewart, while no esthetician, may have sensed that in their movement and immediacy these smaller works were superior to the formal canvases. At any rate, he had them bound into a portfolio and proudly displayed them to his Murthly guests.

So Stewart sat in the cold confines of Murthly castle, basking in memories. Everywhere he turned he found something to remind him of his wild free life on the plains. But Miller's paintings, the buffalo and Douglas fir, and the constant presence of Antoine—gussied up in livery and trained, after a fashion, as a butler—instead of allaying his longing for the West, rather had the opposite effect. In his mid-forties now, he still had an itch to scratch. So, over his family's objections, he sold one of his three estates for the equivalent of $1 million. With the proceeds he paid off the debts inherited from his late brother and put the rest toward a resplendent return to America.

*   *   *

Stewart arrived in the United States in September 1842. After a brief stay in New York and Baltimore (where he commissioned more paintings from Miller), he proceeded to New Orleans. In the Crescent City he made the acquaintance of a cheerful young journalist named Matt Field, a feature writer for the New Orleans *Picayune* who wrote under the pen name "Phasma." Stewart invited Field along to chronicle the expedition and proposed to pay all his expenses. Although recently married and regretting the prospect of leaving his new wife for six months or longer, Field could hardly decline so generous an offer. In St. Louis on the eve of departure, he wrote home to assure his wife that all was well and that "I want for nothing, and shall want for nothing . . . for Sir William will do anything and everything for me."

Sir William's open-handedness was indeed hard to resist, but at least one person managed to regret with thanks his invitation to join the expedition. John James Audubon was staying in St. Louis at the time of Stewart's arrival, preparing for a trip up the Missouri under the aegis of the American Fur Company. His *Birds of America* completed at last, the great painter-naturalist was embarked, at age fifty-seven, on his first western trip to gather material for a portfolio on North American mammals. Audubon was by then an international celebrity, better known perhaps in Scotland and England than in his own country. Stewart would have been honored by his company and presumably wrote ahead from New Orleans extending an invitation, for Audubon called on the Scotsman the night of his arrival. He found Stewart at the Planter's House drying his clothes before the fire—his steamboat had hit a snag and sunk, the sort of hazard routinely faced by frontier travelers. Audubon recalled that his would-be host "was most anxious that we should join his party and offered us every kind of promises," including five mules and a wagon. But the celebrated artist demurred, concluding wisely that "he [Stewart] has too many people of too many sorts" accompanying him.

Sans Audubon, then, Stewart's motley band left St. Louis on May 2, bound up the Missouri as far as Westport, at the site of present-day Kansas City. Fortunately, most of the expedition supplies had been shipped ahead, for the *Weston* never made its destination; several days out, she caught fire and burned to the water's edge. Stewart and most of his party were ashore when the fire started and managed to catch the next west-bound steamer.

Arriving at Westport after a week's passage, they disembarked and pitched camp on the west bank of the river, in a grove of wild cherry and crab apple trees overlooking the sweeping Missouri. Matt Field christened their bivouac Camp William in honor of his patron, "from whom," he wrote to his wife, "I am receiving every courtesy and politeness." It was a tune he would later change.

Westport was the jumping-off place for the overland passage blazed by Ashley's men twenty years before and known by now as the Oregon Trail. Stewart must have viewed with a profound ambivalence the nearby encampment of some two hundred wagons and nine hundred emigrants—men, women, and children bound for Oregon along the route he had come to know so well during the previous decade. This was the first large party of emigrants to make the crossing, and historians would later refer to 1843 as the year of the Great Migration. Successive waves of settlers would soon follow, and by 1847 their annual numbers would reach nearly five thousand. By chance, encamped with the migrants were Stewart's old trail companions, the missionaries Jason Lee and Marcus Whitman. Sir William held these men in the highest regard, while recognizing that the very courage and determination he admired in them were ending forever the fabulous life he had known.

Manifest destiny presented itself in another conspicuous

form at Westport. Lieutenant John Charles Frémont, whom Stewart knew socially in St. Louis as the ambitious son-in-law of Senator Thomas Hart Benton, came through with a surveying party under the guidance of Tom Fitzpatrick and Kit Carson. Over the next fourteen months Frémont would traverse much of the West and emerge as a national hero, the "Pathfinder" whose maps of the region—the first really accurate ones—would serve a generation of emigrants on the passages to Oregon and California. Stewart and Frémont had discussed traveling together for part of the way, but the latter had set for himself a southerly route along the Kansas River, while the Scotsman stuck to his plans to move up the Platte.

Stewart and his party spent several weeks at Camp William, waiting for the prairie grass to thicken sufficiently to feed their horses during the crossing. Ensconced in his spacious crimson tent and waited on by three servants, Sir William presided over camp like a Bedouin sheik. A Persian carpet covered the ground, and his bed of buffalo robes was dressed with sheets of Irish linen and the skins of leopard, otter, and Russian sable. A Turkish incense burner provided the crowning touch of exotica.

The young men of the camp, meanwhile, found various ways to pass the time. They were in the country of the Shawnee, an eastern tribe pushed by white encroachment beyond the Missouri, and for entertainment they could look in on the Bread Dance and other rituals of a local band encamped close by. One night, accompanied by a flute, they waltzed and reeled around the campfire and capped the evening with a Shawnee war dance. On another occasion they staged a "piece of Shakespeare's in the regular Shakespearean style," according to a Savannah correspondent. The play was *Romeo and Juliet*, with a wagon for the balcony and a tin stable lantern for the moon. Matt Field, a Londoner by birth and a former professional actor, took the role of Romeo.

They struck camp during the last week in May, proceeding west through a waving ocean of big bluestem grass. Wildflowers—blackeyed susan, blazing star, aster, and compass plant—flecked this verdant ocean, which in its drier western parts receded into the shortgrass prairie of little bluestem and needlegrass. The gentleman travelers, restless from two weeks' idleness at Camp William, rejoiced at being underway at last. They wore flannel shirts and corduroy pants and rode with rifles astraddle, holstered pistols at the hip. Tucked in the bands of their wide felt hats were clay pipes, and in their belts hunting knives and combination tomahawk-pipes, a standard fur-trade item. Every dude supplied his own horse and man-servant and carried his supplies in red two-wheeled carts, one for every six men, drawn by two mules in tandem.

The mule skinners included Baptiste Charbonneau, the infant "Pompey" of the Lewis and Clark expedition, whom Stewart had probably encountered nine years earlier during his first foray into Crow country. By a "singular coincidence," noted William Clark Kennerly, the son of Sacajawea was headed west again, guiding the son of William Clark just as his mother had guided the Great Captains. Years later, when asked if Charbonneau spoke of his famous mother, Kennerly regretted to report that most of his words were profane ones directed against the recalcitrant mules in his charge.

It did not take long for the expedition to begin living up to its members' expectations for adventure. On guard duty one night, Kennerly fired at and chased off a pair of Osage horse-thieves. A few days later, Stewart personally faced down a posturing band of Osages, fresh scalps dripping from their lances, who were bent on kidnapping a trio of Pawnees riding with the caravan. At night the wagons were drawn into a circle for protection against attack; while Sir William retired to the privacy of his tent, the weary young adventurers dropped off to sleep exhausted beneath the spangled prairie sky. During the day they stood in wonderment at the fury of a prairie thunderstorm—then cursed the discomfort that followed in its wake. Here we sit, one of them lamented, beneath a leaky tent in two inches of rain, "dull, gloomy, weary, and cheerless in the last degrees" as they washed down soggy cracker crumbs with whiskey. "How lucky," another noted ruefully, "for people to have the faculty to fancy that misery is mirth, downright hardship nothing but fun, bitter privation lively amusement, and wild-goose wandering a pleasure excursion."

A pleasure excursion it surely was not, especially for a significant minority who rebelled at both the hardships of the trail and the military discipline imposed by their commander, the autocratic Captain Stewart. After several weeks they reached the forks of the Platte, where a minor mutiny broke out. Thirteen of the company called it quits and elected to turn back. On their return to St. Louis, a newspaper reported the dissident complaints of "fatigues attending the expedition and the overbearing rudeness of Sir William." Some of the company, the paper reported, "threatened to shoot him if he persisted in his tyrannical course."

Others who went the distance with Stewart, however, would later come to his defense. Military discipline was an absolute necessity, and the leader of a caravan on the prairie ocean carried the same responsibility (and authority) as the captain of a ship at sea. A young man named Cyprien Menard forgot this at his peril when, crossing the arid reach between the South and North branches of the Platte, he rode off on his own to find water, disobeying Stewart's strict orders that the caravan stay together. He soon lost his bearings and subsequently his horse, coat, boots, and blanket as he wandered four days in the wilderness. "Every soul of us had given him up as butchered by the Sioux," Field reported, "when he was at length fortunately found," barefoot and exhausted, his ammunition gone, cooking a terrapin in its shell.

There was great rejoicing at finding the lost greenhorn, and shortly afterward their collective spirits were buoyed even higher when they encountered, east of the Laramie Range, their first large herds of buffalo—a sight, Kennerly remarked, "which might well have gladdened the heart of Sir William, who had come four thousand miles to shoot them." The young bloods lost no time in plunging into the primordial prairie experience of the bison run. In Kennerly's account, the horses

> fell readily into the excitement of the chase and seemed to enjoy dashing along beside the shaggy monsters until we could reach over and put the muzzles of our guns almost to the buffalo's shoulders. When one was out of the running, the race was kept up and another singled out, and so on until the prairie was strewn for miles back with the bodies of the dead bison. I must say that a great many more buffalo were destroyed than was necessary to supply our larder, but what man would resist the temptation when the whole earth, it seemed, was a surging, tumbling, waving mass of these animals?

In butchering, they favored only the choicest parts. The meat stripped from along the backbone weighed about eighty pounds, Kennerly estimated, and "together with the tongue and hump, represented the meat taken from a buffalo weighing from fifteen hundred to two thousand pounds; so you may readily understand from this that there was some waste."

When buffalo covered the plains to the limits of vision, however, no one could feel much guilt about their casual slaughter. One morning later in the trip, while preparing for the daily hunt, they gasped at the sight of an approaching herd that in their estimate easily numbered a million. The party was in literal danger of being driven into the Platte, a consequence "averted only by our exerting every effort to turn them off in another direction; and as it took the herd two entire days to pass, even at quite a rapid gait, we were kept busy placing guards of shouting, gesticulating men in the daytime and building huge bonfires at night."

The presence of buffalo gave "our most famous hunter, Antoine Clement" a chance to show off his skills to the pack of greenhorns. In Kennerly's eyes, Antoine was "the most fearless man I ever saw—the only one who would walk straight up to a grizzly bear" and fire at it at point-blank range. On a buffalo hunt one morning, Kennerly recalled, Antoine shot a bull through the shoulder and, thinking the animal dead, was preparing to butcher it when the beast came suddenly to life. Instinctively, Antoine grabbed its tail. Man and beast went round and round in a furious prairie dance, with Antoine cursing and shouting for his companion, a gentleman named John Radford, to shoot. But Radford couldn't shoot from laughing. The buffalo spun like a dervish while Antoine, hanging on for his life and "shouting oaths and imprecations" in French and broken English, at last managed to free his hunting knife and hamstring the beast. With his adversary finally immobilized, the hunter turned his rage on Radford and threatened to kill him, "and it was only after many apologies and explanations on John's part that Antoine was prevented from following his inclination."

(Kennerly's story bears passing resemblance, of course, to Miller's account of Antoine's dance at the nether end of a buffalo back in 1837. Antoine seems to have had better control

Wind River Country. *Miller's landscape may be "Lake Stewart,"
which was later renamed Fremont Lake.*

of the situation then, but he had been absent from the prairie
for five years now and was perhaps out of practice—or simply
getting old.)

Sated with slaughtering buffalo and weary from more than a
month on the trail, the party rested east of Laramie's Fork and
prepared to celebrate the Fourth of July in a grand fashion. A
retired English peddler named Storer, who somehow found
himself in the expedition, spent three days fixing a glorious
plum pudding, raiding Sir William's larder for the necessary
fruits and spices and substituting buffalo marrow for suet.
Others, meanwhile, stitched together a passable rendering of
Old Glory from red silk handkerchiefs, white bandaging, blue
calico, and gold-braided hat tassles. When reveille exploded
with a burst of gunfire on Independence Day morning, the

45

response was immediate—those still slumbering leapt from their blankets and grabbed their rifles on the assumption that Sioux were attacking. But it was only a twenty-six gun salute in honor of the twenty-six states of the Union.

General mayhem followed. The boys fired their guns and danced under the makeshift Stars and Stripes floating beneath the cerulean sky. Wine and juleps lubricated spirits further, although Stewart prudently ordered half the group to stay sober as a caution against Indians. A banquet of sorts capped off the day as the rollicking crew assembled cross-legged on the ground before an oil cloth spread, as Matt Field described, with "buffalo hump ribs, buffalo side ribs, buffalo tongues, buffalo marrow bones, buffalo 'sweetbreads,' and buffalo *et ceteras*"— topped off, of course, by Storer's magnificent pudding. To keep the evening on an elevated plane, Field recited some verse he had composed for the occasion, and in honor of their host they joined in singing, to the tune of the British national anthem, another of Matt's *oeuvres* titled "God Save the Brave."

Ignoring as best they could their wretched hangovers, the party broke camp the next morning and continued on to Fort Laramie, where they spent several days preparing for the final leg of the journey. Elders of a Sioux band camping nearby were astonished at the physical resemblance of red-haired Jeff Clark to his famous father. A select group consisting of Clark, Stewart, and several others were hosted by the chiefs at a sumptuous banquet of chokecherries, bitterroots, and boiled dog—the last item a *piece de resistance*, Kennerly recalled, that he respectfully declined.

After its brief rest, the caravan moved up the Platte and the Sweetwater, past emigrant landmarks like Independence Rock and the Devil's Gate to South Pass and into the Green River Valley, beyond the Continental Divide. It was during this phase of the journey that the expedition suffered its single fatality when Antoine Clement's younger brother, fifteen-year-old Francois, accidently shot himself while pulling a loaded rifle from his tent. The boy was laid to rest in a simple but touching ceremony, with his bier dressed in wildflowers and Matt Field reading another of his poems over the deceased. An itinerant priest who had accompanied the caravan from Westport provided last rites.

On the same day that Francois died, they encountered a trading party returning to St. Louis from the Rockies, led by Louis Vasquez ("Old Vaskiss") and Joe Walker, venerable mountain men whose grizzled, familiar faces must have gladdened Stewart's heart. Both were age forty-five—three years younger than Sir William—but looked much older after two decades in the mountains. Field found Walker "a fine old mountaineer—hale, stout-built, and eagle-eyed"—and took to him as readily as had Miller six years before.

After crossing the Continental Divide the party cut north, skirting the west flank of the Wind Rivers until arriving in the lake region that had been the scene of so many idylls for Sir William in summers past. They set up camp along the shore of "Lake Stewart," whose name went back at least to the summer when Miller had painted it. (Today it is called Fremont Lake.) One of the correspondents found the lake "full of fine trout easily caught," its limpid water tinged with green along the shore and receding to a fathomless indigo at the center. This pristine setting stirred the young men to the depths of their romantic souls, prompting Kennerly to recite from Sir Walter Scott's "The Lady of the Lake," while others poured forth with renderings of various romantic poets as well as Homer, Milton, and Shakespeare. They spent five sylvan days here, catching trout and chasing elk and bighorn sheep on forays into the surrounding alpine meadows, or simply basking in the sun and scenery while floating on the lake in Stewart's inflatable rubber boat. Their montane interlude was punctuated by a visit, at Stewart's invitation, of a band of Snake Indians and a party of trappers that included Sir William's old messmates, Markhead and Black Harris. The reunion put everyone in a celebratory mood, and a kind of mini-rendezvous ensued replete with drinking, racing, wenching, and gambling.

Kennerly took time out from the revelry to stand for measurements by an Indian seamstress, who produced from antelope hide a fancy fringed outfit. He paraded proudly in his new vestments, but the tanning job (which he had done himself) proved unequal to the skillful tailoring. During the first rain, he found, the breeches "began to stretch, and down, down they came over my feet until I was obliged to draw my knife and keep cutting them off every little while. Then, when the sun came out, they began to shrink, continuing to do so until I found myself in short trunks which would have been just the thing for swimming."

They could not, alas, linger longer in the mountains. The nightly frosts and bitterly cold mornings were reminders that winter was coming on fast. Stewart's biographers have suggested the emotions he must have felt the morning of August 17, at "the moment of farewell to a place and a way of life that had fulfilled some deep need within him," a place he would never see or experience again.

The greenhorns had a different attitude. "We have spent 12 days roving about among the famous 'Andes of the West,' " Field exalted, "and now, hurrah!—for two months travel homeward!" As they rode forth from the granite-walled emerald valley, everybody seemed "glad of the move except, perhaps, our friends, the trappers and Indians. We crossed the creek, exchanging parting salutations with the mountain people winding up an opposite hill, and then turned our faces full east, our minds spontaneously filling with thick and enlivening fancies of home."

The young men had to temper their eagerness when a squaw in the party, the wife of a hunter, gave birth on the trail. Hoots of disbelief and general grousing greeted Stewart's decision to tarry several days while the woman recovered. Longing for his wife in New Orleans, Matt Field grumbled loudest of all. *"His omnipotence,"* he slashed in his diary, "in his wisdom has ordered camp *to lay by* on this account. It is, at any rate the first occasion ever known of a mountain journey being delayed *one hour* for such a reason! All the camp swearing at the Old Man—this is the second day now lost to blind and bad management." But Stewart, ever the responsible officer, seems only to have been looking out for the welfare of his command, for the squaw had suffered complications in the birthing and might have died if forced to travel too soon. Stewart paid the Baltimore doctor who presided fourteen dollars for his services.

By September 10 they had reached Fort Laramie. To the exasperation of many of the homesick greenhorns, the caravan dallied another week while Stewart, bidding his leisurely farewell to the West, entertained himself in the company of the Sioux and Pawnee encamped outside the gates. At one point he displayed to a group of Brûlé Sioux the latest in the white man's medicine, an "electrifying machine." The box-like device consisted of a powerful acid battery and metal handles that sent a hair-raising current through anyone grasping them. Field couldn't resist an elaborate conceit when describing the reaction of eight Sioux who held each other's arms to form a closed circuit with the magic box: "The Bull roared, the Dog howled, Little Thunder rumbled, Grey Eyes twinkled, the Flying Bird fluttered, Ni-to-kee (the untranslatable) looked indescribable and the Causes of Eclipses blushed blue at finding himself eclipsed!"

When the party at last got underway again, some of the more impatient members broke off to travel ahead of the main group, while Stewart continued at his maddeningly slow pace. By the end of October they were all back in St. Louis, and any animosities felt toward their autocratic captain were soon forgotten. Kennerly's parents gave Stewart a farewell dinner at the family estate of Persimmon Hill. One can imagine the toasts, the hearty applause, and the singing of Auld Lang Syne. "Sir William was a mighty hunter and prince among sportsmen," Kennerly recalled fondly in old age. "So I will finish this narrative with a toast to his memory: Wherever he may be, good hunting!"

RUXTON'S COUNTRY, 1846

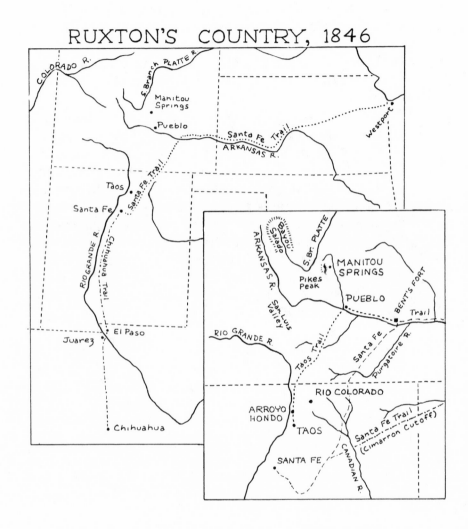

5

Ruxton of the Rockies

George F. Ruxton, the English traveler, with two men, here joined our party. Mr. R. was a quiet, good-looking man, with a handsome moustache. He conversed well, but sparingly, speaking little of himself. He has passed over the burning sands of Africa, penetrated the jungles of India, jogged on patient mule through the Tierra Caliente *of Mexico, and laid down amid the snowdrifts of the Rocky Mountains.*
> —Lewis H. Garrard,
> *Wah-to-yah and the Taos Trail*

SIR WILLIAM returned home to Scotland and the baronial confines of Murthly Castle to take up, once and for all, his family responsibilities. The West he had known would linger in his imagination for the remaining twenty-eight years of his life, however. Drawing on those memories, he set to work almost immediately on a romantic novel of plains life, the first of two that he would write. Stewart's *Altowan* appeared in 1846 and was followed eight years later by *Edward Warren*. Both are terrible novels, written in an impenetrable style and shackled by romantic conventions, and whatever popularity they may have enjoyed would have been due to their exotic subject matter, rather than the awkward way in which the author presented it.

Victorian readers would gain a far more vivid and perceptive impression of western life from a book published in London a year after *Edward Warren*. Its author was a remarkable young man named George Frederick Ruxton, whose *Adventures in Mexico and the Rocky Mountains* describes a journey of two thousand miles from the Mexican port of Vera Cruz to Santa Fe and beyond into the rich beaver country of the Bayou Salado, in the broad valley of the upper South Platte River in what is now central Colorado. Ruxton wrote with great clarity, skill, and enthusiasm, and his observations of the Mexican-American frontier at the close of the trappers' era rank among the classic narratives of the early West.

Ruxton traveled with ragged Mexican auxiliaries or in the company of former mountain men who had married Mexican women and settled down as traders, guides, or distillers of a wheat-based firewater called Taos lightning. Better perhaps than any other writer, he caught the flavor of the mountain man, his patois, and his world, and in the process captured the imagination of his Victorian readers. "It is not often," observed a contemporary reviewer, "that one meets with a hand equally practiced with the long rifle, bowie knife and Colt's revolver and at the same time so apt with the pen." Among Ruxton's memorable descriptions was that of the trappers' rendezvous, that bacchanalian scene of "drunkenness, gambling, brawling, and fighting."

Seated, Indian fashion, round the fires, with a blanket spread before them, groups are seen with their "decks" of cards, playing euker, poker, and seven-up, the regular mountain games. The stakes are "beaver," which here is current coin; and when the fur is gone, their *breeches*, are staked. Daring gamblers make the rounds of the camp, challenging each other to play for the trapper's highest stakes—his horse, his squaw (if he have one), and, as once happened, his scalp. "There goes hos and beaver!" is the mountain expression when any great loss is sustained; and sooner or later, "hos and beaver" invariably find their way into the insatiable pockets of the traders.

Reading Ruxton's account, it is easy to overlook that the mountains had seen their last rendezvous five years before the young Englishman set foot in them. A variety of circumstances—the decline of the beaver from overtrapping, new methods of felting using furs other than beaver, and the passing from fashion of beaver hats in favor of those made of silk—had conspired to end the brief, extraordinary era on which the legend of the mountain man was built. Ruxton's descriptions, then, are to a certain extent reconstructions, and accordingly their vividness is all the more remarkable.

By his arrival in Mexico in the summer of 1846, Ruxton had already packed a lifetime of adventure into his twenty-five years. Like Stewart, he possessed a restless energy that lent itself to a peripatetic life. The third son of a British army surgeon, he enrolled at age thirteen at Sandhurst, the British military academy, where his principal pursuits seem to have been drinking, smoking, snaring rabbits on nearby moors, and devouring The Leatherstocking Tales of Fenimore Cooper. Two years later he was expelled for rowdiness and was soon off to fight as a mercenary in the Spanish war of succession. In his zeal to join in the fray, Ruxton seems not to have cared especially which side he fought on, and it was almost as an after-thought that he took up arms for the Royalists. He campaigned two years in Spain, was decorated for gallantry, and returned to England in 1839 at about the time of his eighteenth birth-day, a veteran combatant itching for more adventure.

Back home, Ruxton was commissioned an ensign in a regi-ment posted first to Ireland and then to Canada, where he spent three happy years hunting deer, wild turkey, and upland birds among the Chippewa Indians in the wilderness north of Lake Erie. "The gun had ever been my delight," he wrote in his notebook, "and my *ardor venandi* had been worked up to the highest pitch by reading the adventures of Natty Bumppo and his friends the Mohegans in the admirable romances of Cooper. I had always longed to pull a trigger in the woods of America, and now the opportunity had arrived." Predisposed toward Indians by Cooper's narratives, Ruxton lamented the sorry state of those tribes debased by civilization but was pleased to find the Hurons in northern Canada living "as primitively as in the days when the Leatherstocking and the Mohegan chief followed the Mingo Trail in the woods of the Susquehanna."

In October 1843 Ruxton sold his commission and, following a winter hunt in Upper Michigan and Ontario, returned home the following spring. His restlessness took him next to South-ern Africa, where his rather haphazard plans to become the first man to cross the continent were frustrated by a lack of cooperation from coastal missionaries who controlled access to the interior. So it was back to England to try, unsuccessfully, to enlist support for a second African expedition.

In the spring of 1846 his attentions shifted to the Western Hemisphere, where deteriorating relations between Mexico and the United States burst into hostilities along the Rio Grande. By July 2 he was bound for Vera Cruz as a representative of British commercial and diplomatic interests to observe the war and to assist as necessary any British subjects caught in the crossfire. With his fluency in Spanish, his military experience, and above all his intelligence, energy, and enthusiasm, he was the perfect man for the mission.

The war had been underway for months by the time of Ruxton's arrival, and it was not going well for Mexico. South of the Rio Grande, Zachary Taylor was marching toward Buena Vista and a decisive victory over a Mexican army that outnumbered him four to one. In California, meanwhile, American irregulars under the command of John Charles Frémont occupied San Francisco and Los Angeles. (Fortuitously for his vaulting ambition, Frémont was leading a cartographic expedition in northern California when the Bear Flag Rebellion broke out, and he lost no time in seizing the opportunity for glory.)

Reeling from these twin thrusts of Manifest Destiny, a desperate Mexican government allowed back from exile the discredited Santa Anna, who disembarked with his young wife at Vera Cruz at about the same time as Ruxton. Observing the former presidente's less-than-triumphal procession through the grimy streets, the Englishman noted that the erstwhile "Napoleon of the West" and victor at the Alamo appeared "a hale-looking man between fifty and sixty, with an Old Bailey countenance and a very well built wooden leg."

> The Senora, a pretty girl of seventeen, pouted at the cool reception, for not one *viva* was heard; and her mother, a fat, vulgar old dame, was rather unceremoniously congeed from the procession, which she took in high dudgeon. The General was dressed in full uniform, and looked anything but pleased at the absence of everything like applause, which he doubtless expected would have greeted him. His countenance completely betrays his

character: indeed, I never saw a physiognomy in which the evil passions, which he notoriously possesses, were more strongly marked. Oily duplicity, treachery, avarice, and sensuality are depicted in every feature.

Ruxton's description, while probably accurate, betrays a strong Anglo-Saxon bias, for in his travels he found almost nothing good to say about Mexicans or their country. As a people, he wrote, they rank "decidedly low in the scale of humanity." He could not wait to get out of Vera Cruz, a pestilential city whose rank streets were strewn with garbage picked over by buzzards, and on the journey overland to Mexico City he noted ruefully the many crosses marking roadside murders. For his own protection against Mexico's infamous highwaymen he brandished a double-barrelled rifle and carbine, a shotgun, and four revolvers. A local *bandito* took one glance at this imposing arsenal and galloped off as fast as his horse would take him.

Ruxton outfitted for the rest of his journey in Mexico City, where he purchased Panchito, a noble steed who would serve him faithfully across two thousand miles of hostile territory and through a winter encampment in the Rockies. Hostility toward *los gringos* was running high in the Mexican capital, and his blond hair and blue eyes stood out like sentinels. In a cantina one night, although dressed in native garb and speaking flawless Spanish, he was singled out by the surly crowd as a *Tejano, Yanqui, burro*—a Texan, Yankee, jackass. But the self-possessed young Englishman quickly defused the situation, rising with hand on heart to declare himself no Yankee but *Yngles, muy amigo a la republica* and to offer a round of *pulque*, the flower-based native firewater. The Mexicans raised a toast to their fair-haired friend and saluted him with cries of *Viva los Yngles!* It was the first of several incidents in which Ruxton would display the quintessentially elegant form of courage that Hemingway called grace under pressure.

From Mexico City, Ruxton traveled across the central Mexican plateau to El Paso, some twelve hundred miles north on the Rio Grande. At one point he lost all his baggage plus three thousand dollars to thieves who broke into his room in the village of Guajoquilla, where he was staying. Fortunately,

Mexican hospitality saved the day when the local prefect, embarrassed by the robbery, tracked down the thieves and ordered them stretched on the rack until they revealed where the booty was cached. "My servant, who witnessed the operation, said it was beautiful to see the prefect screwing a confession out of them . . . until every muscle of the body and limbs was in a frightful state of tension, and the bones almost dislocated. At length they divulged where one trunk was concealed, and then another, and after two or three faintings, one article after another was brought to light."

Lawlessness and barbarity seemed as indigenous to this country as rattlesnakes and mesquite. Entering Chihuahua, Ruxton noted grimly the scalps of recently slaughtered Apaches hanging from the city's portals. Indians and Mexicans were in a continual state of war, with neither side granting any quarter. This particular atrocity had occurred during a brief truce, when a band of Apaches came unarmed into a village to trade and was set upon by a battery of thugs led by a murderous Irishman and former trapper named James Kirker.

> The infuriated Mexicans spared neither age nor sex; with fiendish shouts they massacred their unresisting victims, glutting their long pent-up revenge of many years of persecution. One woman, big with child, rushed into the church, clasping the alter and crying for mercy for herself and unborn babe. She was followed, and fell pierced with a dozen lances; and then—it is almost impossible to conceive such an atrocity, but I had it from an eyewitness on the spot not two months after the tragedy—the child was torn alive from the yet palpitating body of its mother, first plunged into the holy water to be baptized, and immediately its brains were dashed out against a wall.
>
> A hundred and sixty men, women, and children were slaughtered, and, with the scalps carried on poles, Kirker's party entered Chihuahua—in procession, headed by the Governor and priests, with bands of music escorting them in triumph to the town.

Ruxton noted that American traders had been known to act just as savagely against the Indians, and in partial defense of the Mexicans' actions he emphasized that the Apaches "equal their more civilized enemies in barbarity."

The Indians in this desolate region had never been subdued, and they were taking advantage now of the state of near anarchy brought on by the recent invasion of northern Mexico by United States troops. The pathetic inhabitants of Chihuahua and Durango were set upon not only by Apaches but by marauding Comanches, who each fall, like riders out of the Apocalypse, swept down from Texas in fierce raids of devastation and plunder. "So regular are these expeditions that in the Comanche calendar the month of September is known as the 'Mexico moon,' as the other months are designated the buffalo moon, the young bear moon, the corn moon, &c."

Beyond the city of Durango, Ruxton encountered a heavily armed wagon train of traders who had just passed through Comanche territory. They shook their heads in disbelief when the Englishman told them of his determination, despite their warnings, to proceed to Santa Fe, and they were even more incredulous when they learned that he was making the journey for his own amusement. "I thought then, and ever since," one of them would recall, "that no man of common sense who had any knowledge of Indian character, would think of taking such a trip, with such an outfit, for pleasure."

*   *   *

Although appalled by the lawlessness of its human denizens, Ruxton the naturalist and sportsman took bountiful pleasure in the country's wild creatures. Chihuahua's rugged mountains supported grizzly bear and bighorn sheep, as well as elk, deer, and even beaver, while the plains abounded with antelope. He delighted in all aspects of the fauna, from the biggest game to birds, reptiles, and insects. He counted seventy-five varieties of grasshoppers and locusts, "some of enormous size and most brilliant and fantastic colours," and noted with particular fascination a six-inch-long creature that was perfectly camouflaged to resemble a blade of grass carried by ants. The Mexicans informed him that "if horses or mules swallow these insects, they invariably die."

Ruxton struck the Rio Grande at El Paso, a sleepy settlement at a bend in the river where wine grapes were cultivated and whose inhabitants, as elsewhere in northern Mexico, were in a constant state of siege against marauding Apaches. Ruxton noted too that American settlers to the north, many of them former trappers, disguised themselves as Indians and joined in the plunder.

For self-defense the people of El Paso had organized themselves into troops of *auxiliares*, a rag-tag militia that insisted on escorting Ruxton when he left town, bound up the Rio Grande for Santa Fe. To have marched through Coventry with them, he observed, "would have broken the heart of Sir John Falstaff. . . . Armed with bows and arrows, lances, and rusty *escopetas*, and mounted on miserable horses, their appearance was anything but warlike."

Midway between El Paso and Santa Fe he encountered his first large contingent of Americans. A trading caravan encamped in a grove of cottonwoods along the river presented a "picturesque appearance" with its "tents and shanties of logs and branches of every conceivable form, round which lounged wild-looking Missourians, some cooking at the campfires, some cleaning their rifles or firing at targets—blazes cut in the trees, with a bull's eye made with wet powder on the white bark. From morning till night the camp resounded with the popping of rifles, firing at marks for prizes of tobacco, or at any living creature which presented itself."

Ruxton found American troops bivouacked several miles farther up river, and as a spit-and-polish military man he was both amazed and appalled by the appearance of their camp. No one, he wrote, "would have imagined this to be a military encampment. The tents were in a line, but there all uniformity ceased. There were no regulations in force with regard to cleanliness. The camp was strewn with the bones and offal of the cattle slaughtered for its supply, and not the slightest attention was paid to keeping it clean from other accumulations of filth. The men, unwashed and unshaven, were ragged and dirty, without uniforms, and dressed as, and how, they pleased. They wandered about, listless and sickly looking, or were sitting in groups playing at cards, and swearing and cursing, even at the officers if they interfered to stop it."

Ruxton allowed for the bravery of an American in battle but concluded that he "can never be made a soldier; his constitution will not bear the restraint of discipline, neither will his very mistaken notions about liberty allow him to subject himself to its necessary control."

In late December, after five months and two thousand miles on the trail, he arrived at last in "miserable mud-built Santa Fe," which had recently been taken by American forces under General Stephen Kearney representing "the dirtiest, rowdiest crew I have ever seen collected together." The town, whose founding by the Spanish in 1610 made it one of the oldest settlements in North America, was the terminus of two of the West's legendary trade routes: the ancient Chihuahua Trail leading south to the gold and silver mines of northern Mexico, and the Santa Fe Trail east to Missouri. While a few families lived grandly off the trade, most of the region's citizenry subsisted in abject poverty. Having suffered two centuries of neglect under Spanish and lately Mexican rule, they were now forced to contend with the "bullying and overbearing demeanor" of the *Yanqui* invaders. A year after Ruxton's arrival they rose up against their conquerers and murdered American governor Charles Bent at his home in Taos, where Ruxton journeyed after leaving Santa Fe. But the rebellion was quickly put down, and with the quashing of final resistance the United States took possession of a vast territory stretching from Texas to the Pacific and north to Oregon. The loss reduced Mexico's territory by half.

Ruxton's attitude toward the resident New Mexicans resembled Swift's toward the Irish: a mixture of sympathy and contempt. Departing Taos for Rio Colorado (today's Red River), he hired a half-breed Pueblo Indian as a guide, "one of the most rascally-looking of rascally Mexicans," who promptly lost his way through deep mountain snows. They were on the verge of freezing to death when taken in by a measles-ridden Mexican family. Ruxton gratefully acknowledged their hospitality, which saved his life, but he demurred when offered a bubbling potion of "rattlesnake oil" brewed by an ancient crone as a cure for their disease. The name was just a joke, she assured him with a cackle, but he was not persuaded to change his mind.

"No state of society can be more wretched or degrading than the social and moral condition of the inhabitants of New Mexico," he wrote. And the people of Rio Colorado represented "the *ne plus ultra* of misery." They lived at the mercy of the Ute

Indians or Yutas, "who actually tolerate their presence in their country for the sole purpose of having at their command a stock of grain and a herd of mules and horses" for stealing. Moreover, Ruxton observed, "when a war expedition against a hostile tribe has failed, and no scalps have been secured to ensure the returning warriors a welcome to their village, the Rio Colorado is a kind of game preserve, where the Yutas have a certainty of filling their bag if their other covers draw a blank. Here they can always depend upon procuring a few brace of Mexican scalps, when such trophies are required for a war dance or other festivity, without danger to themselves, and merely for the trouble of fetching them."

It was in Rio Colorado that he encountered his first mountain man, an old French Canadian named Laforet, who put him up for several days while he recovered from frostbite. His host—one of the many trappers "who are found in these remote settlements, with Mexican wives, and passing the close of their adventurous lives in what seem to them a state of ease and plenty"—spoke a hopelessly mixed argot of French, English, and Spanish. *"Sacré enfant de Gârce,"* he exclaimed, lamenting for the thousandth time his lack of coffee, *"voyez-vous* dat I vas nevare tan pauvre as dis time; mais before I vas siempre avec plenty café, plenty sucre; mais now, God dam, I not go a Santa Fe, God dam, and mountain men dey come aqui from autre côté, drink all my café."

Laforet was part of a loose colony of trappers who worked the southern Rockies during the beaver era of the 1820s and '30s, trading their pelts in Santa Fe and venturing on occasion as far north as Green River to partake in the festivities of the rendezvous. Ruxton cast a cold eye on these "white Indians" and found much in them to admire: "Strong, active, hardy as bears, daring, expert in the use of their weapons, they are just what uncivilized white man might be supposed to be in a brute state."

Not a hole or corner in the vast wilderness of the Far West but has been ransacked by these hardy men. From the Mississippi to the mouth of the Colorado of the West, from the frozen regions of the North to the Gila River in Mexico, the beaver hunter has set his traps in every creek and stream. All this vast country, but for the daring enterprise of these men, would be even now a terra incognita to geographers, as indeed a great portion still is; but there is not an acre that has not been passed and repassed by the trappers in their perilous excursions. The mountains and streams still retain the names assigned to them by the rude hunters; and these alone are the hardy pioneers who have paved the way for the settlement of the Western country.

With feelings throughout New Mexico running so high against Americans, Ruxton had a hard time of it during his convalescence in Rio Colorado. The local Mexicans recognized him as an Anglo without distinguishing between nationalities, and they hurled epithets and occasional brickbats at him whenever he ventured beyond the protection of Laforet's cabin. As soon as his frostbite subsided he packed his mules and headed north, escorted out of the squalid settlement by his friend, who with a last "God dam" and *enfant de Gârce* warned his young charge to mind his scalp in the mountains. From the crest of a ridge, Ruxton bid an " *Adios, Mejico!"* and surveyed the wilderness before him.

I had now turned my back on the last settlement, and felt a thrill of pleasure as I looked at the wild expanse of snow which lay before me, and the towering mountains which frowned on all sides, and knew that now I had seen the last—for some time at least—of civilized man under the garb of a Mexican sarape.

*   *   *

It was the dead of winter as Ruxton, mounted on his faithful Panchito and leading a string of pack mules in the company of his half-breed guide, descended into the San Luis Valley in what is now south central Colorado. He faced the Rockies at their violent worst: the unspeakable cold froze his hands, and fierce blizzard winds ripped away his bedroll and buried him in snow. He would never forget one night in particular, "marked with the blackest of stones in the memoranda of my journeyings," when the mules groaned and wolves howled on the wind beyond his coccoon of snow. Only the heat of his pipe—an outsized model cut from cottonwood bark and holding a fistful of tobacco—kept him alive, and he smoked it until the bowl itself caught fire and burned to the stem.

Yet Ruxton seemed less to suffer from these conditions than to revel in them. He exalted in the fierce beauty of the mountains and in the game that abounded there. Riding into one valley, they encountered "innumerable herds" of pronghorn antelope. "These graceful animals, in bands containing several thousands, trotted up to us, and with pointed ears and their beautiful eyes staring with eager curiosity, accompanied us for miles, running parallel to our trail within fifty or sixty yards."

Ruxton's observations on western wildlife reveal the fascination of a born naturalist and the skill of a great descriptive writer. "The sagacity of wolves is almost incredible," he wrote. "They will remain round a hunting camp and follow the hunter the whole day, in bands of three or four, at less than a hundred yards' distance, stopping when they stop, and sitting down quietly when game is killed, rushing to devour the offal when the hunter retires, and then following until another feed is offered them."

> If a deer or antelope is wounded, they immediately pursue it, and not infrequently pull the animal down in time for the hunter to come up and secure it from their ravenous clutches. However, they appear to know at once the nature of the wound, for if but slightly touched they never exert themselves to follow a deer, chasing those only which have received a mortal blow.
>
> I one day killed an old buck which was so poor that I left the carcase on the ground untouched. Six coyotes, or small prairie wolves, were my attendants that day, and of course, before I had left the deer twenty paces, had commenced their work of destruction. Certainly not ten minutes after, I looked back and saw the six loping after me, one of them not twenty yards behind me, with his nose and face all besmeared with blood, and his belly swelled almost to bursting. Thinking it scarcely possible that they could have devoured the whole deer in so short a space, I had the curiosity to return, and, to my astonishment, found nothing left but a pile of bones and hair, the flesh being stripped from them as clean as if scraped with a knife.

Ruxton regarded the bighorn sheep as the "game par excellence of the Rocky Mountains." Their sight and smell was better than a deer's, he said, and "as they love to resort to the highest and most inaccessible spots, whence a view can readily be had of approaching danger, and particularly as one of the band is always stationed on the most commanding pinnacle of rock as sentinel, whilst the others are feeding, it is no easy matter to get within rifleshot of the cautious animals. When alarmed they ascend still higher up the mountain; halting now and then on some overhanging crag and looking down at the object which may have frightened them, they again commence their ascent, leaping from point to point and throwing down an avalanche of rocks and stones as they bound up the steep sides of the mountain."

He also ran across buffalo in the mountains, wintering in small groups in the sheltered subalpine meadows, and later in the year he hunted them on the open prairies. Ruxton noted that the buffalo were already in decline along the Arkansas River where it paralleled the Santa Fe Trail. While lamenting their "wholesale destruction" by the hunters, given their seemingly boundless numbers he felt comfortable in prophesizing that "many years must elapse before this lordly animal becomes extinct." No animal, he declared, "requires so much killing as a buffalo. Unless shot through the lungs or spine, they invariably escape; and, even when mortally wounded, or even struck throgh the very heart, they will frequently run a considerable distance before falling to the ground, particularly if they see the hunter after the wound is given."

"It is a most painful sight," Ruxton added, "to witness the dying struggles of the huge beast."

A bull, shot through the heart or lungs, with blood streaming from his mouth, and protruding tongue, his eyes rolling, bloodshot, and glazed with death, braces himself on his legs, swaying from side to side, stamps impatiently at his growing weakness, or lifts his rugged and matted head and helplessly bellows out his conscious impotence. To the last, however, he endeavours to stand upright and plants his limbs farther apart, but to no purpose. As the body rolls like a ship at sea, his head slowly turns from side to side, looking about, as it were, for the unseen and treacherous enemy who brought him, the lord of the plains, to such a pass. Gouts of purple blood spurt from his mouth and nostrils, and gradually the failing limbs refuse longer to support the ponderous carcase; more heavily rolls the body from side to side, until suddenly, for a brief instant, it becomes rigid and still; a convulsive tremor seizes it, and, with a low, sobbing gasp, the huge animal falls over on his side, the limbs extended stark and stiff, the mountain of flesh without life or motion.

William Drummond Stewart poses by the cow buffalo he has shot as Indians take the favored hump rib. Ruxton found buffalo hunting "too wholesale a business to afford much sport."

Although an avid hunter, Ruxton killed only for meat and looked askance at the casual shooting of buffalo by travelers on the plains. "As might be inferred, such gigantic sporting soon degenerates into mere butchery. Indeed, setting aside the excitement of a chase on horseback, buffalo hunting is too wholesale a business to afford much sport—that is, on the prairies; but in the mountains, where they are met with in small bands, and require no little trouble and expertness to find and kill, and where one may hunt for days without discovering more than one band of half a dozen, it is then an exciting and noble sport."

Sport of another sort was practiced on buffalo by the mountain men whom Ruxton came to know at Pueblo, a trappers' settlement on the upper Arkansas. His account of the mountain man's gastronomic jousting was sufficiently graphic for one of his more squeamish editors to expurgate it. On slaughtering a cow," Ruxton wrote, "the hunter carefully lays by, as a titbit for himself, the 'boudins' and medullary intestine," which he prepared by partially cleaning and lightly charring over a fire.

I once saw two Canadians commence at either end of such a coil of grease, the mess lying between them on a dirty apishamore like the coil of a huge snake. As yard after yard glided glibly down their throats, and the serpent on the saddlecloth was dwindling from an anaconda to a moderate-sized rattlesnake, it became a great point with each of the feasters to hurry his operation, so as to gain a march upon his neighbour, and improve the opportunity by swallowing more than his just proportion; each, at the same time, exhorting the other, whatever he did, to feed fair, and every now and then, overcome by the unblushing attempts of his partner to bolt a vigorous mouthful would suddenly jerk back his head, drawing out at the same moment, by the retreating motion, several yards of boudin from his neighbour's mouth and stomach—for the greasy viand required no mastication, and was bolted whole—and, snapping up himself the ravished portions, greedily swallowed them; to be in turn again withdrawn and subjected to a similar process by the other.

The mountain men with whom Ruxton passed the winter in

Pueblo included Markhead, the old trail companion of William Drummond Stewart. The trapper was celebrated throughout the Rockies "for his courage and reckless daring," Ruxton noted, and his body carried innumerable bullet scars from skirmishes with Indians. Ruxton heard from the source himself the story of Markhead taking the scalp of the thief who ran off with Stewart's horse. He considered hiring Markhead as his guide on a trip to the Columbia River, but as matters turned out he never had the chance to employ his services. Markhead went south to Taos to trade pelts for whiskey and was caught up in the rebellion of native New Mexicans against the *Yanqui* invaders. He was captured and shot in the back, then stripped, scalped and castrated, and his body left to the wolves.

From Pueblo, Ruxton journeyed north up Fountainhead Creek to pass some time alone at Manitou Springs, beneath the looming presence of Pike's Peak. He found game abundant in the sheltered valley—"Never was there such a paradise for hunters as this lone and solitary spot." Unfortunately, a band of Arapahoes interrupted his idyll by setting a forest fire that forced him back to Pueblo. Despite its abrupt ending, he would look back on his stay at Manitou Springs and nearby South Park, or the Bayou Salado, as the highpoint of his year in the West: "I never recall but with pleasure the remembrance of my solitary camp in the Bayou Salado, with no friend near me more faithful than my rifle, and no companions more sociable than my good horses and mules, or the attendant coyote which nightly serenaded us."

With the arrival of spring, Ruxton began to think about returning home. He had more than enough material for a book and also felt a family obligation toward his widowed mother. So he joined a trading party bound up the Santa Fe Trail to St. Louis, "one of the dullest and most commonplace cities in the Union," where he booked a room in Stewart's favorite hostel, the Planter's House.

The adjustment to civilization after ten months on the trail was not without difficulty. He went sleepless his first night in a bed, his limbs and body "astonished" by the luxury of a mattress and sheets.

I found chairs a positive nuisance, and in my own room caught myself in the act more than once of squatting cross-legged on the floor. The greatest treat to me was bread; I thought it the best part of the profuse dinners of the Planter's House, and consumed prodigious quantities of the staff of life, to the astonishment of the waiters. Forks, too, I thought were most useless superfluities, and more than once I found myself on the point of grabbing a tempting leg of mutton mountain fashion, and butchering off a hunter's mouthful. But what words can describe the agony of squeezing my feet into boots, after nearly a year of mocassins, or discarding my turban for a great boardy hat, which seemed to crush my temples? The miseries of getting into a horrible coat—of braces [suspenders], waistcoats, gloves, and all such implements of torture—were too acute to be described.

By August 1847 Ruxton was back in England, where he began immediately the writing of *Adventures in Mexico and the Rocky Mountains*. His letters to his mother at this time reveal a concern about his health and the state of his pocketbook—a back injury suffered in the West flared up again, and he was falling behind on his rent even while sending his mother ten pounds a month to help her meet expenses.

Adventures in Mexico and the Rocky Mountains appeared in April 1848 to critical acclaim. He found among Victorians a ready audience for his vivid accounts, for earlier books on the Great West by Washington Irving and their own Murray and Stewart had piqued the curiosity of Britons about life on the plains and in the Rockies. Even before the publication of his first book he was at work on a fictionalized sequel, to be published as *Life in the Far West* by Blackwood's of Edinburgh. It was to pay for another—and, he promised his mother, his last—trip to America that he sold his royalty rights to this book. Shortly before departure he wrote a remarkable letter to his publisher:

As you say, human nature can't go on feeding on civilized fixings in this "big village"; and this child has felt like going West for many a month, being half froze for buffler meat and mountain doins. My route takes me *via* New York, the Lakes, and St. Louis, to Fort Leavenworth, or Independence, on the Indian frontier. Thence packing my "possibles" [personal belongings] on a mule, and mounting a buffalo horse, (Panchito, if he is alive,) I strike the Santa Fe to the Arkansa, away up that river to the mountains, winter in the Bayou Salade, where Killbuck and La Bonte joined the Yutes, cross the mountains next spring to Great Salt Lake—and that's far enough to look forward to—always supposing my hair is not lifted by Comanche or Pawnee on the scalping route of the Coon Creeks and Pawnee Fork.

Sadly, his end would be much more mundane than that. George Frederick Ruxton, mountain man, never saw the Rockies again but made it only as far as the gateway to the West. Ruxton died in St. Louis in the summer of 1848, carried off in an epidemic of dysentery. He was twenty-seven years old.

6

The Solitary Rambler

Do not burthen yourselves uselessly by trying to forestall a thousand imaginary necessities. Beyond your guns and horses ... you will absolutely require nothing on the prairie but your knife, flint and steel, and pipe, an iron ladle for melting lead, a tin mug, and two iron kettles....

Before leaving the settlements, provide yourselves with lead, tobacco, coffee, sugar, salt, needles, one or two dressed skins for making and mending mocassins; and with this equipment, you may pass from Independence to the Pacific Ocean.

—John Palliser's advice to "brother sportsmen
of England, Ireland, and Scotland,"
from the introduction to *Solitary Rambles*

THE WEST THAT George Frederick Ruxton so longed to see again was a region in transition. Victory in the Mexican War and the 1846 settlement, at the forty-ninth parallel, of the Oregon boundary dispute with Britain made the United States a transcontinental nation at last. A near doubling of population in twenty years and the lure of Oregon's lush farmland sent streams of emigrants across the prairies, while the discovery of gold at Sutter's Fort in January 1848 would bring 60,000 fortune seekers to California in a single year.

On the plains, meanwhile, the exploitation of the buffalo began even as the trade in beaver exhausted itself in the mountains. Indian tribes, increasingly dependent on the white man's trade goods, entered the slaughter with gusto, decimat-

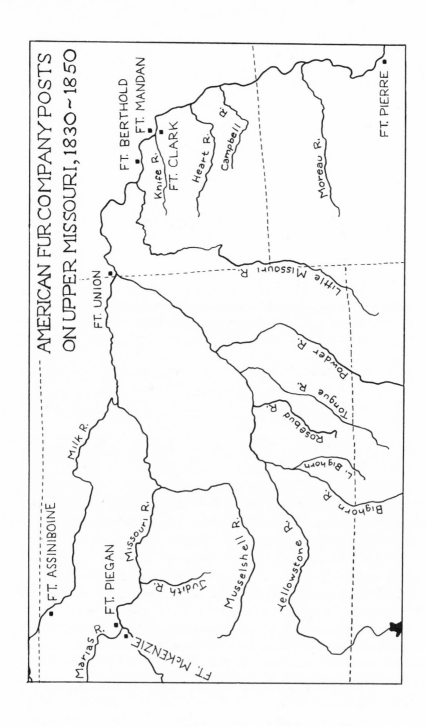

AMERICAN FUR COMPANY POSTS
ON UPPER MISSOURI, 1830~1850

FT. BERTHOLD
FT. MANDAN
FT. CLARK
Knife R.
Heart R.
Campbell R.
Moreau R.
FT. PIERRE

FT. UNION
Little Missouri R.

Powder R.
Tongue R.
Rosebud R.
Lt. Bighorn
Bighorn R.

Milk R.

FT. ASSINIBOINE

FT. PIEGAN
Missouri R.
Judith R.
Musselshell R.
Yellowstone R.

Marias R.
FT. McKENZIE

ing brood stocks by killing, each fall, upwards to 100,000 young cows for their superior hides. Ruxton himself lamented the buffalo's wholesale destruction, which he had noted along the Santa Fe Trail on his return from New Mexico. "It is a singular fact," he wrote, "that within the last two years, the prairies, extending from the mountains to a hundred miles or more down the Arkansa, have been entirely abandoned by the buffalo," with the boundary of their former range now "marked by skulls and bones."

On the northern plains, the expanding trade in buffalo hides was made feasible in part by the introduction, in 1832, of steamboats on the upper Missouri. Prior to this, there existed no economic way of transporting the bulky, heavy hides to market. The advent of steamboats had other effects on the region as well, for in 1837 the American Fur Company vessel *St. Peter's* arrived at Fort Clark with a crewman carrying smallpox. The disease quickly spread, first to the settled tribes along the Missouri—the Mandans, Hidatsa or Minetaree, and Arickaras—and soon to the nomadic Sioux, Assiniboine, Blackfeet, and Pawnees.

The resulting holocaust dramatically changed the dynamics of intertribal relations. To the west, the once mighty Blackfeet were so weakened that their traditional enemies, the Nez Perces and Flatheads, occupied much of their territory on the headwaters of the Missouri. To the east, the Mandans, a people who had figured prominently in the region's history since Lewis and Clark had wintered among them in 1804, were destroyed as a culture and forced to consolidate with the neighboring Minetarees. In their heyday these tribes had contained the warlike Teton Sioux to the northeast of the Missouri. Now the latter were free to cross the river and establish themselves in the rich buffalo country west of the Missouri, a migration that in turn opened up their old territory to other Sioux moving out from their traditional lands in Minnesota. Thus, in a few short years the formidable Sioux nation established its hegemony over the northern plains, setting the stage for the ascendancy of Red Cloud, Sitting Bull, and Crazy Horse and for the climactic confrontation between the United States and its native inhabitants.

As Ruxton neared the Missouri settlements in the spring of

1847, his path would have approached that of a spiritual brother, an Irishman named John Palliser who was bound up the Missouri for a season's adventure on the northern plains. Palliser was a vigorous forty years of age, a captain of militia in his home county of Waterford, where he was raised as the eldest son of a wealthy landowner amid the rugged splendor of the Comeragh Mountains of Ireland's southern coast. An outgoing bachelor, he led a spirited life of travel and sport and spoke fluent French, Italian, Spanish, and German. He came from an equally spirited family—one of his brothers, it is reported, rescued a French lady from pirates in the China Sea, another died exploring the Arctic with Sir John Franklin, and two others traveled with Sir Samuel White Baker (discoverer of the Nile's sources) on shooting trips to Ceylon. Palliser himself would win lasting fame in the annals of British exploration as the leader, a decade hence, of three geographical expeditions in the Canadian West—journeys for which his sporting excursion of 1847 would prepare him well. His lively account of his first visit to the American West, published in 1853 as *Solitary Rambles and Adventures of a Hunter in the Prairies*, would in fact influence the British Colonial Office in choosing him to head the Canadian surveys.

Palliser's desire to visit those regions "inhabited by America's aboriginal peoples" stemmed in part from tales related to him by his brother-in-law, William Fairholm, who had hunted in western Missouri while traveling in the United States in 1840. Departing Liverpool on the steamer *Cambria*, the middle-aged Palliser looked to the open Atlantic and the country beyond it with "all the eagerness of a college student, who casts aside his dull books and duller tutors for a burst after partridges." His fellow passengers included P. T. Barnum and his Lilliputian charge, Tom Thumb, standing a sliver over two feet tall and weighing about fifteen pounds—about the size, Palliser remarked, of "a good-sized leg of mutton." The two took to each other immediately. The diminutive Thumb, as high in spirits as he was small in stature, amused himself by cavorting all over Palliser—"now standing on my shoulder, then balancing himself on my head on one foot, and finally leaping into the pocket of my shooting-jacket until he burst through the lining of it."

In New York, Palliser bid goodby to his little friend and proceeded overland by bone-rattling stage to Wheeling. The gorges and forests of the Alleghenies impressed him mightily, but he held in even greater esteem the stage driver's skill at negotiating a four-horse team over the ruts and tree stumps of the backwoods highway. Careening through hairpin turns and down hemlock-shaded canyons, the American stage, Palliser observed, was "built to accommodate, or rather torture, nine persons inside, and as many outside as have the skill or the courage to sit along with the driver." Palliser himself rode with the driver and found the experience exhilarating, although he seems to have had few regrets about transferring to a steamer at Wheeling for a leisurely voyage down the Ohio and Mississippi.

Following a brief dalliance in New Orleans and some alligator hunting on a nearby plantation, he traveled up river to St. Louis to outfit for his prairie adventure. His plan called for joining a supply caravan of the American Fur Company and crossing overland from Independence to Fort Union, a distance of some eight hundred miles. Situated on the lower Yellowstone five miles above its junction with the Missouri, Fort Union had been for the last fourteen years a principal trading post of the American Fur Company, built at the height of the beaver trade and flourishing now on the burgeoning market in buffalo hides. Palliser's party set out for it on September 2, led by the veteran Missouri trader James Kipp.

"Old Mr. Kipp," as Palliser referred to him, was sixty years old and had been making this annual trek to the northern plains since Fort Union's beginnings. Palliser could not have had a more experienced guide to the country he was about to enter. A Canadian of German extraction, Kipp had been trading on the upper Missouri since 1818 and was reputedly the only white man to have mastered the language of the Mandans. Although Palliser seems unaware of it, he kept two families— an Indian one on the upper Missouri (his Mandan squaw went by the name of Earth Woman), and a white one at his farm near Independence. In the employ of John Jacob Astor's American Fur Company he had supervised the construction of Fort Clark, near the Mandan villages above present-day Bismarck, North Dakota, and of Forts Union and Piegan farther up river.

(Palliser was merely the latest in a long line of distinguished visitors to these parts whom Kipp came to know and befriend. As a senior officer in the American Fur Company's field operations he had played host at Fort Clark to the great German naturalist Prince Maximilian of Wied-Neuwied and to the artists Charles Bodmer and George Catlin. He also collected specimens for John James Audubon during his 1843 visit to Fort Union, the trip made by Audubon in lieu of traveling with William Drummond Stewart to the Wind Rivers.)

There were eighteen men in the caravan—most of them, Palliser observed, "a hardy set of Frenchmen" who were "docile, patient, enduring fellows, with constitutions like iron," each of them mounted and leading a second horse packed with provisions. They traveled along the east bank of the Missouri through a thinly populated country that included, near present-day Council Bluffs, a temporary settlement of Mormons preparing for their heroic trek across the plains. Driven by religious persecution from Illinois, the Mormons had reached the Missouri in the spring of 1846 and were staged now for the last leg of their migration to the promised land of Utah. Brigham Young had led an advance party of them up the Platte several months before, and by the end of the year some 1,600 would be settled by the Great Salt Lake. The followers of Joseph Smith impressed Palliser as "an indefatigable set of men" who personified the spirit of American expansion— "pioneers of a future civilization" that would soon sweep the red men and buffalo off the face of the earth.

Above Council Bluffs they approached a region still beyond the reach of homesteaders. The country took on a primeval character now as the caravan entered an endless sea of tallgrass prairie that took Palliser's breath away. "The vegetation in this part of the prairie was very rank and in some places gigantic," he wrote, "the grass growing over thousands of acres from five to eight feet high. For two days we travelled through this without intermission, occasionally meeting with willows and small spots of timber. Everything around—the huge coarse grass—weeds that I never saw before, rank and tangled in their unchecked growth—and the eternal illimitable sweep of the undulating prairie, impressed on me a sense of vastness quite overwhelming." He imagined himself carried back into some vanished time and place, where the sight of grazing mammoths or mastodons would not have surprised him.

The daily routine of travel and camp chores provided a more than sufficient touchstone with reality, however. The caravan arose before dawn and was underway by first light, riding until late morning before halting for breakfast and a brief midday rest. Stopping again before sundown, they unsaddled and hobbled their horses, gathered firewood for a roaring blaze, and prepared an evening meal of salted meat and boiled beans. Game was scarce, although camping near a prairie kettle one evening afforded Palliser the opportunity to bag several brace of ducks, shooting them on wing to the astonishment of the *voyageurs* who accompanied him. They made coffee by roasting beans over a fire, then wrapping the beans in deerskin and pounding them into grounds with the blunt end of a hatchet. A leisurely pipe followed supper, prior to bedding down between blankets and buffalo robes and sleeping with feet to the fire "as only travellers in the prairie can sleep."

Entering what is now South Dakota, they rested for several days at Fort Vermillion, where Palliser was at last able to observe the "aboriginal peoples" he had come so far to see. Approximately six hundred Yankton Sioux were camped in a village outside the fort, which Palliser found "a miserable little place, tenanted by a few sickly whites" in the service of the American Fur Company. By contrast, the Indian camp proved "a very striking sight" with its tipis spread across the broad floodplain of the Missouri under the deep autumn sky. The braves had just returned from a successful foray against the Otos to the south, and Palliser was able to witness a victory dance around an Oto scalp. The howling and chanting were accompanied by screaming children, neighing horses and growling dogs, creating "such a scene of confusion and uproar as baffled description." Later, the Yankton chief invited Palliser to a feast of boiled dog; he found the canine flesh tasty enough, although his appetite was spoiled somewhat by the grinning skull, propped up before him, of the very animal they were eating. The chief regaled his guest with stories about the Oto raid and boasted of taking a woman prisoner whom they would shortly put to death in ceremonial torture. An appalled Palliser pooled his resources with Kipp and a third white and bought the poor woman's freedom.

The party proceeded northward to Fort Pierre and on toward Fort Union at the juncture of the Yellowstone and Missouri. The sweeping short-grass prairie of the upper plains enthralled Palliser. In the featureless landscape it became impossible to gauge size or distance—a crow might be mistaken for a buffalo, or vice versa. "The atmosphere in these regions is extremely healthy," he declared, "and its effect upon the constitution something wonderful," banishing colds, coughs and other forms of sickness. "I have frequently in the morning risen from a sound sleep, under a down-pour of rain and found my shoulder on the side I had lain in a pool of water, have got up and ridden on, cold and shivering, till the sun rose and his genial rays thoroughly warmed and dried me; and yet have taken no harm." Palliser's rapture was attributable in part to the fine fall season, for he had yet to experience this country under a January blizzard or the baking sun of a summer drought.

The high plains were extraordinary, too, in their ability to support the millions of buffalo encountered around Fort Union. Like Stewart and others of his countrymen before him, Palliser found hunting bison on horseback "a noble sport," whose skills he quickly mastered. Typically, the mounted hunter dispensed with powder horn and bullet pouch altogether. Instead, he carried powder loose in his pockets and ladled it by hand down the barrel of his rifle, chasing it with a bullet spit from his mouth. Then, drawing beside his stampeding target and rising in the stirrups, he leveled the gun at the waist and fired in a single motion. "This is difficult to do at first, and requires considerable practice; but the ability once acquired, the ease and unerring steadiness with which you can shoot is most satisfactory, and any one accustomed to this method condemns ever afterward the lifting of a gun to the shoulder whilst riding at speed, as the most awkward and unscientific bungling."

Palliser spent the next several months at Fort Union. Within days after his arrival the area was hit with the season's first snowstorm. The river froze over, and soon afterward the fort's inhabitants began succumbing to a virulent mumps-like infection. When the disease struck the company hunters, Palliser and the fort physician were pressed into service to provide game—mainly buffalo and venison, which along with pancakes were the staples of the Fort Union diet.

The prairie winter impressed Palliser with its awesome cold, freezing winds, and blinding snows "in which a man could lose his bearings and his life only a few feet from camp." The ice on the river soon increased in thickness to three or four feet. Notwithstanding, he noted, "broken spaces remain open during the whole winter all along the river, at intervals varying two, three, or four miles from one another. These breaks are termed air-holes, and frequently extend their surface of unfrozen waters over acres." Approaching the edge of an air hole could be especially dangerous, "precipitating man or beast into a resistless current of water, quickly forcing them under the ice's opposite edge to a fearful frozen tomb." The weakness of

Ishmah, Palliser's usually faithful companion, from the title page of Adventures of a Hunter in the Prairies.

the surrounding ice, he added, doubtless caused the drowning of "a great many buffalo, elk, and even some few bears, tempted probably by a fine sunny day to leave their winter retreat for an hour or two prowling the ice." Palliser theorized that the gigantic Ice Age elk, whose fossil remains were so often found in Irish peat bogs, might have met similar fates.

His winter on the upper plains gave Palliser ample opportunity to develop his wilderness skills. In forays from Fort Union and on longer treks to outlying posts of the American Fur Company, he learned survival on the harshest terms. He generally traveled alone except for the company of his dog Ishmah, a mongrel acquired at the fort from one of the resident Crow Indians. On one such journey Ishmah answered the call of the wild and ran away with a wolf, dragging off the travois loaded with his master's supplies. A hundred miles from the nearest settlement and with only a few rounds of ammunition, Palliser retreated to a cottonwood grove by the river and contemplated his fate, while "the cold north breeze froze the perspiration which had run down my forehead and face, and formed icicles in my beard and whiskers, that jingled like bells as I shook my head in dismissing from my mind one project after another." Like Ruxton in similar circumstances, he took solace in his pipe, only to find—"climax of misfortunes!"—that he was out of tobacco. He was dreaming of English friends and hearthside when a contrite Ishmah reappeared from his lupine jaunt, dragging the travois with all supplies still attached.

Following a late-winter visit to Fort McKenzie farther up river, Palliser and Ishmah cut overland across "le Grand Detour" at the Big Bend of the Missouri and arrived at Fort Berthold on April 1, several weeks before the ice broke up on the river. With a hint of spring in the air, the peripatetic Irishman decided to return to Fort Union for a trip up the Yellowstone to the mouth of the Bighorn River.

He admired the Bighorn's deeply wooded banks and lush bottom land carpeted in new grass. Journeying a ways up river in the company of several *voyageurs*, he came upon the gnawed stumps of trees—sure sign of beaver. A companion named Boucharville returned to the spot with traps, which he set and baited with castoreum, the musky secretion used by the beaver as a territorial marker. Observing the elaborateness of a beaver lodge and the apparent sagacity it took to build it, Palliser acquired a considerable sympathy for these "industrious little creatures," which he came to view in decidedly anthropomorphic terms. Checking the traps the next morning, they found a "beaver struggling in each; one had been taken by the foreleg, which was fractured high up, the other was caught across the jaws. My companion put them out of pain by striking them on the back of the head with a stick. When I saw the helpless struggles of these poor intelligent little creatures I was seized with remorse, and determined forthwith that there should be no more beaver trapping."

Boucharville, an admirer in his own right of "the wonderful intelligence of the animal," declared the beaver "une espèce de monde."

> Fortunately for these little people, silk, which is now manufactured into hats, has provided an excellent substitute for their fur, previously so valuable; and now that beaver skin has fallen from eight and nine dollars a pound to a dollar and one and a half dollar, avarice and self-interest will no longer ply the instruments of their destruction, and sweep the ingenious little population off their Western waters.

Palliser basked in his prairie freedom and grew sleek off the richness of the spring land. "We lived like fighting-cocks in my little Yellow Stone camp," he would recall fondly. After the long lean winter they gorged on bighorn mutton, the tender hump ribs of buffalo cows, succulent elk meat and venison, antelope's liver, and the delicate flesh of catfish hauled from the river. It was with some reluctance, then, that he drew his Yellowstone idyll to a close. The year was advancing, and his plans called for meeting the American Fur Company steamer at Fort Berthold in July for the return to St. Louis and home. They descended the river in bullboats, makeshift vessels of buffalo skin stretched over willow frames, and along the way corralled a pair of buffalo calves for transport back to Ireland.

Fort Berthold proved a disagreeable place. Their stay got off to an inauspicious start when the fort factor, the ailing Francis Chadron, dictated his will to Palliser and subsequently died. The smell of death literally permeated the fort. In the adjacent

Minetaree village, the Indians mounted their dead on scaffolding, and the stench of rotting flesh grew steadily worse as the season progressed. Palliser blamed the ghastly ambiance for the dysentery he suffered. He noted that near each body hung the deceased's medicine—"any little thing that during his lifetime he may have deemed a preservative against danger, or a charm against sickness, or miraculous agent assisting him to find buffalo."

> A strange anomaly seems, however, to prevail, and one inconsistent with this great apparent respect for the dead, namely, that an Indian will not hesitate to appropriate any part of the dead man's paraphernalia, provided he replaces it by an article of the same kind no matter how inferior or how much previously injured; for instance, if an Indian has an arrow without feathers or headless, he does not scruple to exchange it for the best arrow in the deceased's quiver.

The Minetaree village included among its residents that summer of 1848 old Etienne Provost, a legendary figure in the fur trade, who eleven years earlier had accompanied Stewart and Alfred Jacob Miller to the rendezvous at Green River. Palliser's reference to Provost is cryptic, but we can imagine this "man of the mountains," as he was universally known, entertaining the Irish dude with extravagant yarns of the trapper's life. He was sixty-three years old and on his last visit to the upper Missouri. Stewart would describe him in *Edward Warren* as a "burly Bacchus," ruddy of face and "bearing more the appearance of a mate of a French merchantman than the scourer of the dusty plains." To the trader Bartholomew Berthold he was the very soul of the mountain trapper. Provost would be retiring from the trade at the end of this season and was awaiting the same company steamboat as Palliser for the return to St. Louis.

The old man engaged Palliser in a discussion of grizzly bears, a subject of which he bore more than a passing acquaintance, describing in detail a struggle he had witnessed once between Ephraim and a bull buffalo in which both combatants fought to the death. Palliser's single meeting with a grizzly to date had occurred on the Yellowstone, where he and a *voyageur* named Dauphin had shot and killed a young and rather smallish boar.

Provost's stories whetted the Irishman's desire for bigger sport; with arrival of the steamboat still several weeks away, he set off on an expedition up the Little Missouri to find grizzly.

Palliser's destination was a region known since at least the days of Lewis and Clark as the Turtle Mountains. The trappers also referred to this rugged territory of buttes, ridges and coulees as the "mauvais terrains," or Badlands. Some thirty years later, a young eastern blueblood and gentleman rancher named Theodore Roosevelt would still find it a hunter's paradise. In Palliser's day the region was a no man's land between the country of the Minetarees, Sioux, and Crow, and he attributed the abundance of game there to the scarcity of Indian hunting parties. The expedition did not disappoint him, for within a day of their arrival they encountered a large sow grizzly with cub. Palliser dropped the bear with a bullet through the heart. On a later occasion he was hunting alone on foot when he came upon the putrid carcass of a buffalo surrounded by the fresh paw prints of a monster bruin.

Palliser's "close quarters with a grisly bear," as illustrated by a nineteenth-century artist.

I drew my shot charges, rammed down a couple of bullets, and followed the tracks over an undulating prairie, till at a distance I descried a very large bear walking leisurely along. I approached as near as I could without his perceiving me, and lying down, tried Dauphin's plan of imitating the lowing of a buffalo calf. On hearing the sounds, he rose up, displaying such gigantic proportions as almost made my heart fail me; I croaked again, when, perceiving me, he came cantering slowly up. I felt that I was in for it, and that escape was impossible, even had I declined the combat, so cocking both barrels of my Trulock, I remained kneeling until he approached very near, when I suddenly stood up, upon which the bear, with an indolent roaring grunt, raised himself once more upon his hind legs, and just at the moment when he was balancing himself previously to springing on me, I fired, aiming close under his chin; the ball passing through his throat, broke the vertebrae of the neck, and down he tumbled, floundering like a great fish out of water, till at length he reluctantly expired.

The animal was so large that, after skinning it in a pouring rain, Palliser found its hide too heavy to carry back to camp.

Palliser's bag of grizzlies totaled five by the time of his return to Fort Berthold. During his absence a delegation of Sioux had appeared at the fort to parlay with the Minetarees, among them a chief who recognized Palliser as one of a group of whites he had seen earlier that summer hunting along the Missouri. The chief's war party had threatened to attack, and as Palliser recalled, only a "timely retreat into the timber" had saved them. "We could have killed you all," the chief told him now, "but you should have killed several of us while running from behind the trees, for white men shoot far." Palliser ruminated on this while sharing a pipe with his would-be assassin. Later, he made the chief a present of tobacco, and "we parted excellent friends."

Several days following the departure of the chief and his delegation, a band of Teton Sioux appeared to challenge the Minetarees in battle. Palliser was invited to join the village warriors riding out to meet the Sioux but prudently declined, instead posting himself with a telescope on the highest point of the fort to view the combat from a safe vantage.

82

Far away along the plains, at a great distance from the Fort, the hostile parties met (if drawing up at a respectful distance of two or three hundred yards can be called meeting), and the firing began on both sides. The sight was very picturesque. From my post I could see the strong puffs of smoke issuing from either line—the result of the double charges which Indians universally use in battle, under the erroneous impression that they give superior efficacy to the bullets, as well as to strike terror into the hearts of their enemies—while at intervals the braves rushed backwards and forwards on horseback, appearing and disappearing by turns through the clouds of smoke. At last, in rode one of the Minetarees with a scalp in his hand, and was instantly surrounded by a crowd of women and youngsters triumphantly screaming and yelling. This battle, however, did not entirely terminate in favour of the Minetarees, as they had one man slain on their side and carried off by the Sioux horsemen, who dragged him ignominiously along the ground by leathern thongs till they reached their own party, where they scalped him in safety.

The Minetarees, meanwhile, had killed another Sioux warrior and dragged his body back to the village to exact an even more gruesome revenge. Palliser watched in disgust as the village boys used the corpse for some impromptu archery practice; his feeling turned to revulsion when the squaws took over the riddled remains, carving off chunks of flesh which they broiled and ate.

When the steamboat *Martha* arrived in late July, Palliser— accompanied by a menagerie of four buffalo, two deer, an antelope, a black bear, and his faithful Ishmah—bid a regretful farewell to the upper Missouri. Although steamboats had been plying this stretch of the river for sixteen years, the annual appearance of the American Fur Company vessel still evoked awe on the part of the Indians who saw it. The Minetarees crowded the bank to watch the *Martha's* approach and scattered in pell-mell flight when she emptied her boilers in a roar of steam. Palliser confirmed the observation, made by the artist George Catlin more than a decade before, concerning the Indian's sense of wonder toward this "big medicine canoe" that could uncannily choose "the deepest part of the river, and keep in the channel and avoid the snags."

Not all Indians, however, gave the wonders of white man's technology such respect, for a few days prior to her arrival at Fort Berthold a member of the *Martha's* crew had been killed in an attack on the vessel by the Arickaras. Palliser noted that the death went unrevenged by the company agents, "who preferred silently submitting to the loss of their follower sooner than run the risk, as they themselves expressed it, 'of spoiling the trade.'"

7

Wretched Excesses:

- **The Wild E. Poore**
- **A Sportsman Among Thousand**
- **The Short, Unhappy Hunt of Grantley Berkeley**

The Western hunter will tell you he never knew one of "them thar English lord chaps' 'outfits,' them top-shelfers who come over a'hunting, to be without 'bear-coated wipes' (rough towels), rubber baths, string-shoes (laced boots), and a corkscrew in their pocket-knives."
—William Adolph Baillie-Grohman,
Camps in the Rockies

IF PALLISER and Ruxton represented the very model of the gentleman adventurer—intelligent, thoughtful, competent in the out-of-doors, and respected by all who met them—then their opposite number was surely Sir Edward Poore.

We know regrettably little about Sir Edward. Most of the sketchy documentation on his "strange career," as a newspaper titled his obituary, comes from a series of hilarious letters to his mother, chronicling his miseries and misadventures on a trek across the American continent in 1849. The "wild E. Poore," as he signed at least one of these missives, was a dilettante and a kind of proto-hippie who joyously adopted the looks and dress of his *voyageur* guides, including greasy buckskins, greasier hair, and ear rings. In his eccentricities and disregard for the opinions of others he represents, at least in degree, a new kind of

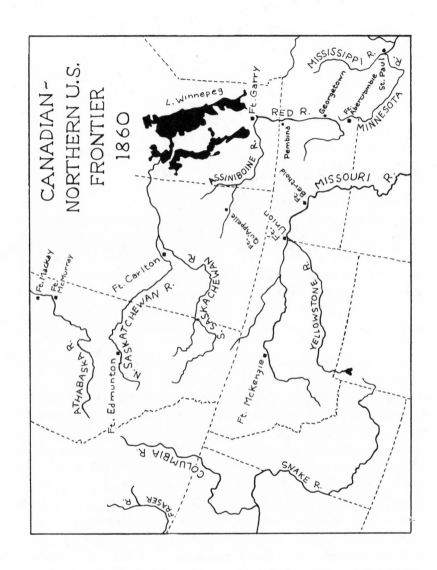

CANADIAN ~ NORTHERN U.S. FRONTIER 1860

L. Winnepeg
Ft. Garry
RED R.
ASSINIBOINE R.
Pembina
Ft. Berthold
Qu'Appelle
Ft. Union
MISSOURI R.
MISSISSIPPI R.
Georgetown
Ft. Abercrombie
St. Paul
MINNESOTA
YELLOWSTONE R.
Ft. McKenzie
Ft. Carlton
N. SASKATCHEWAN R.
S. SASKATCHEWAN R.
Ft. Mackay
Ft. McMurray
ATHABASKA R.
Ft. Edmunton
COLUMBIA R.
FRASER R.
SNAKE R.

western adventurer from those we have seen before. Poore's excesses would find their ultimate manifestation during the next decade in the hunts of Sir St. George Gore and Grantley F. Berkeley.

*   *   *

Poore was just twenty years old when he arrived in Canada in 1846, a restless young officer in the Scots Fusilier Guards and a refugee from love seeking solace in the American wilderness. After visiting relations at Cobourg on Lake Ontario, he headed for St. Louis to outfit for a hunting excursion on the prairie. Of this first adventure in the West we know almost nothing. It apparently did not last longer than a season, and like Murray a decade before, he probably did not venture farther than what is now eastern Kansas—far enough, in any event, to give him a taste of the heady freedom to be found on the plains. Returning east, he lost his jacket and purse to a thief and was reduced to pawning his pistols in Buffalo, New York, to pay for the rest of his passage home. He arrived in Cobourg with one dollar in his pocket. Poore was a survivor, although just barely, and the incident was revealing of how the rest of his life would proceed.

The young baronet settled down in his fashion, buying a house at nearby Grafton and turning his energies to polo. He soon tired of this, however, and by the spring of 1849 he was headed west again, this time with the Canadian artist Paul Kane, who had been courting one of the young ladies in the Cobourg social set. Kane was a protégé of George Catlin and had assembled a rich portfolio of Indian paintings on a trans-Canadian odyssey, completed the previous fall, along the trade route of the Hudson's Bay Company. He was itching to make another trip west and eagerly accepted Poore's offer of 200 pounds to serve as "conductor, guide, and interpreter" on a journey they would make together.

We can imagine how Kane must have whetted Poore's appetite for western adventure, relating stories of the great buffalo hunts he had seen on the prairies east of Fort Edmonton and of the spectacular gorges and mountain passes near the headwaters of the great Columbia River. His expedition of the year before had taken him through Rupert Land, the vast western region controlled by the Hudson's Bay Company, and across the mountains to Fort Vancouver at the mouth of the Columbia.

The company was phasing out its operations throughout Oregon, which by the treaty provisions of 1846 was now part of the United States. Kane found the region swarming with American immigrants and relations with the loyal Cayuse Indians and other tribes at tinderpoint. Accompanying the waves of white settlers in their covered wagons, as one observer noted caustically, were "their pleasant travelling companions the Measles, Dysentery and Typhus." Epidemics raged throughout the native population, killing 1,500 Indians in one summer along the Columbia and wiping out entire villages, leaving no one to bury the dead. Near Walla Walla he spent four days as the guest of Stewart's old friends, Marcus and Narcissa Whitman, and sketched portraits of Cayuse residents at the Waiilatpu Mission. In an incident symptomatic of the tense racial atmosphere, the artist nearly came to blows with one of his subjects, a brave named Tomakus, when the latter tried to throw Kane's sketch of him into the fire. The massacre, in a native uprising, of the Whitmans and eleven others at the mission occurred just four months after Kane's visit there.

Accompanying Poore and Kane on their journey west were a pair of greenhorns named Franklin and Philips, who were evidently partners in idleness with Poore at Cobourg. An Ohio River steamer, the *Franklin II*, took them to St. Louis and up the Mississippi and Minnesota rivers as far as St. Peter, where they disembarked for an overland crossing to the Red River flowing north into Canada.

The year was an especially bad one for cholera, and one of the passengers succumbed from the dread disease before they had reached Cairo, Illinois. "It was a miserable thing to see a man die" in such circumstances, Poore wrote to his mother, for the victim had left his family only four days before on a trip to purchase cattle. They deposited his body in a makeshift coffin and put it ashore for burial under a tree in which someone cut a cross. "Some kind of parson said a kind of sermon over him and we left again," Poore observed dryly, adding in the same breath that they had "met and passed about 70 or 80 men going to California, everyone seemed to be mad after gold."

At St. Peter they transferred their supplies to several carts and a string of pack mules and set off on horseback toward the Red River. The spring rains had turned the trail into a quagmire and the many streams they had to ford into swollen brown torrents. What might have been, under benign conditions, a bucolic ramble through the rolling edge of the Minnesota prairie became instead a daily ordeal that frayed tempers and threatened lives. In attempting to cross one creek, a cart was upset and most of their provisions washed downstream. When the pack mules and most of the horses bolted for freedom in the general confusion, Poore and Franklin rode off in pursuit, ignoring Kane's warnings about unfriendly Sioux. After an exhausting chase they managed to find the wayward animals and round them up, returning at dark to a demoralized camp and a dinner of warmed-over tea leaves sprinkled with sugar.

So it went. "Since we left St. Peaters [sic] we have had nothing but bad luck," Poore complained to his mother in a letter posted from Fort Garry (present-day Winnipeg) on the lower Red River. Other misfortunes befell them. When Philips, a particularly inept outdoorsman, attempted to cut down a tree, the axe slipped and cut his foot nearly in half. And one of the horses kicked Poore in the mouth, resulting in the loss of several teeth and jaw fragments, which he dutifully mailed home to Lady Poore.

The rigors of the trail quickly eroded the relationship between Poore and Kane, and by their arrival at Fort Garry they were barely on speaking terms. Abandoning the notion that Kane might instruct him in sketching, Poore dismissed the artist prior to his departure for the Pacific. "Kane we are going to send back," he reported to Lady Poore, "for he is *of no use whatever* so I *suppose* all the drawing I shall ever do you might stick in your ear."

Poore and Franklin idled fifty days at Fort Garry, waiting in vain for Philips' foot to heal before they started overland. It was a frustrating period, made more so by the absence of game. During the long wait, Poore must have heard many accounts of how different it had been only a few years before. Until 1840, Fort Garry was center for the famous Red River hunt, an

Paul Kane 1846

Half-breeds running Buffalo

Paul Kane painted metis (French-Indian halfbreeds) chasing buffalo on the plains west of Fort Garry in 1846, three years before he accompanied Sir Edward Poore to the same territory.

90

annual spectacle in which more than 650,000 buffalo were killed over a twenty-year period.

Each June, the Red River settlers—descendants of a hearty band of Scottish highlanders who had colonized the region in the early 1800s—moved out on the plains to meet the great herds following the ripening spring grasses north. Men, women, and children took part with their "Red River carts," outsized versions of the *charette,* or peasants' cart of France. A bloody orgy ensued, and when the slaughter ended some weeks later the ungainly vehicles groaned under the weight of thousands of pounds of buffalo hides, dried meat and pemmican. The last item was a staple in the diets of Indians, mountain men, and *voyageurs* throughout the history of the frontier—a nearly indestructable (some might say indigestable) concoction of powdered buffalo flesh, fat, tallow, and berries. Wrapped in an airtight parfleche bag, pemmican would keep for years. It was rich in nutrients and "could be eaten," according to Bernard DeVoto, "uncooked or fried, roasted, or boiled, by itself or in combination with anything you had in hand." Red River pemmican was regarded as a particular delicacy.

During the long wait at Fort Garry, Poore cultivated the looks and manner of the colorful frontiersmen surrounding him. "You ought to see me now," he boasted to Lady Poore, "with *long hair, earrings,* leather *trousers fringed* & all the other fixings belonging to a half breed." He beamed with pride in his newly gained proficiency with a lasso, which "by incessant practice" he could now throw as well as "any Indian." To provide Lady Poore with a literal taste of plains life, he shipped home 150 dried buffalo tongues and tenderloins, advising her to soak them for twenty-four hours before cooking.

Like many a son before and since, the wild E. Poore took an innocent pleasure in worrying his mother half to death. In his last letter from Fort Garry he bid her a cheerful farewell, reassuring her that he would write again as soon as he reached Fort Vancouver—provided, of course, that he didn't get scalped along the way. "We shall have to pass through the Black feet country," he said, "*the* worst in all America."

Poore survived the crossing, arriving at the mouth of the Columbia "in a state of high preservation but *very thin,*" as he assured his mother in his promised letter from Fort Vancouver.

They in fact had seen few Indians, the Blackfeet having already moved through the area, and the closest Poore came to getting himself killed occurred while running rapids on the Columbia, when his boat smashed against a rock and broke in two. With the other passengers he managed to crawl onto a sunken rock, where they huddled together in the freezing current for four hours until finally rescued.

With the exception of such incidents, the expedition failed to live up to his expectations for adventure. "This country is *not what it is cracked up to be*," he groused. Buffalo were scarce throughout the eastern prairie—a direct result of overhunting by the Red River colonists—and they did not encounter them in significant numbers until nearly at Fort Edmonton, an important way station on the Hudson's Bay Company trade route to the Pacific. The chief happenings of note were further misadventures—a man washed overboard while fording the Athabaska River (Poore jumped in and saved him), and the accidental shooting death of the bourgeois in charge. The victim was relaxing around the campfire at the end of a hard day when a gun discharged in front of him, blasting a hole in his chest. They made him as comfortable as possible, but the wound was mortal. After two hours of delirium, Poore related, the unfortunate man "sat up & looked round wildly & banged down and died." The next morning they rolled him in three blankets and buried him beneath the prairie sod, erecting a small log structure over the grave to protect it from wolves.

Poore dallied at Fort Vancouver, where his renegade appearance became the subject of much talk. The British officers stationed there refused to believe he was a gentleman, while the fort's factor, Peter Skene Ogden, in a letter to Kane expressed his amusement at Poore's eccentric behavior. He was, Ogden remarked, "truly a free young Man."

While tongues waggled, Poore and Franklin pondered what part of the world they might visit next. The Sandwich Islands looked appealing, as did California, where they considered either joining in the gold rush at Sutter's Fort or setting up in the cattle business. Circumstances of the heart soon intervened, however. Poore's lady love in England sent word that she was ready for a reconciliation, and before too long he was back home and married. Two years later he returned to

Cobourg, where his son was born, but soon after this he redeposited his family in England and set off by himself for Australia. He remained Down Under for the remainder of his bizarre life and died, broke and alone, in Adelaide in 1893, en route to the South Australia gold fields.

*   *   *

Poore's aberrant ways were more than matched five years later by another baronet, Sir St. George Gore. A man of virtually unlimited means—the annual income from his estates came to $200,000, the equivalent of millions today. Gore indulged his lust for sport in a manner not seen in the Rockies since William Drummond Stewart's last, sentimental journey to the Wind Rivers. Gore's safari through what is now Colorado, Wyoming, Montana, and the Dakotas rivaled any ever staged on the Serengeti. It lasted three years, cost $500,000, and took what even then was regarded as a profligate toll of wildlife. In the course of his wanderings, Gore by his own estimate slaughtered more than 2,000 buffalo, 1,600 elk and deer, and 100 bear. The magnitude of his hunt assumed legendary proportions even before it ended, and over the years accounts of the Gore saga became increasingly embellished until they passed into the realm of fantasy.

Gore was the eighth baronet of Gore Manor, County of Donegal, in northern Ireland, an indulged only son and Oxford-educated bachelor with an unquenchable passion for shooting and fishing and the means to pursue it. He was forty-three years old at the start of his expedition and described in a contemporary account as "a fine built, stout, light haired and resolute looking man." Later writers would also characterize him as flush-faced, bald, with straw-colored Dundreary whiskers and in personality "mercurial, wrathful, effervescent and wreckless." He could also be generous to a fault. Once, on purchasing a horse for the asking price of $150, he tested the animal and found it such a bargain that he gave the seller an extra $100, "which makes the cost nearer its true value."

Stewart's Wind River hunt of a decade earlier seemed modest by comparison. When it left Fort Leavenworth in the spring of

1854, Gore's baggage train comprised twenty-one Red River carts, four six-mule wagons and two three-yoke ox wagons. One wagon was filled entirely with arms—countless pistols, more than a dozen shotguns, and seventy-five rifles, most of them the product of England's finest gunsmiths like Purdy, Whestley Richards, and Joe Manton. Two wagons were laden with fishing tackle, while a professional fly dresser accompanied the expedition to keep the baronet supplied with lures. There were also 112 horses, 18 oxen, 3 milk cows, and an unrecorded number of mules. Gore's 50 greyhounds and staghounds impressed one observer as "the most magnificent pack of dogs there were ever seen in this country." Years later, Fort Kearney on the Oregon Trail was reportedly overrun by the mongrel descendants of Gore's canine corps.

This extravagant outfit included as well a large green-and-white-striped linen tent, a rug, a washstand, and a portable iron table and brass bed. His personal wagon was built with a collapsible roof that popped into place with the turn of a crank—a veritable Conestoga convertible. Among the more than forty men in the party were cooks, secretaries, hunters, stewards, and dog-tenders.

Accompanying Gore on the first leg of his expedition was another titled gentleman, Eton-educated Sir William Thomas Spencer Wentworth-Fitzwilliam, Sixth Earl of Fitzwilliam, a former member of Parliament and future aide-de-camp to Queen Victoria, who chased coyotes and timber wolves over the rolling terrain in the company of Gore and his hounds. Lord Fitzwilliam had dropped by Oregon on a round-the-world trip in 1853, and his account may have inspired Gore to go west himself. An amateur astronomer, he brought along a telescope with a six-inch lens for gazing on the panoply of stars in the prairie sky.

William F. Cody was a boy in Fort Leavenworth when Gore passed through there. Later, as the famous Buffalo Bill, he would look back on this titled nimrod as "a sportsman among thousand" whose good fellowship made him a favorite among the townsfolk. Doubtless his popularity had as much to do with purse as with personality; Gore did much of his hiring and outfitting at Fort Leavenworth, and his stay there was an economic windfall to the merchants.

As might be expected from a man who boasted of killing more than 4,200 buffalo as a professional hunter, Cody viewed uncritically Gore's excesses in the field. In the 1850s, game was still plentiful enough throughout the West to be taken entirely for granted, and the overwhelming attitude toward Gore was one of puzzlement that a gentleman "would come all the way across the ocean, and make the tedious journey from the seaboard to the frontier, with no other end in view than the chase."

The caravan got underway in June. At its head, along with Gore, rode Henry Chatillon, a former trapper and one of the best Oregon Trail guides. The "brave and true-hearted" Chatillon was in his late thirties, five years Gore's junior, and had already achieved an immortality of sorts as a principal figure in Francis Parkman's classic narrative of the early West, *The Oregon Trail*. He had guided Parkman a decade before, when the fledgling historian and recent Harvard graduate visited the frontier to gain experience for his life's endeavor, a definitive history of French colonial America. Parkman reasoned that a taste of real Indians and frontiersmen would be useful in his scholarly pursuits, and while his exposure to the West lasted only a few brief months, it more than matched his expectations. The handsome, rawboned Chatillon displayed great natural leadership and a vast knowledge of plains life. In his buckskins and drooping felt hat and with his extraordinary wilderness skills, he seemed in Parkman's romantic eyes the apotheosis of frontier self-reliance. Since *The Oregon Trail* was first published in 1849, it is possible that Gore had read it and that its idealized portrait of Chatillon had influenced him in his choice of guide.

Gore's party crossed overland and followed the North Platte to its junction with the Laramie River, where they stopped at Fort Laramie for rest and reprovisioning. The fort had been built twenty-one years before by Bill Sublette and Robert Campbell as a way station on the supply route to the trappers' rendezvous. Stewart had stopped here on his Wind River odyssey in 1843, and since 1849 the fort had functioned as an Army post protecting emigrant wagons along the Oregon Trail. During his stay at the fort, Gore must have heard stories about the Great Council at Fort Laramie, held three years earlier under the direction of Stewart's old comrade, Tom Fitzpatrick. Acting as official agent of the United States government, Fitzpatrick had called together delegations of the various plains tribes for a major peace conference. In the Treaty of Fort Laramie, each tribe agreed to restrict itself to a defined territory, to cease warring with one another, and—most important to the government—to stop harassing the emigrant trains on their way to Oregon and California. While most of the treaty's provisions were soon violated, it succeeded in bringing a measure of peace to the Powder River country to the north, allowing Gore to hunt there for most of the following season with few Indian troubles.

Henry Chatillon's brother, Joseph, guided Gore from Fort Laramie for a summer's hunt in what is today the northern Colorado Rockies. Like Ruxton before him, Gore seems to have taken special pleasure in the splendor of the mountain-rimmed upper valleys, or parks, with their sagebrush plains and gentle slopes teeming with elk, deer, and other game. He snatched gleaming cutthroat trout from their broad clear streams and banged away at antelope and mountain sheep in the secluded reaches of North and Middle parks. Gore preferred shooting from a standing position, his rifle resting in the fork of a stick and with a gunbearer at the ready to hand him a freshly loaded weapon.

Gore's rambles through the Colorado Rockies are memorialized today in a series of place names in the region southeast of Steamboat Springs. Besides Gore Canyon on the upper Colorado, there is Gore Creek near present-day Vail and the rugged Gore Range to the west of Highway 40. According to a persistent legend, Gore hired a band of eight hundred Indians to cut a wagon road across the range so he could reach the numerous elk reported on its western slope. More likely, as writer Forbes Parkhill points out, he left his wagons behind and packed across the mountains at 9,527-foot Gore Pass. As the season progressed the party moved farther south and to lower altitude, camping in the vicinity of Pike's Peak late in the waning season before returning to Fort Laramie for the winter.

The following April found Gore and his caravan on the trail again, moving up the North Platte and crossing overland to the Powder River, a tributary to the Yellowstone. The Irishman was guided this time by none other than Jim Bridger, another of Stewart's trail companions and perhaps the greatest of all the mountain men.

Gore had met Bridger the previous spring in St. Louis, where Old Gabe had been paying a rare visit to civilization. The sportsman doubtless knew of his legendary status and would have picked up immediately on the keen intelligence behind the illiterate drawl and rude mountain argot. Bridger was in his fifties now and had spent a third of a century in the Far West. In 1822, at age eighteen, he had penetrated to the dangerous Three Forks region of the upper Missouri as one of William H. Ashley's original "enterprising young men." Bridger went the next seventeen years, as he often boasted, without once tasting bread. He roamed the vast interior of Western America from Fort Union to Taos to dreamy California, absorbing its topography and committing its features to his near-photographic memory. He discovered the Great Salt Lake (whose waters he reportedly tasted and spat out with the exclamation, "Hell, we are on the shores of the Pacific!"), and explored the fantastic geyser country of the upper Yellowstone. He knew Indians as well as any white man who ever lived and could keep a party of Sioux entranced with an hour-long narrative delivered entirely in sign language. Since the collapse of the beaver trade a decade before he had buried two Indian wives and married a third and had built a trading post—Fort Bridger—on Black Fork of the Green River, in the old rendezvous country, before Brigham Young and his Mormon colonizers chased him out in 1853.

Bridger had an affinity for British gentlemen (perhaps because he was a natural aristocrat himself) and despite their extraordinary differences in background and education, he hit it off with Gore as easily as with Stewart twenty years before. Old Gabe's account of Gore's Powder River expedition is preserved in the reminiscences of Army General Randolph B. Marcy, who met Bridger at Fort Laramie in 1857. According to Marcy, Bridger commended his titled charge as "a bold, dashing and successful sportsman, a social companion, and an agreeable gentleman."

> Sir George's habit was to sleep until about ten or eleven o'clock in the morning, when he took his bath, ate his breakfast, and set

out generally alone for the day's hunt; and Bridger says it was not unusual for him to remain out until ten o'clock at night, and he seldom returned to camp without augmenting the catalog of his exploits.

His dinner was then ordered, to partake of which he generally extended an invitation to my friend Bridger, and after the repast was concluded, and a few glasses of wine had been drunk, he was in the habit of reading from some book, and eliciting from Bridger his comments thereon. His favorite author was Shakespeare, which Bridger "reckin'd was a leetle too highfalutin for him"; moreover, he remarked that he "rayther calculated that thar big Dutchman, Mr. *Full-stuff* was a leetle bit too fond of lager beer," and suggested that probably it might have been better for the old man if he had imbibed the same amount of alcohol in the more condensed medium of good old Bourbon whiskey.

Bridger, Marcy related, was skeptical about the published adventures of Baron Munchausen, noted for his fanciful accounts of travels to the moon and stars. He dismissed the baron as "a durn'd liar," although on further reflection he acknowledged that some of his own experiences among the Blackfeet would be equally marvelous, *"ef writ down in a book."*

During one of these cultural sessions, Sir George read to Bridger the account by Sir Walter Scott of the Battle of Waterloo—unaware perhaps that, around another campfire in another time, the veteran mountain man had heard the same battle described by one of its participants, William Drummond Stewart. When Gore finished his reading he asked Bridger his opinion of the battle. "Wall, now, Mr. Gore," he replied upon reflection, "that thar must'a bin a considdible of a skrimmage, dogon my skin if it mustn't; them Britishers must'a fit better thar than they did down to Horleans, whar Old Hickry gin um the forkedest sort of 'chainlightnin' that prehaps you ever did see in all yer born days!" When Sir George suggested to Bridger that perhaps he overrated the decisiveness of this battle, the latter added, "You can jist go yer pile on it, Mr. Gore—*you can*, as sure as yer born."

Under Bridger's able guidance, Gore spent a happy summer on the plains in pursuit of buffalo, elk, antelope, and bear. By that following fall of 1855 he was encamped on the Tongue

River, eight miles above its confluence with the Yellowstone, near the site of present-day Miles City, Montana. At some point during the ensuing months the expedition suffered its only loss in the death, by natural causes, of a hand named Uno. The men planned to bury him in a blanket according to prairie custom, but Gore ordered that a coffin be built from floorboards taken from one of his wagons.

In preparation for winter each man gathered 125 pounds of cottonwood bark as forage for the horses and other animals. Gore's personal mount, a Kentucky thoroughbred named Steel Trap, was exempted from such base fare, however. The noble steed passed the snow months in a cabin shared with his master, who fed him exclusively on corn meal. Amid the snow-hushed cottonwoods, with the black river gliding past, the winter lodge was a peaceful respite from the activity of summer. Deer and elk, seeking the same wooded cover along the river, offered both meat and sport; if boredom still threatened Sir George, there was always Jim Bridger to entertain him from his fathomless repertoire of trapper tales.

The local "hostiles" provided another antidote to cabin fever when a raiding party of Blackfeet pilfered twenty-one horses. On discovering the loss, Gore's men pursued the thieves for sixty miles before a snowstorm turned them back. Later that winter, more Blackfeet raiders descended on the camp, but this time Gore's men were ready and drove them off without losing any horses. One of the Blackfeet wounded in the skirmish was a brave named Big Plume, who turned out to have relatives in high places.

Big Plume's sister was married to Alexander Culbertson, the American Fur Company's chief factor at Fort Union and, like Kenneth McKenzie before him, the most powerful man on the upper Missouri. Although an Englishman by birth, Culbertson had spent most of his adult life beyond the frontier and was as tough as his Indian kin—he shocked John James Audubon during the artist's 1843 visit to Fort Union by killing a buffalo, then splitting the animal's skull and devouring the raw brains.

Culbertson and the regional Indian agent, Alfred J. Vaughan, took a dim view of Gore's cavalier slaughter, for mere trophies, of game that the Blackfeet and other tribes depended on for survival. There was also the matter of Gore illegally trading with the Indians—an offense compounded by the fact that the articles exchanged included powder and ball. As to the wanton killing, reported Vaughan to his superior in St. Louis, "The Indians have been loud in their complaints." But he added, "What can I do against so large a number of men coming into a country like this so very remote from civilization; and doing & acting as they please?" Another observer wrote directly to the Secretary of Interior, pointing out that "We punish an Indian for killing a settler's cow for food. How can such destruction of their game be permitted by their friends in the Government of the United States?" Government officials, in fact, considered taking legal action to seize Gore's thousands of trophies as reparations but decided it would not be worth the cost.

The profligate Gore spent his last summer in the field oblivious to the controversy swirling about him or to the rumor, prevalent at Fort Union, that he and twelve of his men had been killed by a joint force of Sioux and Blackfeet. The rumor may have stemmed from a raid on the expedition by a party of Sioux in which the Indians succeeded in running off with a number of horses, although the only casualty in the incident was Gore's pride. According to a story related years later by Cody, the red men's thievery prompted a choleric response from Gore, who "proposed to Uncle Sam" to raise a private army that would "whip the entire Sioux nation" in thirty days. The historian Clark C. Spence dismisses this story "as simply another bit of folklore that has become a part of the Gore saga." Apocryphal or not, Gore's boastful threat sounds very much in character.

Another persistent piece of lore surrounding this hunt of hunts arose from Gore's visit that summer to the Black Hills, where two members of the party reportedly found gold in the icy currents of the Belle Fourche. Greatly excited, they returned to camp and showed their "nuggets" to Gore, who cooly announced that they had found nothing more precious than mica. Only later did they learn that the gold was indeed real, but that Gore had duped them to prevent the wholesale desertion of his men. So, the story goes, the Black Hills had to wait another twenty years before gold—real gold for certain—was discovered there. The Black Hills belonged by treaty to the

Sioux, and the resulting rush of prospectors precipitated one of the last great Indian wars on the upper plains—a war forever remembered for the folly of George A. Custer and the slaughter of his command at the Little Bighorn.

With fall approaching, Gore cut short his romp in the Black Hills and descended to the plains, where he picked up the Little Missouri and followed it north toward Fort Union. After two and a half years in the field, it was time to think about dismantling the expedition and returning home.

Major Culbertson must have greeted Gore cooly at Fort Union, but he agreed nonetheless to build him two Mackinaw boats for the trip down river to St. Louis. (Mackinaws were the sturdy, flat-bottomed vessels that served as a mainstay of the river trade in furs for more than half a century.) Culbertson also promised to purchase Gore's surplus wagons and equipment. A misunderstanding over terms caused Gore to cancel the deal, however, and in an extraordinary fit of pique to burn most of his gear—including three wagons, twenty carts, and leftover trade items—in a great bonfire in front of the fort. To prevent salvaging, the petulant Irishman ordered his men to sift through the ashes and throw any iron into the river. Gore sold off his horses and livestock to the fort's motley assemblage of halfbreeds, Indians, and traders. With the expedition "now decimated by mutual consent," he took his trophies and remaining supplies by flatboat down river to Fort Berthold.

Gore's troubles with the locals did not end with his departure from Fort Union, however. Word of the wealthy sportsman's approach preceded him to Fort Berthold, where the merchants quickly boosted their prices in anticipation of his arrival. Gore responded by refusing to deal with any of them beyond purchase of the barest necessities. Out of spite, perhaps, he spent most of the winter apart from the fort, living in the quarters of a hospitable Hidatsa chief named Crow's Breast. With ice-out the following spring he was bound down the Missouri to St. Louis, and from there to the more congenial confines of his Irish estate in Donegal.

So Gore passed out of the country and into legend. It is unfortunate that he left no personal narrative of his three years' wandering, which might at least have added something to the documentation of a remarkable adventure. General

Marcy, who met him in St. Louis in 1857, viewed Gore uncritically as "an enthusiastic, ardent sportsman" who "had seen something of life out of the ordinary beaten track of the great mass of other tourists." Yet, as the historian Clark Spence has noted, except for some place names on the map, "he contributed little that was tangible to the unfolding drama of western development. If his exploits represented the adventuresome spirit of the times, they also showed man's wasteful and destructive nature at its worst."

*   *   *

Gore's single-minded destruction of wildlife must be judged, of course, in the context of his times, when a seemingly inexhaustible supply of buffalo and other game still ranged the prairie. And despite his imperious manner and troubles with regional officials and Missouri River traders, he seems, like Stewart, to have genuinely admired the Indians and former trappers whom he encountered during his three years' wandering in the West. It was an attitude in marked contrast to the arrogant disdain shown later in the decade by Grantley F. Berkeley, who swaggered onto the plains for a fall hunt in 1859. Berkeley's expedition was brief, lasting only a few months, but it capped a colorful and occasionally notorious career as a not-always-so-gentlemanly gentleman in early Victorian England.

George Charles Grantley Fitzhardinage Berkeley, sixth son of the Fifth Earl of Berkeley, was trained at Sandhurst and commissioned at age sixteen in the Coldstream Guards. By his twenties he had retired on half pay and was living the life of a gentleman sportsman, riding to hounds across the lush green hills of his native Bedfordshire. Ambitious in an unfocused way, Berkeley launched a political career that would span three decades, beginning with his election in 1832 to Parliament. He cut a flamboyant figure in public—flaunting throughout his life, as one chronicler has described it, "a coarser kind of buckish coxcombry." He sported multiple layers of gaily colored satin shirts and "around his throat three or four gaudy silk neckerchiefs, held together by passing the ends of them through a gold ring." In 1836 he "raised a laugh that ladies should be admitted to the Gallery of the House of Commons. The same day he was cheered along Rotten Row by the fashionable concourse, and in 1841, on the concession of the privilege, received a piece of plate from grateful ladies."

Berkeley Castle, the first of two historical romances he would write, appeared in 1836 and exposed a less-than-savory aspect of the author's character. When the three-volume tome was harshly reviewed by one of the literary journals, the stoutly built Berkeley accosted the diminutive publisher and beat him unmercifully. Berkeley boasted of having learned boxing from the same instructor who had taught Lord Byron, but on this occasion he took his revenge with the butt end of a gold hunting whip rather than with his fists. Later he challenged the reviewer to a duel and wounded him slightly, escaping unscathed himself and with his honor restored. Incredibly, Berkeley would later criticize Americans for what he saw as their overfondness for dueling.

Defeated for reelection in 1852, Berkeley retired from political life and devoted himself to field sports. He became a master breeder of dogs, and four of his animals—a terrier named Smike, the bloodhound Druid, the mastif Gumbo and the retriever Smoker—were famous in hunting circles throughout the British Isles. He also kept a trained cormorant, named Jack, who was celebrated for his angling abilities.

In 1859, at age fifty-nine, Berkeley determined to test his hunting skills on the American plains. As he would emphasize in *The English Sportsman in the Western Prairie*, the account of his visit published three years later, one of his aims was to refute the commonly held notion that a sportsman had to devote at least a year to such an expedition; Berkeley managed it in a little more than three months, leaving England at the end of August and returning by early December. While Berkeley may have accomplished his American adventure in record time, he did so at the expense of seeing very much country—his excursion was limited to a visit to Fort Riley, some four hundred miles beyond Kansas City, where he hunted buffalo in the company of American officers stationed there.

Berkeley's account of his travels amounts to a prolonged sneer at the majority of American manners and institutions.

Notwithstanding this illustration from Berkeley's The English Sportsman in the Western Prairie, buffalo seldom attacked their pursuers.

New York shocked him with the "barbarous cookery" of its hotels and the city's "miserably paved" streets festering with unspecified "rotting horrors." (A visitor today might be similarly impressed.) While conceding the natural aristocracy of the American upper class, he was repelled by the country's urban poor. "There is nothing so dangerous," he sniffed, "as liberty insufficiently restrained, or suffrage so universal that property and life lie at the mercy of an irresponsible multitude." In its "unwashed depravity," he added, the American proletariat was comparable in wretchedness to the lowest inhabitants of Billingsgate—except that London's poor at least knew their place and were undeluded by the "revolting assumption" of equality.

The rudeness of Americans was supremely manifest in the nearly universal vice of spitting. Had they been "half the shots with firearms they proved to be with the juice of tobacco," Berkeley declared, "I should have gone home a defeated sportsman." On arrival in Kansas City he was approached by a sharp-eyed huckster and *soi-disant* "bloody arm of the Rocky Mountains" who offered to guide the "English lord" on the plains; for some reason he mistook Berkeley's valise for a spittoon and during the course of his sales pitch hit it with six consecutive bull's eyes.

After bidding a hearty farewell to New York, Berkeley traveled to St. Louis by train—the first of our British sportsmen to do so—and pronounced American rail service a "surfeit of horrors." Like Stewart and Ruxton before him, he checked in at the familiar Planter's Hotel. During his stay there he made the acquaintance of Robert Campbell, Stewart's friend and the longtime business partner of Bill Sublette. Berkeley kennelled the quartet of hunting dogs he had brought with him in a warehouse owned by Campbell, who advised him on prairie travel and extended him credit when the Englishman realized that he had "immensely underrated" the cost of his trip.

In outfitting for the expedition, Berkeley to his profound dismay encountered the American (that is, western) saddle. He found it a beastly device and "at least a hundred years behind the modern or English improvement." In his critical eye the bulky but eminently practical stirrup was a "coalbox-looking or clog-like thing" and the pommel a "huge upstanding crutch" that could impale the rider in a fall: "Of all the unsightly, hideous, and dangerous things on a saddle this excrescence is the worst." Climbing aboard one of these atrocities of leather and wood, he asserted, was like mounting "a deal board, with the bowsprit of a ship ready to rip up the buttons of my waistcoat, or penetrate my waist to the impossible arrangement of any future dinners."

Like other cultivated travelers of his day, Berkeley was struck by the forwardness of frontier folk, who on the trail did not hesitate to approach him and ask all manner of questions about his outfit and purposes of travel. He even came to enjoy these exchanges in a condescending way. Noting the westerner's propensity for tall tales, he "soon began to see that veracity was very far from an object of veneration, and that if any man had been as far across the desert as the Rocky Mountains, it was impossible to believe a word he said." He further regretted that two things—tobacco juice and whiskey—"forever keep pace" with westering man, while "religion and roads are left far behind." His advice went unheeded to "leave off chewing that mouthful of poisonous tobacco" and to refrain from drinking "the stuff you call whiskey, and instead of spirits buy calomel and quinine, and grow some fruit and vegetables in your never half-cultivated garden." Berkeley attributed the fevers and "agues" (malaria) that westerners complained of suffering each summer to excessive imbibing.

The expedition—comprising Berkeley, his four dogs (Druid, Brutus, Bar, and Chance), eight hands, and a "worthless guide" named Canterwell—left Kansas City on September 26 and proceeded overland toward Fort Riley, an Army post built six years earlier to protect settlers and travelers on the Santa Fe Trail from marauding Indians. The Missouri frontier had pushed westward into Kansas during the previous decade, and by the time of Berkeley's visit there were 100,000 Americans occupying the former range land of buffalo and elk. Kansas had been a United States territory since 1854 and two years hence, on the eve of the Civil War, would be admitted as the nation's thirty-fourth state. It was the era of the sod buster and also of "Bleeding Kansas," for the territory was torn by factional fighting over slavery. Berkeley professed to despise the peculiar institution, but most of his comments reveal the typical racism of his time. He found free Negroes in Pennsylvania "the idlest, most ill-looking, discontented, hang-dog ruffians that ever made a man uneasy as to his watch," while the enslaved blacks he saw in Missouri conformed to the carefree stereotype of the plantation darkie.

As the expedition proceeded up the Kansas River it passed near the settlements of Lawrence and Pottawatomie, scenes of some of the bitterest fighting between freesoilers and proslavery forces. Berkeley, however, ignored the slavery issue as he popped away at grouse, blue jays, hawks, and owls—all the while dreaming of bigger game beyond the rolling hills. "Oh! what a country for an English pack of fox hounds and a thorough-bred horse!" he exclaimed. At night, he removed his wagon from the rest of the caravan to avoid listening to the "objectional conversation" of the men.

They were a week on the trail before encountering their first Indian, a desultory brave who approached the caravan on horseback, dead drunk and begging for whiskey. Prolonged contact with white men had by now thoroughly debased local tribes like the Kansas and Oto, although farther out on the plains the fierce Kiowas and Comanches remained formidable barriers to westward movement. Berkeley had reason for concern about the chances of Indian attack. Throughout the summer, braves led by the truculent Satank had been harassing wagon trains on the Santa Fe Trail, whose traffic had recently swelled as a result of the Pike's Peak gold rush. The Indians had also plundered the government mail, killing the three men guarding it, and Satank's 2,500-man force was still in the region of Pawnee Fork on the Arkansas—exactly where Berkeley was headed. Concerned about the reception he might receive there, he prudently altered course and redirected the party northward to Fort Riley. He reached the post on the Kansas River without incident and settled in to a month of sport with the small herds of buffalo grazing within a day's ride of the fort.

Like others before him, Berkeley found that the excitement of the bison hunt made up for the discomfort and inconvenience suffered in reaching the plains. Stalking a huge lone bull, he and a companion crawled on hands and knees through the grass, ducking down motionless whenever the beast lifted its

Stalking buffalo, as shown here in an illustration from Berkeley's book, was easy sport on the open prairie.

great shaggy head to peer around. Observing their prey only a few yards away, he "could not help thinking what mere frogs we were in the grass when compared to our giant foe." Later, on horseback, he pursued a wounded animal on a rollicking chase. "Oh! it was *so* lovely, that wild ride over the plains, the mighty game in view!" As he closed the gap, the buffalo slowed to a canter, then a trot. "His huge head, as well as his tail, was raised; he drew himself up to his full height, and facing suddenly with a sort of side swing right about, he offered his shaggy head to me as I came on, and at once stood stock-still prepared for battle," fifty yards away. The bison made a dash at Berkeley, "flinging the rent turf of the plains far behind him with his short and immensely powerful hind legs; but on the snaffle, faster still away flew [my horse] Taymouth." When the bull stopped, Berkeley walked his lathered, panting horse around him like a proud toreador. He was so impressed by the "huge animal at bay, unscathed and savage and robust in the wildest beauty," that he considered sparing him. This charitable mood quickly passed, however, and after steadying his horse he dropped the beast with two shots from his John Manton double-gun. Berkeley's grandiloquent account concludes: "The monster swayed for a second to and fro, and as he fell dead on his side upon the plain the English death halloa rang aloft."

Berkeley felt it imperative to stay on his best sporting behavior during his prairie adventure, for the eyes of America's fourth estate were upon him. He had heralded his arrival in the United States by writing, for publication in American newspapers, an open letter to the "sportsmen of the New World." Now, as he concluded his stay at Fort Riley and prepared to return home, accounts of his adventures were filtering back to civilization and making their way into print. The articles were not always kind. Berkeley railed against the "General Chokes" and "Jefferson Bricks"—derisive terms for American editors applied by Charles Dickens, who had also run afoul of the press during an earlier tour of the United States. The newspapers, Berkeley charged, libeled him by claiming he suffered from "what they vulgarly called the buck fever" and that he had "failed with the larger game."

Leaving Fort Riley in late October and returning to the settlements, he tried to set the record straight in a lecture on his travels at St. Joseph, Missouri. Among the various notions he sought to dispel in this and subsequent talks was the American misperception that a corn-reared horse, when fed on prairie grass, could not run down a buffalo—Taymouth, he bragged, had conducted himself faultlessly in the chase. He also disputed the advice of Captain Randolph Marcy (whom he had met in New York) that at least fifty men were needed for a plains expedition; Berkeley survived with only ten, "many of whom could scarcely be depended on, and all of whom were badly or insufficiently armed."

In his book *The English Sportsman in the Western Prairie*, Berkeley took to task his countryman Charles A. Murray for his "inflammatory description" of the "romantic pleasure of his association and life on the prairies with the Pawnees." Murray, he asserted, must have been describing the wrong tribe, "for such are the degraded and thievish propensities of that abominably filthy and squalid race, that any white man would not only have been robbed and murdered, but ere his death he would most assuredly have had to submit his head to the will, or at least the inspection, of the chiefs on summer days, in their camps, to have afforded them the pastime of refreshment, entomological capture, and food, for the Pawnees are the only tribe who deem the most revolting insects a luxury."

All of which was a fastidious and long-winded way of saying that the Pawnees—like many aboriginal peoples—groomed each other by picking lice from their hair and eating them, and that Berkeley disapproved of the custom.

8

Envoys from the Great White Mother

The West rejoices in the absence of "nobs" and "snobs"–worshipped
lords and those that worship them.

—William Adolph Baillie-Grohman,
Camps in the Rockies

GRANTLEY BERKELEY'S reaction to Murray, span-
ning as it did a quarter century, reminds us that by 1860 the
British sportsman had been a presence in the West for a generation. On the eve of the Civil War the worst of his breed had
become a thoroughly recognizable type, supercilious and aloof
and viewed by frontier Americans—who on occasion included
émigrés from his own country—with a mixture of awe, resent-
ment, and ridicule.

J. S. Campion, an Englishman who spent most of the 1860s
wandering across the southern plains and Rockies, tells of an
encounter he had at Leavenworth, Kansas, with a party of
British gentlemen bent on prairie sport. Campion had gone to
the local hotel where he noticed in the lobby

> a pile of gun and rifle cases, saddles sewn up in canvas covers,
> boxes and packages of every shape and size, all unmistakably
> English, and suggesting strongly a hunting party. I stepped up
> to the desk, bid good-day to the hotel clerk, and asked him what
> was up. "Tell you what's up? There is a parcel of English
> a-*ris*tocrats arrived, who are going to kill all the game in the
> country. They have brought their dogs, their weapons, and their

mountebanks with them, and they have got a kit of everything in the universal world that is of no earthly use in this country. They are in No. 8, and there is nothing good enough for them in this 'blarsted hotel!' "

The gentlemen's "mountebanks" turned out to be their liveried servants—"two grooms, a gamekeeper, and a body-servant; clean, smart-looking, well-appointed, good-style retainers." Campion forwarded his calling card to the titled guests with the innocent idea of advising them on properly outfitting for their expedition. He was soon shown to their room and duly announced by the black bellhop.

A small party of men of unquestionably British cut were standing together before the spot where, in an English room, the fireplace would have been. The centre one stood with his feet wide apart, his left hand in his trousers' pocket, and his right one extended with my pasteboard between its thumb and first finger. He bowed stiffly, waved the hand holding my card towards a chair, and said: "Mr. Er--r--r"; then he glanced at the card and addressed me properly; "take a chair, and state your business with us."

Campion sat down and was somewhat discomfited when his hosts remained standing, "hands in their pockets, balancing themselves forward on their toes, and then back again, and staring at me." They listened cooly as he explained his purpose—"my best advice was theirs to command"—then dismissed him curtly. "Thanks very much, ah! very much indeed," their spokesman replied. "Most *disinterested* of you—but, ah! we never take advice from an *entire stranger*. We have letters to the first banker here. We shall rely entirely upon him in the matter. He will have our full confidence, Ah! Good-morning. Ah!"

Not even the isolation of the American frontier, it seemed, could breach the wall of English class division. As a chagrinned Campion bowed out of the room, he realized that the gentlemen had taken him for either a "Galvanized Englishman" or a "Whitewashed Yankee"—a mere tradesman, in other words, scheming to make a commission on their purchases. The situation was both ludicrous and pathetic. A dismayed Campion

112

"felt morally certain I should see them made the laughing-stocks of the whole country; hear them described as 'Cockney sportsmen,' as 'Battue lordlings.' Why, even the hotel clerk had already begun to ridicule them." Worse, as a fellow Englishman he would be identified with them and inevitably forced into defending the honor of queen and country: In every barroom and public place, he lamented, "I should have them and their doings flung in my face."

The typical "English tourist-sportsman," Campion advised, "necessarily carries with him his habitual British manner; unconsciously he treats at their first interview his supposed social inferior—that is to say the man who is worse dressed than himself—with abruptness, hauteur, or condescension, according to his individual disposition or the temper he may be in; but whatever way he may treat him, he permits it to be plainly seen he considers himself very much the superior being." Such a manner, Campion added, is "the natural result of the construction of English society, and in England is not offensive. But the true frontiersmen will allow no such pretension."

Given this attitude of disdain, it was no wonder that the West's "unprincipled border idlers and roughs" found the foreign sportsman such an easy mark. Blinded by class assumptions, the typical British sportsman, in Campion's view, could not tell a good man from a bad one and invariably picked his retinue from the dregs of frontier society—and with predictable results. "Most of these men have during their roving careers been many times across the Plains," he said. "To loaf round camp-fires is their delight. It is to them as the blacksmith's shop is to the idlers of many an English country village." Versed in oft-told tales of hunting, trapping, and Indian warfare, they are "thoroughly qualfied to cajole, humbug, and impose on an open-hearted, ardent English sportsman who, knowing nothing of what he is about to undertake, thinks he knows it all."

Campion seems to have known whereof he spoke regarding the character of the British upper class. While the hunting party in Leavenworth viewed him as *declassé*, he apparently came from a well-to-do background. His posthumously published *On the Frontier: Reminiscences of Wild Sports, Personal*

Adventure, and Strange Scenes is lamentably skimpy on biographical details but suggests that his family was of more than modest means. He had hunted in England, France, Albania, and Canada before testing his sporting skills in the American West. His status as a permanent expatriot would even suggest that he might have been a "remittance man," one of those second sons, like Stewart, paid by their families to stay away.

The Campions were prominent enough, at any rate, to be visited by George Catlin, the Pennsylvania lawyer-turned-Indian-artist whose traveling gallery took England and France by storm in the early 1840s. The young Campion listened "with delighted attention" to the artist's anecdotes of plains life and spent hours poring through his portfolio of drawings. The vision of Mandan chiefs in full regalia and of the fabulous landscapes of the upper Missouri inspired him to see the West at first hand. Shortly before the Civil War, he at last realized that ambition with a trip to Fort Riley to shoot buffalo.

Campion wrote in an engagingly self-deprecatory manner and was never afraid to poke fun at himself. As a greenhorn on his first buffalo hunt, he and a companion pursued an old bull for several miles, emptying their revolvers into the beast's flanks but ultimately abandoning the chase when their exhausted ponies would go no farther. The buffalo disappeared over a hill in a "staggering role," Campion recounted, its tongue lolling and sides streaked with gore. "It was quite evident we had yet to learn *where* to hit a buffalo, and by practice acquire ability to strike him there."

Setting up their "Camp Gibralter," the Englishmen made additional forays and quickly improved their hunting skills. When Campion finally downed a buffalo, however, he was faced with the formidable task of skinning it:

> I went to work with confidence, but soon found that if I had not an elephant on my hands, I had the next thing to one. I could not lay a buffalo-bull on the flat of his back as I could a specimen dormouse; and if I could, his hump would not let him stop in such a position.

He managed to get half the skin off and then realized he had to turn the bull over to remove the other half. "I pushed, I pulled; tried one leg, tried another. I perspired and I strained. I sat down and felt very small indeed." Removal of the tongue proved equally tasking. Campion took the animal's "upper lip in one hand and his beard in the other and pulled with all my might, but open his mouth I could not. Grim death had shut it too hard and fast for my strength to avail. I broke the point of my good bowie knife between his jaws, trying to pry his mouth open with it, then a corner off the blade of my tomahawk." At last he cut the bull's throat, "put my hand into the opening, pulled his tongue through, cut it off, and gathering up my spoils and tricks, went to camp rejoicing in success."

The Britishers enjoyed their "free, jolly life" in the field until a lone Indian appeared to disturb their idyll. Assuming a war party might be in the area, they beat a hasty retreat back to Fort Riley. There was good reason for their concern, for the Kiowas and Cheyenne had been raiding the mail stations along the overland route between the Kansas settlements and the Colorado gold fields all that summer. On the sportsmen's return the Fort Riley officers—who had given the dudes up for lost—lifted their glasses to them, toasting "The hair on your head, long may it wave."

Campion's arrival in the West coincided with the start of a bloody decade in Indian-white relations as the pace of emigration quickened. The 1858 discovery of gold near the junction of Cherry Creek and the South Platte—site of present-day Denver—fueled an orgy of prospectors and settlers to central Colorado. Pony Express riders began carrying mail between St. Joseph and Sacramento in the spring of 1860; by the end of the following year the continent had been linked by telegraph, and it was possible for the first time to cross the central plains, Rockies, and Great Basin to California by stage. The Homestead Act of 1862, which promised a 160-acre tract to any man who would settle it, brought more emigrants, and by 1865 most of the West had been organized politically into U.S. Territories.

To its native inhabitants the country was changing at an alarming rate. Recognizing a common enemy at last, the plains tribes made peace with one another and sought to stem the swelling paleface tide. The Comanche, Kiowa, Arapaho, Cheyenne, and Sioux went on the warpath in a bloody arc of terror from Texas to Montana.

With most federal troops fighting Confederates east of the Mississippi, the territories relied heavily on militia for protection. In the typical Indian-white engagement, no quarter was asked and none given. Campion recalled a friendly stopover at a wagon station on the Denver road where, for a dollar, he purchased a coon hound from the station master. "Poor fellow," he would recall later, "it was doubtless the last dog trade ever made by him."

Not many days after I left his station the great Sioux and Cheyenne outbreak occurred. In one night, without warning, for a distance of three hundred miles, every road station but two on the Platte and Big Blue rivers were rushed and captured by them, and, except some few almost miraculous escapes, their inmates were massacred—men, women, and children, even babes.

Following the trail back to Leavenworth, he "daily saw the smouldering ruins of burned and gutted stations—busy scenes, when we had last passed that way, of life and motion. At one place the bodies of a family of sixteen strewed the ground, looking ghastly and horrid in the bright light of day."

There they lay, all, from the gray-headed old grandfather to the last infant—the corpses of the sons, their wives and little ones; their sisters, the old man's three marriageable girls; an orphan grandchild—all lay there, stripped, mutilated, partly charred. Decently and reverentially we put them "below wolf smell."

Although verging on the bathetic, Campion's description reflects the risk and horror faced by anyone venturing on the Colorado frontier in those days. The white response to such atrocities could be equally ruthless, as when a brigade of Colorado militia slaughtered at least two hundred defenseless Cheyenne in the infamous Sand Creek Massacre of 1864. Despite a general sympathy towards Indians, Campion developed in time an attitude nearly as hardened as any sodbuster's. Some years later, as a captain in the Colorado militia recalling the mutilated corpses he had seen along the Denver road, he would order his sergeant on the eve of an engagement to "pass the word quietly amongst the men that we can *not* be troubled with prisoners to-morrow."

* * *

The scenes of devastation witnessed by Campion in Colorado were mirrored to the north in the bloody Minnesota Uprising. There, the Santee—the most sedentary and least warlike of the three branches of the greater Sioux nation—had done their best to accommodate the influx of whites into their territory throughout the previous half century. Now, confined to reservations along the Minnesota River, they were dependent as wards of the state on food provided by the Bureau of Indian Affairs—a federal agency notorious, throughout the history of American expansion, for its venality and corruption. In the summer of 1862 the agent for the Santees delayed delivery of their desperately needed supplies, pending receipt of his accustomed kickback from government contractors. Facing starvation, the Santees under Little Crow broke out of their reservations and went on a rampage, killing at least four hundred whites before federal troops quelled the uprising.

As shock waves from the Santee outbreak spread throughout the northern plains, another Britisher arrived on the scene to record the impact. He was Charles A. Messiter, a sportsman bound for the Canadian prairies west of Fort Garry. Years later he would write an engaging account of his *Sport and Adventures Among the North-American Indians*. Messiter spent a total of eleven years in the West between 1862 and 1875, and the book resulting from his experiences is one of the outstanding travel narratives of the frontier; in its vividness, pacing, and eye for arresting detail it ranks nearly with Ruxton's *Adventures in Mexico and the Rocky Mountains*.

Messiter's travel companions included several other sportsmen and a bloodhound sired by Grantley Berkeley's celebrated "Druid." His itinerary took him by steamer across the Great Lakes, and from there overland to St. Paul and to Georgetown on the Red River of the North. As the head of practical navigation on the upper Mississippi and capital of the young state of Minnesota, St. Paul was a bustling commercial center and an important way station for *émigrés* en route to the northern frontier and western Canada. Messiter was surprised to find there thirty Englishmen, "tempted by a bubble company to subscribe forty pounds apiece on understanding that they should be transported to the gold mines of British Columbia." When the bubble on this particular venture had burst, most of them were cast adrift in St. Paul without money and wound up "sweeping the streets, chopping wood, and doing any work they could find, some of them being broken-down gentlemen, and none of them ever having done any manual labour before."

St. Paul and the entire Minnesota frontier were astir with talk of the Santee uprising. Arriving at Georgetown, Messiter found its dozen or so log cabins mostly deserted, their inhabitants having fled down the Red River in flatboats for fear of Indian attack. Forty miles upstream, federal troops at Fort Abercrombie had temporarily repulsed the first of a succession of raids by Little Crow's forces, but the fort would remain under seige for most of the next two months. Messiter heard the usual stories of Indian atrocities from the few people who had remained behind. "Some of the settlers," he relates, "had been murdered under circumstances of awful barbarity, and one poor woman crawled seven miles into Fort Abercrombie with her nose, ears, and both breasts cut off."

With the situation *in extremis*, Messiter and his companions lost no time in quitting Georgetown. Because the steamboat they had expected to take to Fort Garry had ceased operations on account of hostilities, they purchased bark canoes for the run down the Red River—"one of the most crooked and, I should say, muddiest streams in the world; there being hardly a place on its banks which you could land without sinking to your knees in black mud." When they reached Pembina on the U.S.-Canadian border they unexpectedly found a waiting steamer that would take them the rest of the way to Fort Garry, at the river's junction with the Assiniboine.

*　　*　　*

After outfitting at Fort Garry, Messiter crossed overland to Fort Carlton, a Hudson's Bay Company post on the Saskatche-

118

wan River due north of present-day Saskatoon. He spent the next seven months at the fort and in its vicinity, rejoicing in the abundance of buffalo and other game. His guide, a hearty *voyageur* named Laronde, advised him on the best and safest methods of hunting buffalo—advice that Messiter, in his enthusiasm for the chase, was quick to ignore. "In the excitement of a run, who can think of all this?" he asked. Besides, "it would not be half so much fun if you could remember all your instruction; the getting into scrapes and out of them in your own way being the best part of it."

When the snows descended for the long subarctic winter, Messiter took to himself in a cabin in the nearby Thickwood Hills, which became his base for hunting lynx and moose and running a trapline on five-foot-long snowshoes. He enjoyed a Christmas feast of buffalo hump rib and plum pudding with a local band of Cree Indians and raised his cup with them in a toast to Victoria, "the Great White Mother." Messiter lived for a while among the Cree, learning their ways while successfully resisting an elderly headman's overtures that he marry one of his daughters.

The Englishman's relations with Indians were not always so friendly. On his return to Fort Garry the following spring, he nearly lost his scalp in a run-in with a Sioux chief of particularly ugly disposition named Little Fox. Messiter's account of this incident and his derring-do escape would read as great western fiction were it not true.

He was making the two-week journey with a halfbreed named Badger when they entered an Indian encampment of perhaps sixty warriors and nine lodges, elaborately painted in the manner of the Sioux. They noticed immediately that the camp seemed unnaturally quiet due to the complete absence of dogs—an indication, they quickly surmised, that the Sioux were poaching in Cree territory and therefore traveling light for a speedy getaway if caught. Following Indian protocol, they went to the headman's tipi, recognized by its large size and by the spear and scalps adorning the entrance. Inside, Little Fox—a "very tall, black-looking Indian"—sat with several of his lieutenants glowering at the fire and refusing to acknowledge their visitors' presence. Worse, Little Fox declined Messiter's offer to share his pipe—"no greater insult can be offered a man." The Englishman kept his cool and helped himself to some boiled buffalo meat from the community pot; but as he ate, "a curious feeling" swept over him as "old stories of Indian atrocities came back to me in a very unpleasant manner."

As soon as it seemed prudent to do so, they excused themselves and went outside to mount up. Badger was already on his horse, and Messiter had his foot nearly in the stirrup when he found himself surrounded by a sullen crowd of warriors. An angry exchange followed between him and Little Fox. The latter postured for a while, declaring his hatred of all whites, and proceeded to take the reins of Messiter's horse and lead it away. When the Englishman responded by grabbing Little Fox, the headman pulled a war club from under his blanket and smashed it across the white's upraised arm, breaking it above the elbow and laying a gash across his skull.

With his good arm, Messiter drew his Tranter revolver and fired twice at point-blank range. Hit in the chest and neck, Little Fox collapsed in the dust. Messiter jumped on his horse and galloped off with bullets whizzing past his head. Badger had already made his escape in the confusion; by the time the Sioux had collected their horses and started in pursuit, their quarry was several miles ahead. But between them and Fort Garry lay three hundred miles of open prairies—a "fearfully long ride for one's life on grass-fed horses."

Maintaining a healthy distance from their pursuers, Messiter and his companion rode hard from early afternoon until nightfall, when the absence of a moon afforded them a few hours' rest. At midnight they remounted and continued on, following a rocky ridge for several hours so as to leave no tracks.

Messiter's fractured arm, meanwhile, had grown swollen and excruciatingly painful, with the bone sticking through the skin. They bound it as best as possible with leather strips cut from a hunting shirt, but "the pain was now very great, and nothing but the certainty of being tortured if caught kept me going." Their hopes of shaking the Sioux were dashed the next morning when Little Fox's warriors appeared again, three miles in the distance, "running the trail like bloodhounds."

For the next three days the routine never varied. "Our plan of traveling was to halt soon after sunset, when Badger rubbed down the horses and staked them out, watering them when cool; we then slept, or tried to do so for about three or four hours, when we mounted and rode at a canter till nearly daylight. The horses had then two hours more rest and were rubbed down again, working the sinews of the legs well with the hands, after which we mounted and rode all day, getting off now and then for a few minutes. By these means, we had gained a good many miles on the Indians, who sometimes did not come into sight till nearly twelve o'clock, when the fast riding began."

On the morning of the fourth day they came to a small settlement some twenty miles west of Fort Garry. They were safe at last, the Sioux beating a hasty retreat when the men of the community rushed out to greet them with blazing rifles. The exhausted riders were covered with dust and sweat and their clothes in tatters. Messiter's greasy hair, unwashed and uncut for a year, hung to his shoulders, and his color was that of "light mahogony." After a woman dressed his arm, he collapsed in bed and slept for twenty hours.

Following a hearty meal, they bid their hosts goodby and rode the rest of the way into Fort Garry, "where we attracted a good deal of attention, our horses being mere bags of bones." Messiter's first stop was at the local bakery to purchase a loaf of bread hot from the oven and a pound of butter. "I ate them in about equal proportions, and do not think I ever enjoyed anything so much in my life." During his winter encampment, he had subsisted partly on a prairie staple called *galette*, an unleavened concoction made of flour, water, and baking soda formed into flatcakes and fried. "It is not bad when hot," he observed, "but only fit for making bullets when cold."

Later, on his return to St. Paul, Messiter learned that Little Fox, the man he had killed, was a renegade with a $1,000 price on his head. He made no attempt to collect his bounty, however, as he had no witness except Badger, whose halfbreed status made his testimony worthless in the eyes of frontier whites.

*   *   *

Surfeited with adventure, Messiter went home to England to recover completely from his summer on the plains. He returned to the American frontier in 1866, this time to St. Joseph to outfit for a hunt on the Kansas prairie beyond the Republican River.

His narrative here reveals something of the pitfalls faced by any gentleman sportsman preparing for a season in the field. Even a seasoned frontier traveler like himself was not immune from those "specious men who offer to buy horses, mules, and outfit for them, on the plea that they know the people and their ways, and can save them a lot of money." Frontier charlatans like "the Colonel," who approached him in St. Joe, were the linear if slightly more polished descendants of Berkeley's "bloody arm of the Rocky Mountains." When Messiter commissioned him to procure "a good span of mules, and four horses suited to the West," the results might have been predictable. One of the mules purchased by the Colonel was manifestly lame and had evidently been so for months. Of the four horses, one was "a confirmed bolter," while another "ate up his bridle, reins, or anything else with which he might be fastened." The third horse was "touched of the wind" and useless, therefore, in a chase. Only the fourth—a "race-mare" that could reportedly "do a mile in some wonderfully short time"—appeared satisfactory. But events showed otherwise. The mare turned out to be hopelessly gun-shy, "jumping many feet" if the rider so much as raised his rifle.

Messiter's concern with his animals was more than justified, for he knew from firsthand experience that a good horse could make the difference between life and death on the plains. Finding a reliable mount was never easy, however, and looks alone could be deceptive. One "very handsome animal" purchased the following season seemed excellent in all respects, but the rigors of the field soon revealed its defects. An initial gun-shyness proved curable, but its master had not figured on another phobia. At the end of a successful buffalo chase, Messiter butchered his prey and packed the meat on the horse's back.

I was standing in front of him, putting on my coat, when he turned his head round and smelt the meat, seeming to take in for the first time what it was, and then began as desperate a struggle as I ever had with a horse. He kicked and reared and jumped. I was holding on to the bit, and was often taken off my feet, the meat flying about and hitting him and driving him nearly mad.

A battered Messiter managed to hang on until the buckskin strap gave way and the meat fell to the ground. Immediately the horse went quiet. Leading him back to the butchered buffalo, Messiter hitched the horse to the buffalo's head, blindfolded him with his coat, tied on the meat again, and remounted and removed the blindfold "for the second act of the performance." The horse began bucking violently, but Messiter got him turned in the right direction and they were off in a gallop. After a heart-stopping ride the terrified animal flew into camp, nearly stampeding the picketed horses before Messiter could rein him in.

"Complete Summersault," from John Palliser's Solitary Rambles.

Sometimes the best horse flesh was found far from the usual sources of procurement. Messiter exchanged the gun-shy mare purchased in St. Joe for a plains-hardened pony he came across in a small Kansas settlement. Like Ruxton's faithful Panchito, she was a tough little mount who made up in sure-footedness, wind, and speed whatever she may have lacked in size and pedigree—"by far the best animal that I have ever sat on in America."

The pony quickly proved her mettle on the open prairie when Messiter, hunting alone, encountered seventeen mounted Sioux spread out in a line between him and camp.

The Indians sensed an easy scalp, but once again Messiter—aided by his ready wits and a trusty steed—commanded the day. He rode along the line of Indians at a hard gallop, keeping parallel and slightly in front of them, "gradually increasing the pace till I had dropped the slow ponies, and had about eight of the fastest opposite to me." After another two miles a gap of three hundred yards had opened between the first group of Indians and the second. Messiter let the faster party get within a hundred yards of him. Then he wheeled, lying flat on the pony's back and spurring her on with the butt of his rifle as he charged through the gap in the Sioux phalanx. With bullets flying overhead he rode for his life, firing his pistol in a prearranged signal of distress as he approached camp. When the other members of his party came out firing, the Sioux beat a hasty retreat, flashing insulting gestures as they disappeared over the hill.

*   *   *

Messiter spent two seasons on the Kansas prairie and seems to have loved every minute of them. Although it would not remain so much longer, the rolling country beyond the Republican River was sufficiently removed from the emigrant trails that it still boasted an abundance of game—not only buffalo but deer, elk, antelope, and wild turkey. "I do not think I was ever in a more perfect hunting-ground than this," he declared, "the danger from Indians giving it that dash of excitement which is always needed to make any life really perfect."

124

In contrast to the attitude of Grantley Berkeley and other gentlemen sportsmen, his enthusiasm for the country also extended to the hired hands. Messiter had an eye for character and could spot a good man behind the most unpromising exterior. One of the best he engaged was a hard-bitten type named Fox, "who seemed by all accounts to fear nothing." Fox was barefoot when Messiter found him digging a well along the Republican. When he offered to buy him boots in the nearest town, however, Fox demurred, explaining that he had killed two Germans in a gambling row there and was wanted by the sheriff. He also volunteered that he carried a price on his head in Texas. "He was evidently a first-class desperado, but as our trip was a dangerous one, his pluck more than counterbalanced everything else."

Fox performed admirably through the 1867 season but was murdered before Messiter could take him on again for the following year's hunt. In his place he hired—out of the local jail—a St. Joe butcher named Douglass, "who had fought seven others in the market and had strewn them all over the place." His services were put to good use almost immediately outside a saloon, when he cowed a gang of rowdies who tried to pick a fight with his new employer.

It was in St. Joseph that Messiter also found "Billy Breeze," an ex-London bobby dismissed for drinking, who had emigrated to America, fought in the Civil War, and wound up in Kansas as a professional hunter. Taking a chauvinistic fancy to a fellow countryman, he took him on as a dog-keeper and general factotum.

Messiter had reason aplenty to hire the toughest and most experienced men available, for Indian hostilities had reached a new apogee of violence in the years following the Sand Creek Massacre. On the central and northern plains the Cheyenne, Arapaho, and Sioux had formed an alliance creating a daunting barrier to westward expansion. Their harassment of emigrant trains and constructon crews along the route of the Union Pacific rail line provoked a ruthless response from Civil War veterans like General Philip H. Sheridan and Colonel George A. Custer, who employed the same uncompromising tactics against Indians as they had against the South a few years before. In late November of 1868, Custer's Seventh Cavalry, riding to the fife and drums of the "Garry Owen," attacked at dawn a Cheyenne encampment along the Washita River in present-day Oklahoma. Sheridan had ordered Custer to trap the hostiles in winter quarters and "to destroy their villages and ponies, to kill or hang all warriors and to bring back all women and children." Yellow Hair—the dashing "boy general" of the Civil War, who was still not yet thirty—followed his orders faithfully, destroying the entire stock of Cheyenne horses (he shot many of them himself) and taking no male prisoners older than eight. .

Over the next ten years, despite the occasional and dramatic Indian victory, the government's relentless and often brutal tactics wore down and ultimately subdued the plains tribes. Taking advantage of traditional Indian rivalries, the Army found it expedient when possible to employ Indian auxiliaries in plains warfare. Crow scouts often guided U.S. cavalry columns, while a Pawnee battalion under the command of Major Frank North won fame for its valuable service protecting the Union Pacific as it made its way inexorably toward Promontory Point. The Pawnees' fierceness in battle earned the respect of the professional military men under whom they served in a series of campaigns against hostile plains tribes. Bernard DeVoto has commented on the Pawnee "renaissance" during this period, while noting caustically (and perhaps unfairly) that the Army's use of them against the Sioux "permitted us to destroy two tribes in one righteous cause."

*   *   *

Another English sportsman, Frederic Trench Townshend, spent several weeks in the company of Major North and his Pawnee troops during an excursion up the Platte in the fall of 1868. Townshend's purpose in visiting the West was to pursue the "noble sport of buffalo hunting," but the story he relates in *Ten Thousand Miles of Travel, Sport, and Adventure* is more interesting for what it tells us of the lives of Indians and soldiers on the post-Civil War frontier than for its predictable tales of the bison hunt.

Townshend was a military man himself, a captain in the

Second Life Guards on leave from his duties, and he was accompanied throughout his travels on the central plains by cavalry with a twofold mission: to protect the Union Pacific from Indian attack, and to locate any roving bands of Sioux who by treaty belonged on their new reservation in the Black Hills. The Union Pacific had been under construction since 1865 and was proceeding westward—despite attacks on the labor gangs by parties of Sioux, Cheyenne, and Arapaho—at the phenomenal pace of a mile a day.

Around the nightly campfires, Townshend listened with rapt attention to the tales of Indian atrocities told by the horse soldiers in whose company he traveled. A survivor of Major George A. Forsyth's recent stand against a force of five hundred Arapaho and Sioux raised the Englishman's hair with an account of the fate of captured troopers: "Some had their entrails pulled out and fastened to a tree, round which they were driven until their whole interior was wound round it. Others were hoisted up on sharp stakes and left to die a lingering death, while many were skinned alive and mutilated." With such stories abounding, it is little wonder that many troopers followed the cavalryman's maxim to "save the last bullet for yourself," chosing suicide over capture. After getting his fill with such tales of torture, Townshend returned to his tent, "quite satisfied with the justice and necessity of the orders which our party were prepared to carry out, viz., to kill every Red Skin we should meet—man, woman, or child." When the howling of wolves awakened him that night, a feeling "as though an Indian was scalping and skinning me made me think that the life of an American soldier, when scouting on the plains of the Far West, was one which I should not care to exchange permanently for the less exciting, but decidedly safer, occupation of mounting guard at Her Majesty's Palaces in London."

Tales of Indian brutality notwithstanding, Townshend enjoyed and respected the Pawnee auxiliaries he came to know during his prairie passage. Indian ponies were "wonderfully tough little beasts" in his view, and the Pawnees themselves were splendid riders. "It is commonly said in the West that, when a white man has ridden a horse to a standstill, an Indian will jump on his back and gallop him seventy miles farther." A

Pawnee scout named Bob told him that he had visited Washington and New York; he didn't care for the capital because, as he put it, there was "too much nigger there," although New York dazzled him with the skill of its pick-pockets.

The Pawnee, Townshend wrote, "are great gamblers, and having nothing else to play for stake their clothing. An Indian who has been fortunate will sometimes appear wearing trousers, mocassins, two or three coats, blankets, and an old felt hat while another who has been unlucky in play has nothing left but an old blanket thrown round his shoulders, over which the long black hair is streaming." He found the latter "far more natural and stately than his lucky comrade, who, dressed up in his extravagant European garments, with his face painted red and yellow, and an eagle's feather stuck in his wide-awake hat, is simply a ludicrous object, more suggestive of the monkey than of the noble savage." The Pawnees, he added, were made to camp at least a hundred yards away from the troops "for fear we would suffer from the vermin which abound on their persons."

Of the Army's regular soldiers, Townshend was surprised to find that so many of them—as well as a few of the officers—were Irish. During the march he "sometimes heard songs decidedly anti-British, such as 'The Wearing of the Green,' which seems to have been adopted as a sort of Fenian anthem."

As a soldier himself—even a pampered one in the Queen's Guard—Townshend could look with sympathy on the cavalryman's lot. His life was far from enviable. A soldier or officer on frontier duty might go three years without leave, although married officers at least had their wives and families with them and could take advantage of "exceptional opportunities" in land speculation along the Union Pacific route. Like all soldiers in wartime, the troopers suffered through interminable bouts of boredom and suffocating routine, punctuated by moments of terror.

Given the cruelty of the enemy, Townshend could understand the soldier's hatred of Indians and the prevalence of this attitude throughout the white population. As an outsider, however, he could also sympathize with the Indian's plight. He was shocked by accounts of the "horrible outrage" at Sand Creek four years earlier. The atrocity occurred, Messiter noted, with the Cheyenne at least nominally at peace and with most of their braves off hunting, when a thousand Third Colorado Volunteers descended on their village south of Denver. A former Methodist minister, the notorious Colonel John Chivington, led the attack in the certain conviction that God had placed him on earth to rid it of heathen redskins. Like Custer at the Washita, he attacked an under-defended village at dawn. In both episodes the Cheyenne had retired to winter encampments and tragically assumed that a truce existed in Indian-white hostilities. (Townshend heard the story of Sand Creek from the officers and men at Fort McPherson at the same time that Sheridan was planning the winter campaign that would result, only a month later, in the Custer atrocity.)

The village along Sand Creek, Townshend related, was attacked by Chivington's forces "and every soul put to the sword, old men, women, and little children—none were spared. The work of scalping and mutilating the bodies then began, and not only the scalps of the men, but also the bosoms and other parts of the women were cut off, and hung to the saddles and belts of the volunteers as they rode back in triumph to Denver." Although a Congressional inquiry would later condemn the treachery of Chivington's attack, Townshend added, it was hailed a "great victory" by westerners. "Most of the lower classes—the hunters, trappers, ranchkeepers, &c.—to whom I afterwards spoke about the business, considered it a justifiable and meritorious act, saying that an Indian ought to be killed whenever he can be found. When such is the treatment the Indians receive at the hand of the whites, it is no wonder if they kill any white they can catch, with every cruel torture known to the savage."

*   *   *

Townshend's description of white and Indian brutalities are sufficiently graphic to make us forget that they are second-hand observations, for during his period of travel with federal troops the Platte River country was spared any major attack. Most of the action during this and the previous season occurred to the north, along the Bozeman Trail through the Powder

River country, and to the south along the Republican, where his compatriot Charles Messiter hunted in the summer of 1867.

Messiter had taken to the field from his base at Fort Kearny without escort, despite the considerable risk of encountering one of the several hostile bands of Sioux, Cheyenne, or Arapaho spreading terror throughout the region. Riding alone near the Little Blue River one day, he came upon the remains of an Indian camp so recently broken that the marrow bones strewn about it were still moist. Later, along the Republican River, he noticed what appeared to be an abandoned wagon in the bankside bushes and went to investigate: "On reaching it, I found it had been plundered, while round it lay the bodies of five men and four horses, all of the former being scalped, and one who lay under the hind end of the waggon had had the top of his head chopped off down to the eyes." Messiter later learned that the mutilated remains belonged to an Army major and several of his men who had gone hunting to escape the tedium of fort life. By the time he came upon them, the victims had probably been dead a fortnight and were partially eaten by wolves.

A shaken Messiter made camp a mile from the scene of carnage and spent a fitful night, dreaming of the butchered soldiers and worrying that Indians might still be roaming in the area. He had hoped to winter in the mountains later that year. As he pondered the grisly remains on the Republican, however, discretion won over his quest for further adventure. It was not the best of times to be a white man in country that the Indians, for a bit longer at least, could still claim as their own.

9

Hell on Wheels

Around us, in front of us, at our side, is the immeasurable nothing of the sagebrush desert. The streets of the settlement begin in it, and end in it with the same startling abruptness. Built yesterday–inhabited to-day–deserted to-morrow, is written on everything.
—William Adolph Baillie-Grohman,
Camps in the Rockies

CHARLES MESSITER retired to New Orleans for the fall of 1867. He found on his arrival there that the old French colonial capital, while offering a sensuous respite from the rigors of prairie life, posed special dangers of its own. A raging epidemic of cholera—a disease that could act with devastating swiftness—was killing two hundred people a day. Messiter made the acquaintance of one young man who seemed healthy enough when he accompanied him to a local fairgrounds. On their return to the city his companion complained of feeling ill; to Messiter's astonishment, he was dead and buried less than twelve hours later, despite the Englishman's efforts to nurse him through a night of fever.

It was not long after his young friend's demise that Messiter came down with the dread disease himself. It fortunately proved a mild case, and after a convalescence of several weeks he was up and about again partaking in the city's pleasures. These included high-stakes poker at a fashionable casino, where he passed the night in the company of a party of former Confederate generals, among them P. T. Beauregard, a sur-

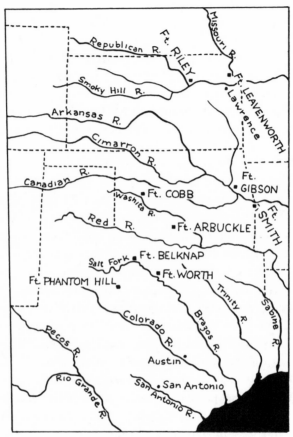

TEXAS~OKLAHOMA~KANSAS
FRONTIER, 1865

vivor of Pickett's Charge at the Battle of Gettysburg.

After taking his fill of the comforts and companionship of urban society, Messiter was ready for further adventures afield and set off for East Texas to hunt bear, turkey, and snipe.

Texas, of course, had been a slave state and a member of the Confederacy. Sultry, bayou-laced East Texas was deeply southern in the attitudes that prevailed there in the years following the Civil War. In his travels, Messiter observed firsthand some of the bitterness and adjustment that went with Reconstruction. Lynchings were a common occurrence. A Galveston man related to him the story of one of his servants, a former slave, who had been charged with beating and robbing two white women. The man was escorting the accused into town to await trail in the local jail when, as he expressed it, "The boys met me and we put him up." When Messiter naively asked what he meant by the term, the man pointed to his horse and asked if he could see the rawhide lariat on the saddle. "Well, that is what we put him up with."

The Texan went on to explain that "since the war it had been almost impossible to get a Negro punished, the usual plan being to send any who had committed a crime to a black regiment, and that therefore in this case they had taken the law into their own hands. He added that when we had been longer in the country we should often hear of the troublesome Negroes having disappeared, and of having gone on a visit to their friends in the north, which meant in reality that they had gone underground."

Messiter found a similar kind of vigilante justice prevailing against horse thieves of any color. In San Antonio, he noted, the stolen horse frequently served as passive executioner. The thief was placed on the horse with his hands tied behind him and a rope around his neck. The other end of the rope was tied to the branch of a tree, "it being then merely a question of time as to when the pony would move off to feed and leave the man hanging. Since this became the unwritten law of the land, horse-stealing has gone out of fashion."

Like men everywhere in the West, East Texans placed special value on horse flesh and the skills of a seasoned horseman. Messiter was surprised to find that many of the best riders were Negroes, who excelled in the dangerous and demanding job of breaking wild horses. When a wrangler mounted a wild mustang for its first ride, he observed, the bucking might go on "for a half an hour or more, the rider bleeding at the nose and mouth when it was over." Few men could break wild horses for more than two years, he was told, "and they then are wrecks for life." Many of them did not even last that long but were "killed or maimed by horses falling on them."

(The East Texas counties had supported big cattle operations since before the Civil War, and the black cowboys whom Messiter observed breaking wild mustangs were now doing for pay what they had formerly done as slaves. The black cowboy played a significant if unheralded role in the great postwar trail drives from Texas to Abilene, Dodge City, and other Kansas railheads. Virtually every outfit on the Chisholm Trail had its share of black cowboys, and a few of them were all black.)

At the end of March 1868 Messiter headed north from San Antonio, following a string of Army posts that would eventually take him to Fort Arbuckle in the Indian Territory of Oklahoma. His ultimate destination was Denver and the Colorado Rockies. There were several other sportsmen in his party, which also included the ex-London bobby, Billy Breeze.

In what by now had become his *modus operandi*, Messiter survived several more of his Perils-of-Pauline escapes from bellicose Indians lusting for an easy scalp. The first of these incidents occurred along the Brazos River. Messiter was riding alone one morning when he surprised a party of braves camped for a meal along the river. The inevitable chase ensued. With the Indians gaining ground on him, Messiter spied a lone rock in the grass, reined in his horse and took position behind it. When the lead pursuer galloped within range of his 12-bore double rifle, he squeezed off a shot that blasted a fist-sized hole in the Indian pony's neck. The horse collapsed in the dust and pinned the rider, who was "some moments in extricating himself" from beneath the dead animal.

The other Indians, meanwhile, had turned tail at the report of Messiter's gun. When the horseless brave at last managed to free himself and hobbled away in the direction of his companions, the Englishman resisted the temptation to take advantage of his situation. "I could easily have shot him in the back as he limped off, but it seemed so like murder that I could not do it." So he let him go, contenting himself to shouting and waving his arms to hurry him along.

Messiter's party rested at Fort Belknap, a post located north of present-day Abilene, on the Salt Fork of the Brazos on the overland mail route between Fort Smith, Arkansas, and Santa Fe. Four companies of cavalry were billeted at the fort, and camped outside it was a band of Tonkawa Indians who invited Messiter to a buffalo dance in honor of his "Great White Queen."

The Tonkawas lived on the margins of the Texas prairie and had coexisted in an uneasy relationship with whites for more than three hundred years. Their day in the sun—if it had ever existed—had long since passed. By the time Messiter encountered them they were "much thinned by smallpox" and had been ravaged as well by neighboring tribes in Oklahoma and Texas. The Tonkawa headman invited his English guests to join in the buffalo dance, but as their would-be female partners "were not sufficiently tempting," they respectfully declined. The festivities began with a prayer to the Great Spirit for success in the hunt and protection against their enemy, the Comanches. "One old fellow whom I sat near had a necklace made of the finger-and-toe-joints of a Comanche he had killed some years before; and he was evidently very proud of it, refusing to sell it to me, though I offered what to him was a long price. Killing a Comanche seemed a very rare event, for they had divided the man amongst them—one having the scalp, another the ears, which he had dried and hung round his neck."

Messiter would soon have experience of his own with the fearsome Comanches, who for two centuries had been the scourge of the southern plains. Although weakened in recent years by smallpox and cholera, this southern race of the Shoshones remained a formidable presence in Texas and Oklahoma and had lost none of its truculence or consummate skill in horse thievery. Seeking a guide to head his party north to Fort Cobb in Oklahoma, Messiter hired a surly Comanche chief named Asahabe—"an immense man, standing six feet four and broad in proportion, with a very ill-tempered and treacherous face, the hair growing close down to the eyebrows."

Asahabe proved as unreliable as his appearance suggested, for they were just two days out from Fort Belknap when he deserted. Messiter knew that Comanches were in the area and suspected that Asahabe, who had slipped away during the night, would reconnoitre with them and return to plunder his party. They had to get to an Army post fast. The nearest one—Fort Arbuckle, in southern Oklahoma—was an estimated two and a half days away; losing no time, they set out for it early the next morning across the rolling prairie.

As expected, within hours Asahabe appeared on their trail, leading forty Comanche braves. Advancing ahead of the others, their erstwhile guide approached carrying a branch as a signal to parlay. Give up your wagon, outfit and all extra horses, he demanded of Messiter, and in return the whites could keep a horse and rifle apiece and would be assured safe passage to Fort Arbuckle. When Asahabe added that his terms were non-negotiable, Messiter gave him two minutes to get out of camp or be shot.

Rebuffed, Asahabe rode off in a rage to rejoin his band. The Comanches might have attacked then and there but for the vastly superior firepower of Messiter and his companions. While outnumbered better than four to one, they carried Winchester repeating rifles capable of firing fourteen rounds at a clip. Their complete armory would give pause to the most truculent warchief. It totaled nine Winchesters with three thousand rounds, four double breechloaders with several hundred rounds, and an eight-gauge double shotgun, "which loaded with about two ounces of buckshot in each barrel would be grand at close quarters." The Comanche arms, by contrast, probably consisted of old muzzle loaders and bows and arrows.

Jettisoning several sacks of flour to lighten their load, Messiter and his companions continued on their journey. The Comanches kept out of sight for the rest of the day, appearing only once to issue some inconsequential harassing fire. The whites drove till nearly dark, "filling buckets and kettles at a pond we passed and watering all the animals, so that we might camp in the middle of the prairie, where there was no cover of any kind to hide a crawling man."

Messiter's defensive tactics reflect his native good sense and past experience at evading Indians. To avoid ambush whenever approaching a wooded creek bed, he and one or two others would ride ahead of the wagon and, once within rifle distance, gallop parallel to the timber, lying Indian fashion on the side of their horses to draw any fire. This gambit paid off on the second morning of the chase when they were shot at by a lone Comanche who had gone ahead of the others. Messiter and two companions set off in pursuit and managed to kill him with a lucky shot. Examining the body, they found that the hollow-point Metford shell had blown a hole the size of a hat crown in his back, nearly cutting him in half.

They were now faced with the squeamish decision of making good on a boast to scalp any dead Indian whose body they might recover. When the opportunity actually presented itself, how-ever, "each one tried to get out of it" until the driver of the wagon, "asking why we made such a fuss about such a trifle, took it off at once, removing merely the scalp lock and skin under it, about the size of, and in the same position as, the tonsure of a priest." The driver's grisly trophy, Messiter added, was modest in contrast to what the Comanches might do to them if given the chance. "When Indians have plenty of time, they like to take the whole skin of the head, beginning behind, skinning the head and the whole face, including the ears; and the scalp when thus taken presents a ghastly appearance when stretched."

Discovery of the mutilated remains of their fellow warrior sent the Comanches into a rage. Messiter's party had by now forded the stream, and from the opposite side they could hear their pursuers howling in protest beyond the wooded banks. Scrambling their horses and plunging across the creek in pur-suit, the Indians overtook the wagon, "yelling their war-whoop, and placing their closed fists against their foreheads and then opening and shutting them, which means 'war to the knife.' " The whites responded with a fusillade that cut down three of the Comanche ponies.

Towards evening a formidable group of reinforcements ap-peared, swelling Asahabe's ranks to an estimated two hundred. Outnumbered now by more than ten to one, Messiter and company fortified themselves in a copse of timber at the top of a rise, a position that gave them command of the surrounding prairie. Over the next twelve hours the Comanches prudently stayed out of range of the deadly Winchesters and restricted their actions to taunts and harassing fire. The only casualty in this Mexican standoff, which went on through the night, was a gut-shot mule.

The Comanches gradually worked themselves into a fury and the next morning rushed to within several hundred yards of the redoubt before retreating in a hail of lead, losing five more horses and a warrior. Next, Asahabe himself galloped up the rise in a lone attack but was stopped when his black stallion was shot from under him. The whites rushed the fallen rider in hopes of collecting another scalp and a fifty dollar bounty placed by Messiter on Asahabe's head, but the Comanches successfully covered their chief's retreat.

Messiter could take grim satisfaction in having held off, for more than two days, an overwhelming force of the plain's fiercest fighters. Yet they could not hold out indefinitely, and if they were to save their scalps they would have to reach Fort Arbuckle soon.

The situation showed signs of improvement when they heard shouting and musket fire and watched three horsemen appear over the ridge, running the Comanche gauntlet. The riders turned out to be friendly Caddo Indians who had been hunting out of Fort Arbuckle. Messiter was cheered to learn that the fort was only a few hours' ride away. One of the Caddos took the fastest horse available and rode hell-for-leather to rally reinforcements.

Knowing that troops would be arriving soon, Asahabe decided to risk an all-out assault. In the fury of the ensuing attack the Comanches closed to within buckshot range, but after fierce fighting they were driven back with the loss of two more braves and seven horses. The whites suffered six wounded, one of them mortally. The wagon was awash in blood. Messiter himself had taken an arrow under the knee and a bullet in the shoulder, which a companion later cut out with a razor.

The repulse of the Comanche attack broke Asahabe's will to fight any longer. Messiter proceeded on to Fort Arbuckle; although his pursuers lingered on the trail, they remained well out of range of the Winchesters. Several miles from the fort, the Comanches turned tail as two companies of cavalry came riding over the hill. Messiter and his exhausted party completed their harrowing journey under escort and were safe at last within the walls of Fort Arbuckle.

*　　*　　*

Recovering at Fort Arbuckle, Messiter reconsidered his plan for continuing north across the prairie to Denver. They were certain to encounter other tribes on the trail whose disposition was likely to be no better than the Comanches'. His goal was to hunt that season in the Colorado Rockies, and there were safer if less direct ways of getting there. So he headed east to Memphis, took a steamboat to Omaha, and boarded the Union Pacific for its terminus at Julesburg, Colorado.

The Union Pacific had been under construction since 1865 and was still a year away from its rendezvous with the Central Pacific at Promontory Point, overlooking the Great Salt Lake. In the last furious year of constructon as much as seven miles of track were laid in a single day. A string of boom towns grew up along the route to satisfy the basic needs—drink, sex, and food, more-or-less in that order—of the labor gangs. Julesburg, in the extreme northeast corner of Colorado just over the Wyoming line, was one of the most notorious of these towns, a ramshackle collection of shacks filled largely with gamblers, prostitutes, and their clients. "This place," a stranger told Messiter during his first night in town, "is only removed by the thickness of a sheet of writing paper from a certain hot place." The floating populations of Julesburg, Cheyenne, Laramie, and the other railroad boom towns referred to them with a certain perverse pride as "hell on wheels."

Messiter had every reason to agree with this appellation. While walking along the street shortly after his arrival, he and his companion, another Englishman identified only as "F--," were soon presented with "an opportunity of seeing what kind of place we were in." Across the street, the doors of a saloon crashed open and disgorged two of its customers in advanced stages of inebriation. As the two tumbled out into the street, one of them grabbed the other and pressed a revolver to his head. The two men grappled for the gun while Messiter and F-- looked on in horror. Instinctively they started across the street to break up the fight but were stopped immediately by another bystander, who "told us not to be fools, but to remain where we were, as the more of such men there were shot the better."

The streets were composed of small one-story wooden houses of all shapes, and placed anyhow, some projecting many feet further into the street than the others—no two being alike—and the intervals between them were filled with empty tins, broken crockery, old boots, broken bottles, and all kinds of rubbish. Some men had put a short piece of board sidewalk in front of their houses, and some had not, which made the walking at night very awkward, especially as there were no street lamps, and the only light came from the lanterns hung in front of saloons.

Since there were no bona fide hotels available, Messiter and F-- moved into an "eating-house" with attached sleeping quarters. The accommodations amounted to a long lean-to attached to the outside wall of the building and partitioned into cubicles. Guests were assigned two to a bed, which with a chair and washstand took up almost all of the floor space.

The first night we were there it began to rain, and almost immediately F-- and I felt water pouring on us; so we lit the candle, and then found that the roof was only composed of boards laid side by side, the chinks not being stopped in any way, and that consequently there was nothing to keep the rain from coming through. Having a mackintosh sheet with us, we put it over the bed, but it was not quite large enough, and, besides, the water collected on it so rapidly that there was soon a small lake in the middle, and in shooting it off from time to time we at last shot one lot into the middle of the bed.

To escape the deluge, Messiter and F-- gathered their clothes and bedding and retired to the "eating room," where they found most of the other guests, "of all ages and both sexes, in similar dress, or rather undress, looking very miserable." With the rest of the clientele they retired under and on top of the tables for the remainder of the night.

Taking meals at the establishment could be a novel experience in its own right. The people who came to dinner were "a very miscellaneous collection" of ox drivers, mule skinners, railway workers, store clerks, dancehall girls and saloon keepers. The last group seemed primarily composed of ex-prize fighters, according to Messiter, and along with the professional gamblers made up the brahmin class of this boomtown society. The elite gamblers "seemed always to have plenty of money, with which they were continually treating their friends, and they generally drove a fine pair of trotting horses and had some good dogs." The gamblers had easy pickings among the town's itinerant population, which besides railroad men included miners from the gold and silver fields of the Colorado Rockies. It was not uncommon for one of these rubes to be cleaned out of a season's wages in a single night.

If the workers and miners had any money left after an evening of poker or faro, they could spend some of it in the ubiquitous dance halls. Messiter visited one of these establishments and observed there "three females, two of whom were smoking cigars, and you had to pay half a dollar to dance round the room with one of them, standing drinks afterwards." Music was provided by a street organ.

Each place worked hard at attracting customers. One oddly popular come-on was the marathon distance walker who—for a fee, of course—could be observed treading his paces in the back room. A typical advertisement outside the premises might read: "Walk in, gentlemen, and see John Smith, the champion long-distance walker in the world, who is doing one thousand miles in one thousand hours, and is now fresher than when he began last week.—N.B. Don't be taken in by the shams at the other houses." It cost a shilling to have a look at Smith, who always appeared "wonderfully fresh." This was not surprising, noted Messiter, "as he went comfortably to bed on the house being closed, and resumed operations when it opened at eight the next morning."

"Almost every night," he added, "there were fights in these saloons, a good many men were shot, and no notice was taken of it, as there were only three policemen in the place, who took particularly good care to get out of the way as soon as a row began."

In lieu of statutory law enforcement, peace of a sort was maintained by the local vigilance committee. Staying in Cheyenne, which Messiter and F-- used as a jumping-off point for an elk hunt in the Wind River Mountains, they awoke one morning to find four men hanging from telegraph poles outside their boarding house. Another man convicted by the Cheyenne vigilantes was placed against a telegraph pole for a summary execution by firing squad. The committee members, as it turned out, simply wanted to put the fear of God in him and fired only blanks. The man died of fright.

The vigilantes also took care, in their fashion, of a desperado named Hughes, who was reported to have murdered at least five men. The gentleman's wife was alleged to be "as bad as himself" and reportedly had assisted her husband in several slayings. After hanging Mr. Hughes, the vigilance committee gave his widow twenty-four hours to get out of town or meet a similar fate. Messiter went down to the station to help see her off and found a large crowd assembled for the same purpose. When Mrs. Hughes appeared—wearing "a great deal of jewelry," Messiter noted—rather than being cursed as he might have expected, she was instead mobbed by well-wishers. The good lady "joked and laughed with them as if she was going to a ball. After getting into the train she alternately cursed the vigilance committee and sang snatches of comic [read bawdy] songs, and was kissing her hand as the train disappeared round a curve."

*   *   *

Vigilante justice would make an equally vivid impression on Messiter's compatriot, F. Trench Townshend, when he visited the Union Pacific towns of Laramie, Benton, and Bryan later that year. Townshend had journeyed by rail to Laramie from South Platte, Nebraska, after completing his summer tour of the prairies in the company of Major North and his Pawnee battalion. Arriving at Laramie in the morning, he was greeted by a lineup of corpses—ten in all—hanging from such makeshift gallows as telegraph poles and the timbers of a frame house under construction.

Laramie was a town of two thousand inhabitants, he observed, consisting of "four or five streets with brick or wooden buildings, though the favourite material for the construction of the stores is frame and canvas mixed. Drinking and gambling saloons, and brothels, compose the majority of the houses. . . . The population is at present a floating one, comprising some of the vilest scum of the earth." On a more positive note, Townshend added that the "embryo city" could at least boast of "a really fine railway hotel just opened, and a bank," although "of church or chapel I saw no sign."

Members of the merchant class made up Laramie's vigilance committee, which typically carried out its business at night. While condoning lynch law as "a stern necessity in these western towns," Townshend observed that many of those acting as judge, jury, and executioner were scarcely more principled than the scoundrels they condemned in secret session; a bribe of a few dollars, he was told, could and frequently did change a "guilty" vote to innocent. Perhaps the worst failing of vigilante justice was its capriciousness. "It would occupy a volume to relate all the tales of murder, violence and crime that were told me," he said. Every man "goes about with a pair of revolvers and a bowie knife in his belt" and uses them on the slightest provocation, "knowing well that the chances are fifty to one he is never punished for his crime."

Townshend left sordid Laramie behind him for a brief, bracing excursion into the high country. With a party of cavalry from nearby Fort Sanders commanded by Colonel John Gibbon, he climbed the Laramie Plain under a cloudless Indian summer sky and crossed the Laramie Range into George Gore's old stomping grounds of North Park, Colorado. The mountains were blanketed in the season's first snow and showed everywhere the tracks of bears, panthers, and wolves. Townshend took particular note of the huge footprints of a grizzly. Old Ephraim, who thirty years before had played such a commanding role in the campfire tales of the mountain men, could still be found in the remoter parts of the Rockies but had largely disappeared from the plains and foothills.

Another rare but not wholly extinct species was the mountain man himself. Although the fur trade era had been history for a quarter of a century, Townshend found in the snow-hushed alpine valleys a breed of men following the independent life of the solitary hunter. These "great tall sinewy fellows" in fringed buckskin might have served as models for Cooper's archetypal frontiersman. Townshend liked them at once and wound up lifting "many a glass of whiskey ... To these bearded nimrods; each of us addressing to the other the

Indian salutation of 'howgh' as we swallowed the fiery liquid."

The Rocky Mountain hunters lived off the land and generated a modest cash income from the sale of antelope and deer skins. While doing some trapping, they largely ignored the animal, *Castor canadensis*, that had lured their spiritual forebears to the Rockies in the first place. The beaver had made a strong comeback in these parts since the collapse of the fur trade in the early 1840s. Most of the streams encountered by Townshend's party "swarmed with them, often making us go ten miles out of our way before we could cross their dams." But a prime beaver plew would fetch only fifty cents at market— less that a tenth of the price in the 1830s and far too low for the effort expended in procuring it.

Townshend returned to Laramie later that fall and caught the Union Pacific west to Benton, Wyoming, (a town "inhabited by a more lawless set of ruffians than even Laramie") and thence to the railroad terminus at Bryan, west of Green River in the heart of the old rendezvous country. His immediate destination was Salt Lake City, a Wells Fargo stagecoach journey of 180 bone-crunching miles up the high plains and across the Wasatch Range into Utah.

> These coaches are made to hold nine people inside, three on each of the front and back seats, and three in the centre; and as there is just room for four to sit comfortably, the sufferings of the unfortunate nine—when that number are crammed into the inconvenient vehicle—can only be understood by those who have endured the torture. The body of the coach is hung on leather springs; and the wheels and under-carriage are built very strong, to stand the horrible road, or track, over which they have to run. The lumbering machine is drawn by six horses, which are changed about every twelve hours.

The stage traveled at an average speed of four miles an hour, with the six passengers "crowded together, with a lot of mail-bags and heavy packages of goods, which occupied the whole of the back seat and most of the floor of the vehicle. These were the cause of many bitter execrations from us unfortunates, as we vainly strove to stretch a limb or get into a more easy position, while we jolted along over the hills, rivers, and swamps."

A fresh snow covered the eastern slope of the Wasatch, rendering the road treacherously slippery. To lighten the load sufficiently for the horses to make the grade, the driver ordered everyone out to walk. As Townshend and his fellow passengers trudged up the hill, the snow soaked through their boots, while falling flakes clung to their beards and eyelashes and quickly turned to ice. On returning to the stage they rubbed their faces and feet to ward off frostbite.

Climbing another hill, Townshend found the contents of a mail bag scattered about the snow and dutifully retrieved them to carry on to the next station. However, "nobody else troubled himself about them [the lost pieces of mail], and I was told it was an affair of frequent occurrence." Confronting a swamp, the driver again ordered everyone out to walk. The passengers went ahead and quickly sank up to their knees in mud and snow while the stage, following behind, settled into the muck to its axils and refused to budge. The only recourse was to wade back to the stage and lighten it by unloading the baggage—"a fearfully cold operation, in which we spent the best part of two hours."

Free at last from the freezing mire, the stage continued on for an all-night ride to Fort Bridger. An important way station on the old Oregon Trail, the fort had been established by Jim Bridger as a trading post in 1843. For the last ten years it had served as an Army garrison. Townshend was grateful to be received hospitably by the fort's officers, who ignored the fact that he was "cold, wet, dirty, and travel-stained, and altogether in appearance most unlike 'an officer and a gentleman.' "

To cope better with the road conditions, they switched here to a "mud wagon." This was a lighter stagecoach with canvas sides that were "rolled up during the day and let down at night, but utterly inefficient to keep out the bitter blasts which sweep across these desert plains and mountains." On the next leg of the journey the wagon skidded off the path and overturned, tossing its passengers into a snowbank.

Beyond Bear River—a town only recently sprung up as a vanguard to the advancing Union Pacific—they came to a stream spanned by a crude bridge. It was night, the swollen current washed over the planks, and the bridge "shook and groaned" under the onslaught of ice floes. Crossing the bridge under such perilous conditions would be madness, a teamster at Bear River had warned them. Ignoring this advice, the driver ordered the passengers out to cross the icy span on foot. Then, whipping his horses to a frenzy, he sent the team crashing across it with the stage in tow.

*   *   *

It was a thankful and bone-weary group of passengers who arrived, twenty-four hours later, "in the famous city of the Saints." With a population of twenty thousand, Salt Lake City was by western standards a major metropolis. To Townshend's eyes it seemed nothing less than a manicured Garden of Eden in the middle of the wildest and crudest country on earth. From his hotel balcony he looked down on boulevards edged by irrigation canals and shaded by acacias and cottonwoods. The streets were lined with neat houses set amid orchards of peach and other fruit-bearing trees. The soaring Wasatch Mountains, brilliant white in their snowy cloak, formed a spectacular backdrop under the winter sky. The Englishman noted approvingly that the town contained but one saloon, which was owned by a "gentile" or non-Mormon. "The absense of gambling saloons and drinking shops, with the quiet and orderly aspect of the place and people, strikes one forcibly as a wonderful contrast to the attractive bars and gambling establishments, with the hard-drinking gamblers and dissolute ruffians who inhabit the other cities of the plains and make them perfect Pandemonia."

Townshend's reaction to Salt Lake City and the mores of its citizenry was mixed. Like most visitors, he expressed grudging admiration for the industry and vision that had built this oasis in the wilderness. At the same time, he was appalled by the polygamy inherent in Mormon religious doctrine and by the rigidity of male-female relations. He sensed as well a puritanical suppression of spirit throughout the population.

In a town where nearly every woman is married as soon as grown up, and where any infraction of the seventh commandment on the part of a Gentile and a Mormon woman, is punished by the death of the former, it is perhaps fortunate that the women should be in general remarkably plain, both in looks and dress. They have also a subdued air about them, and a way of looking down, as though ashamed of themselves. They do not appear to be treated by the men as at all equals, but rather as beings whose duty it is to serve their husbands, and add to the population as many little Mormons as possible. Nearly every woman I met in the streets had either a baby in her arms, or was in an interesting situation. None of the women I saw at Salt Lake appear to belong to the rank of those whom we call in England "ladies." Neither male nor female Saints were apparently above the middle class.

The gentile attitude toward Mormons, he noted, had softened not a bit since Brigham Young had led his people to this desert Canaan twenty-one years before. They were looked upon by Yankees, said Townshend, "as very little better than the original inhabitants of Sodom and Gomorrah, and should a similar fate overtake them, it would at least relieve the American government of a serious difficulty."

During his stay in Salt Lake City, Townshend had occasion to call on the great Mormon leader himself. Brigham Young looked a decade younger than his sixty-eight years and resembled "an English farmer or provincial tradesman," with a "broad and honest countenance. He must possess the greatest tact and executive ability, as his power is supreme and unhesitatingly obeyed, though he is now only head of the church and no longer governor of the territory, both of which offices he formerly held."

*   *   *

From Salt Lake City, Townshend continued on to California and home. Charles Messiter also returned to England that year, but like others before him he had trouble getting the West out of his blood. His friend, the enigmatic "F--," was bitten by the same bug and chose to stay in the States, settling in northern Texas and writing Messiter enticing letters about the profusion of game along the Red and Wichita rivers.

Never one to take his adventures vicariously, Messiter returned to the frontier twice in the 1870s, his enthusiasm for the rough-and-ready life as strong as ever. Visiting F-- in Henrietta, Texas, he found the cowboys there "very rough fellows, being in many cases men who had to disappear for a time, yet they were kind-hearted and hospitable, and would give a passing stranger anything he wanted, or shoot him, should a quarrel arise, with equal pleasure." When a raiding party of a hundred Cheyenne warriors stripped the local homesteaders of all their stock and chickens, Messiter gave money to the county judge to distribute among them.

Although familiar enough with the polyglot nature of western society, Messiter could still be astonished by the most unlikely match-ups of people and circumstances. Hunting deer in the Dakotas, he encountered on the trail "a rough-looking cowboy" who in typically laconic fashion barely responded to the Englishman's greeting. They rode together for several miles without speaking. The day was exceedingly hot, and Messiter wondered if he was hallucinating when he heard his companion ask, "Would not some iced champagne-cup be nice now?" The cowboy, it seemed, was a native-born Englishman who had once lived in South Kensington and gone about in a stovepipe hat and frock coat.

On another occasion, Messiter was traveling by steamboat up the Missouri for a season's hunt in the Judith Basin of Montana. The boat would moor each night, and in the mornings he would set off up river on horseback hunting deer and grouse and reconnoitering with the vessel in the evening.

One day when making my way through a dense thicket on the river's bank, into which I had driven some grouse, I came upon a hunter's cabin made of brush, and so placed that if I had not gone in as I did I should never had suspected its existence. The occupant was a curiosity, and was dressed in an old leather shirt and trowsers, almost black with age and dirt, his hair hanging down fully six inches below his collar, and his face one mass of wrinkles and very like old brown parchment. This old fellow had led a solitary life on the river for years, only going into town twice a year to buy ammunition and sell his pelts.

In conversation with the ancient trapper, Messiter learned

that he had grown up in St. Louis and had gone up river at age sixteen in the early days of the fur trade. He had joined a brigade led by Jim Bridger, spent many winters in the mountains, and was twice wounded in Indian skirmishes. "When he was twenty he married a Bannock squaw, and he assured me that an Indian wife was worth several white ones, and they could do more work, and you could always beat them when they did not obey you, and send them back to their place when you were tired of them." Messiter and his grizzled host supped that evening on beaver tail, "but I fear I did not appreciate it, though it was considered a great delicacy, as it was almost solid fat." A month after their encounter, Messiter learned later, the old man was found dead outside his cabin, the victim, apparently, in a fatal quarrel with another trapper living along the river.

Continuing up the Missouri, Messiter entered Palliser's old territory around Fort Berthold. Here he found a pitiful remnant of Santee Sioux who had been forcibly removed from Minnesota to the Dakotas after the quashing of Little Crow's rebellion during his first visit to the West in 1862. Now, sixteen years later, the Santee's numbers had been reduced mainly to a few old women. Within two years following their removal to the Missouri, noted Messiter, most of the tribe's seven to eight hundred members had been killed off by the Cheyenne and Blackfeet.

Messiter could forget for a time the sorry plight of the western tribes once he entered the Judith Basin. By this time—1878—the plains tribes had been assigned to reservations, and with the buffalo swiftly nearing obliteration they were dependent to varying degrees on the white man's largesse for subsistence. Yet the Judith Basin seemed largely untouched by the advances of civilization, existing as a kind of time capsule in which Stewart or Ruxton would have felt at home. Here Messiter found Crow and Bannock camped by crystal streams running with cutthroat trout. Enclosed by timbered mountains, the valley teemed with wildlife. A remnant herd of buffalo dotted its rolling plain. Deer grazed on streamside willows, elk bugled from the sagebrush hills, and mountain sheep jumped nimbly from granite outcrops. Grizzlies patrolled the creek beds and made for heart-stopping sport—he killed several during his stay here, including one that he foolishly chased into a thicket and shot at point-blank range. Messiter declared the Judith Basin to be "one of the most perfect hunting grounds" he had ever seen.

Messiter became fast friends with the Crows, who in his honor staged a mock battle on horseback with the Bannocks. In his turn, the Englishman entertained them with a display of white magic in the form of some "Pharoah's serpents" he had brought with him. These are the familiar Fourth-of-July pellets that, when lit, billow forth a long ash worm. When Messiter demonstrated one of these black powder snakes in one of the Crow tipis, it caused "a regular stampede—men, women and children tumbling over one another in their hurry to get out of the lodge. In a few minutes a number of heads appeared, looking cautiously in at the door, and seeing that I was unhurt they gradually returned and made me do it again and again, till I refused to light any more, wishing to keep a few for the Bannocks."

On another occasion he watched the Crows entertaining themselves with a shell game called "hand."

> The game consisted of holding a shell in one hand, then placing both hands under a buffalo-robe, which is lying in front of all the players, who kneel in a circle, moving the hands about rapidly, changing the shell from one to the other and then holding them both up closed, your adversary having to say in which of them the shell is, losing a peg if he is wrong. . . . These pegs represent so much, and everything an Indian possesses is valued at so many pegs—a wife, so many, a horse so many, and so on. An Indian will frequently lose all he has in one evening—wife, children, horses, and lodge—and will leave with nothing but what he stands up in, when his friends will lend him a gun and some ammunition, with which he will in time get skins enough to fit himself out again. Many of those present lost heavily on this occasion, but they all took it very quietly, and you could not tell from their faces whether they were winning or losing. I was told that when a man lost his wife and children they generally went to the lodge of the winner without showing any feeling at all.

Messiter's sensitivity and obvious sympathy toward his Indian hosts were in striking contrast to the attitude of most other whites with whom the Crow and Bannock had dealings. The year before, he remarked in disgust, another British sportsman had passed through the valley and had stolen the head of a dead Crow chief from a funeral scaffold. Furious at this desecration, the Crows threatened to go on the warpath but were pacified by the legerdemain of the local Indian agent, who "retrieved" what he purported to be the stolen trophy. In fact, the head returned to the Crows had been hastily procured from the burial ground of another reservation.

As shocking as it was, this incident paled next to the systematic plundering of tribes by their government-appointed "protectors." Messiter gained firsthand insight into the venality of Indian agents through conversations with a man named Reed, a former agent who now operated a trading post in the Judith Basin and openly boasted of cheating his tribal charges out of their due.

> He [the agent] certainly opened my eyes to the way in which the Indians were treated, telling us that though an agent's pay was only three hundred a year, yet he must be a fool (or an honest man, which terms he considered synonymous) if he did not make twenty thousand pounds during the five years for which he held his appointment. He told us that he had often landed one half of a steamboat load of flour on the bank of the river, bringing on the other half and giving it to the Indians, as all that had been sent, and then had returned and fetched the second half, and sold it as his own, always selling as well half of the coats, blankets, socks, &c., which were forwarded for them.

Reed's cynical attitude toward his duties was typical of all too many agents throughout the sorry history of Indian-white relations. It is little wonder that, when the Oglala Sioux were relegated to reservation life, their wise leader, Red Cloud, requested they be assigned a wealthy agent who would not feel compelled to steal from them.

10

Wonderland

I think a more confirmed set of skeptics never went out into the wilderness than those who composed our party, and never was a party more completely surprised and captivated with the wonders of nature.
— Cornelius Hedges, member of the
Washburn Expedition of 1870, the first
to explore the Yellowstone plateau

WHILE LAMENTED by Messiter, the frontier's passing was inevitable in the westward rush of civilization following the Civil War. As railroads penetrated ever farther beyond the Missouri, the Great American Desert became increasingly accessible, and a journey across the plains that had taken weeks only a decade before could now be accomplished in little more than a day. The advent, too, of fast trans-Atlantic steam service meant that a British sportsman could be hunting grouse on his favorite moor at the beginning of one week and stalking elk on the Front Range at the end of the next.

Fanning interest in the West, meanwhile, was a steady flow of narrative accounts describing the exotic sights and adventures to be found there. By 1870 there were so many Britishers—whether sportsmen or rough-and-ready tourists—wandering about the plains and mountains that it becomes difficult to keep track of them all. To British publishers the popularity of the travel narrative must have seemed inexhaustible, for they issued book after book by peripatetic gentlemen authors, whose western escapades were often merely one leg in globe-girdling journeys.

Many of them reported their adventures in the preeminent sporting journal, the *Field*, employing gentlemanly pseudonyms like "Oliver North," whose magazine pieces were later collected in a volume titled *Rambles After Sport*. North, whose real name was Mullen, entertained his readers with condescending tales about the locals he encountered on his excursions for elk and grizzly in the California Coast Range in the late 1860s. One of his contemporaries, Parker Gillmore, chose the more suggestive *nom de plume* of "Ubique" in recounting his adventures in North America and South Africa. Ubique may have indeed been ubiquitous, but he could as easily have written under the name "Prolix"—he produced nineteen books in all and must have been one of the more popular outdoor writers of his period, even if his work is largely forgotten today.

Gillmore's *A Hunter's Adventures in the Great West* links together a string of vignettes on the sport, climate, zoology, and botany of the Montana prairie. He was one of the few of our sportsmen to show very much interest in angling. Ubique was at heart a meat fisherman who fished mostly with bait such as grubs and lizards; once, however, in a more refined mood he fashioned a makeshift fly from a bit of scarlet yarn yanked from his shirt and caught with it a twelve-pound cutthroat trout. His observations on natural history run the gamut from prairie chickens to moose to the "effluvium" of an Indian squaw, whose smell struck his fastidious nose as "peculiar, indescribable, sickening—strongly impregnated with the odour produced from bruised limbs or foliage of dwarf cedar."

His Anglo-Saxon prejudice notwithstanding, Gillmore's view of Indians was mainly benign, at least when contrasted to the expressions of Henry Astbury Leveson. "The Old Shekarry," as Leveson called himself, concluded from his single season on the plains that "The noble savage or the Red Indian as portrayed by Fenimore Cooper was a very interesting kind of being, but unfortunately he never existed save and except in a sensational novel." To Leveson, the true Indian resembled in character "the prairie wolf, being sneaking, cowardly, and revengeful, with scarcely a redeeming quality." It was by "a very wise dispensation of Providence," he concluded with smug approval, "that they are gradually disappearing from off the face of the earth before the advancing strides of civilization."

At least the Old Shekarry could feel some empathy for the land itself, if not for the people being dispossessed from it. He found the Gallatin Valley, north of what would soon become Yellowstone National Park, "too beautiful for description," its surrounding peaks enveloped in morning clouds and its basalt cliffs reminding him of ruined castles in Germany and Italy. Leveson and his party—a total of five Englishmen, four former Confederate officers, five ex-slaves to handle the cooking and washing, and three halfbreed guides—camped for several weeks in "this romantic valley," where "the days flew serenely by, whilst at night we gossipped, played whist, told yarns, and sang around a roaring camp fire of glowing embers until the drowsy god made his visit."

By the early 1870s the West had become so popular among Britishers that many of them took up semi-permanent residence as ranchers. (Of 311 ranch owners in 1880 Wyoming, according to the census that year, 52 were British.) Making a living off the sparse prairie grasses was a secondary motive, at best, for gentlemen like Moreton Frewen, whose home on the range—a 128,000-acre spread on the Powder River—set a standard for rustic elegance. Frewen, a future brother-in-law to Mrs. Randolph Churchill, entertained the cream of British and American society in a ranch house costing $40,000, an extraordinary sum for those days. Built of pine logs cut from nearby hills, the Home Ranch boasted interior woodwork of imported English hardwoods and a solid walnut stairway. The house doubled as a hunting lodge for Frewen and his wealthy guests, whose forays into the Bighorn Basin produced scores of grizzly bear, mountain sheep, and puma proudly recorded in his guest book. (Frewen's definition of a proper game animal did not include the "tame and unsporting" buffalo or elk, which were shot only for meat.) In addition to shooting, his guests enjoyed spectacularly easy fishing in the virgin streams coursing through his property. When Frewen's brother and sister-in-law camped for two days on nearby Trout Creek, they caught cutthroat by the bushel: "not often less than a pound and often three."

Frewen epitomized the dilettante rancher for whom the cattle enterprise was largely a backdrop for his leisure pursuits. "If the stockman has the faculty to select good men," a magazine writer advised any would-be gentleman homesteader, "he need not make himself a prisoner in his ranch, but may treat himself to a month's hunting in the mountains, or even a trip to England." Frewen in fact was much too sociable to be trapped in such splendid isolation, and during the years he operated his Powder River Cattle Company (known familiarly as the "76 Outfit"), he was frequently absent on visits home to England and to the fashionable salons of New York and Chicago. He traveled in the most rarified circles and seems to have known everyone who was anyone on both sides of the Atlantic—his list of friends and acquaintances, he later claimed, included every U.S. president from Buchanan to Wilson as well as the Prince of Wales and sundry dukes, generals, artists, and writers.

Of all his encounters with the great and famous, perhaps none was more memorable than his meeting on the Little Bighorn with Sitting Bull. Frewen had been hunting along the Tongue River in 1884 when he learned that the legendary Sioux headman was camped with a small party only a day's ride away. Sitting Bull and his companions had pitched their tipis on the "Greasy Grass," as they called the Little Bighorn, within sight of the place where eight years before a combined force of five thousand Sioux, Cheyenne, and Arapaho warriors had wiped out George A. Custer and five troops of his vaunted Seventh Cavalry. By now, Sitting Bull had long since made his reluctant peace with the white hordes and had joined the rest of his people on the Standing Rock Reservation. (The following year he would leave the reservation to tour as a top-billed attraction in Buffalo Bill's Wild West Show.)

Pacified or not, Sitting Bull symbolized in the Englishman's fevered imagination all the ferocity and romantic savagery of two centuries of wilderness fighting between red men and white. Tethering his horse at a respectful distance, he walked with heart in mouth to the four lodges shaded in a grove of cottonwoods. "I was about to meet," he recalled later, "the great protagonist of the Custer Massacre, the Indian whose name and deeds filled the dime novels and made the flesh of good boys and girls creep. There, too, but a quarter mile away on the gently rising ground, was the obelisk which marked all that was mortal of the 7th Regiment of Cavalry. It would have been strange indeed had I met this grisly warrior at such a spot without some rise in temperature."

His apprehension was not assuaged when he entered Sitting Bull's tipi and found the old warrior gnawing on what at first appeared to be a baby's head. To his relief, Frewen quickly realized that it was just a dog's skull. Lionized by the American and British press for nearly a decade, Sitting Bull was apparently used to such curious visitors and barely acknowledged Frewen's anxious "How-How." Although neither spoke the other's language, the Englishman managed to convey his desire to tour the battlefield with the great Indian strategist. To his surprise, Sitting Bull agreed—"I suppose inwardly as exultant as Callimachus contemplating Marathon."

Lacking an interpreter, Frewen made what little he could of his historic opportunity. "I could, however, from his signs divine at least this much, that when the Indians fired the first shot from the dense belt of timber and brush on the river, the sun was high in the heavens; that when the last shot was fired, and the last trooper killed, it was dipping below the Horizon."

As Frewen wandered the battlefield where more than two hundred Blue Shirts had died, he recalled an earlier visit to the Little Bighorn made in 1879, three years after the battle, "when the relics of this Homeric fight had not been entirely effaced by time's pious hand. Ribs of horses, picked white by timber wolves, and here and there brass buckles and fragments of saddlecloths, still remained to bid the traveler pause." Surveying the scene now, Frewen philosophized on Custer's passing and asked rhetorically, "Was it not all a part, and a splendid part, of 'the winning of the West' for our common civilization?"

Frewen's assumptions about the rightness of the Indians' passing were shared by Sir Rose Lambart Price, a professional soldier who served with the Royal Mounted Light Infantry in India and China before taking early retirement and touring the Western Hemisphere. Price's ramblings, described in *The Two Americas; an Account of Sport and Travel*, took him to the heart of the contested Sioux country in 1874. The discovery of gold that year in the Black Hills, a sacred hunting ground promised to the Sioux in perpetuity, had triggered a rush of miners to the region in flagrant violation of the Fort Laramie Treaty of 1867. Ironically, it was Custer himself who caused the stampede; the Boy General had reconnoitered the Black Hills with his Seventh Cavalry and returned to tell of gold lying "at the roots of the grass."

As Price correctly noted, the Black Hills invasion spelled the beginning of the end for the Sioux nation: "Gold, the great civilizing agent of the world, is hard at work—and nothing can now stop the tide of adventurous and desperate men flocking in on the coveted possessions. These forerunners of civilization, though in themselves unscrupulous, vindictive and cruel as the savages they are destined to replace, will soon become possessed of a firm footing. The legitimate trader will rapidly follow in their footsteps; the settler will gradually appear; and in time railroads and a distinct form of municipal government will render the at present dangerous and formidable Sioux as innocuous and peacable as the few remaining Indian tribes so rapidly becoming extinct."

In fact, the Sioux had been doing rather well relative to most other tribes west of the Mississippi. In the years immediately following the Civil War, the great Oglala chief, Red Cloud, had led his people to a stunning victory against the whites, driving them from the Powder River country and closing a series of forts that the Army had built along the Bozeman Trail to protect miners and settlers moving north into the Montana gold fields. In his short, decisive campaign and in the ensuing negotiations, Red Cloud displayed his brilliance as both a military tactician and diplomat, forcing the cavalry to fight on terrain that negated their superior firepower, then refusing to bargain with the Blue Shirts until the forts were completely abandoned. He later led a delegation of Sioux to meet with President Grant in Washington and went on to visit New York City, whose citizens were sufficiently removed from the threat of Indian attack to give him a thunderous ovation at the Cooper Institute.

For all his skills as a military strategist, Red Cloud was no warmonger and wished to live in peace with the white men. He and Spotted Tail of the Brulé Sioux settled down to reservation life and did their best to control their truculent younger braves, who regarded the reservation as a convenient staging ground for raids against white settlers on the fringe of the Indian territories. As Price noted, "The older Indians are content to stay in comfortable lodges and behave themselves, but the young men scorn such effeminancy, and long for the day when they may meet their foemen (no matter who) in the shock of battle." The Black Hills invasion, following on the heels of a railroad survey through the Powder River country, proved the final straw in the rapidly deteriorating relations between the Sioux nation and the United States. Both sides prepared for the major confrontation that would culminate in the debacle at the Little Bighorn.

After a season's hunt in the Laramie Range of Wyoming, Price went east to New York in the late fall of 1875. There he met none other than the celebrated Indian fighter himself—George A. Custer, on leave from field duties and epitomizing in Price's view the verve and spirit of the American professional soldier.

Custer came off as "a fine, dashing, gallant officer" who shared with Price a love of hunting and the out-of-doors. The two military men became instantly chummy, and when Custer promised his English friend an unpaid staff job on an expedition that spring to the Yellowstone, Price quickly accepted. Custer downplayed the Indian threat and guaranteed plenty of opportunity for shooting bear, elk, mountain sheep, and buffalo. With keen anticipation Price readied his gear, but his dreams of riding with the glorious Seventh were dashed when President Grant, for mainly political reasons, took the promised command away from Custer and placed him in a subordinate position under General Alfred Terry. As Custer explained apologetically in a letter posted from Fort Abraham Lincoln in May 1876, his reduced role in the expedition precluded any staff, and he had no choice but to retract his invitation.

"The rest," Price noted, "is a matter of history" as Custer rode off, *sans* his English aide-de-camp, to glory and immortal controversy at the Little Bighorn.

*　　*　　*

Confined as they were to a single season, Price's frontier travels were less extensive than Townshend's or Messiter's and his observations more limited. Nonetheless, he had a good eye for detail and a nice sense of the absurd, and some of the descriptions he has left us are memorable. Riding an over-crowded railroad car from Lake Tahoe to Virginia City, Nevada, he and a companion abandoned the crush of passengers in the coach for the exhilarating openness of a platform over the cowcatcher: "Our billet had certainly the sensation of novelty to recommend it, and after confidence became restored by getting over the first half-dozen miles in safety, we lighted our pipes, and began somewhat to relish our queer ride." Later, in Laramie, Wyoming, he witnessed the arrival by train of President Grant and was astonished at the crowd's indifference: "I never saw less enthusiasm at the reception of any distinguished individual than was displayed here. For some moments the crowd seemed undecided as to who was the President, and a man near me shouted out, 'Which is Grant?' 'I guess he's that red-faced coon in a plug hat,' replied another, in a by no means *sotto voce*; and this information seeming to be sufficient, the mob shortly afterwards raised a faint cheer." Grant for his part responded in like fashion, leaning from the platform and extending his hand mechanically for the obligatory pressing of the flesh. "Every one so disposed gave it a wring," Price observed, "but during the entire operation, which lasted for several minutes, I never once saw his Excellency open his mouth."

Grant was the first U.S. president to travel beyond the Missouri. The presence, however brief, of the nation's chief executive in a rawboned town like Laramie suggests the swiftness at which civilization was overtaking the West. After two and a half centuries of battling the wilderness and subduing it for their ends, Americans were at last in sight of final victory. In a few more years, the historian Frederick Jackson Turner would declare the frontier closed and a unique shaping force in the American pageant gone forever. As an inevitable consequence of such "progress," buffalo and other game were disappearing at an alarming rate, provoking an incipient conservation movement. In California, the state legislature had already moved to protect Yosemite Valley; and two years prior to his

Laramie visit, President Grant had signed into law an act making the headwaters of the Yellowstone the nation's—indeed, the world's—first national park.

Straddling the Continental Divide, this wild and forbidding territory of bubbling hot springs and geysers had been known by a few score white men since the early days of the fur trade. Jim Bridger had dined out for decades on fantastic tales about the wonders of Yellowstone, where one could find "peetrified trees a-growing, with peetrified birds on 'em a-singing peetrified songs." It was easy to dismiss the stories of notorious liars like Old Gabe, but in 1871 an exploring party led by the respected geologist Ferdinand V. Hayden, director of the U.S. Geological Survey, brought back the first documentation—including photographs—of this extraordinary region. After an intensive lobbying effort by Hayden and others the following winter, Congress set aside the Yellowstone in perpetuity as a public "pleasuring ground" for the "preservation, from injury or spoilation, of all timber, mineral deposits, natural curiosities, or wonders within."

Pleasuring ground or not, the upper Yellowstone would remain a remote place, with the most rudimentary of tourist accommodations, for at least a decade after Grant's conferral of national park status. Among the earliest and most enthusiastic visitors to Yellowstone was an exhuberant Irish blue-blood named Windham Thomas Wyndham-Quin, who carried a list of titles longer than a cavalry mule train: Fourth Earl of Dunraven and Mountearl in the Peerage of Ireland, Second Baron Kenry of the United Kingdom, Knight of the Order of St. Patrick, and Companion of the Order of St. Michael and St. George. Dunraven passed the fall of 1874 exploring Yellowstone with his physician and traveling companion, Dr. George Henry Kingsley, and engagingly described his visit in *The Great Divide*, one of a half-dozen books of travel and reminiscence he wrote during a long and illustrious life. (He died in 1926 at age eighty-five.)

Born in the "good little old County of Limerick" to a Roman Catholic father and a Low Protestant mother, the future earl—despite, or perhaps because of, his parents' attempt to instill in him a stern religious view—evidenced from youth a most worldly outlook on life. After schooling in Rome and

160

Paris, he idled at Oxford, passing much of his time there at horse racing and cricket. Later, he played briefly at soldiering as a cornet-of-horse in the First Life Guards, dallied with spiritualism under the celebrated medium Daniel Dunglas Home, and as a foreign correspondent covered the war in Abyssinia for the *London Daily Telegraph*.

What he wanted to do more than anything, however, was visit the American West. His head had been filled since boyhood with fabulous tales of frontier adventure. He had read Cooper, of course, and an uncle who had personally known Sir St. George Gore regaled him with stories of the old game hog's exploits in Colorado and Wyoming. Even better were the firsthand accounts of Missouri trappers and Minetarees related by family friend John Palliser, "a Tipperary man, and a mighty hunter before the Lord." Palliser was a frequent guest at Adare, the Dunraven estate, on whose grounds he pitched tipis and jacklighted deer in games of trappers and Indians with the future earl. By young adulthood, wrote Dunraven, "My boyish brain-cells were stored to bursting with tales of Red Indians and grizzly b'ars; caballeros and haciendas, prairies and buffaloes, Texans and Mexicans, cowboys and *voyageurs*."

His opportunity to experience the Far West at first hand came at last in 1871. Having assumed, on his father's recent death, his hereditary earldom and the thirty thousand acres in Ireland and Wales that went with it, he found himself with enormous means for indulging his wanderlust. He was also married now, although to a remarkably understanding woman who, during this and subsequent trips, never begrudged him his long absences from home.

Dunraven and Kingsley were guided that summer by Buffalo Bill Cody and Texas Jack Omohundro, a pair of colorful characters who might have stepped from the pages of a dime novel. Indeed, the writer Ned Buntline had already chronicled Cody's adventures as a cavalry scout and Indian fighter in the Cheyenne wars. A year later, Cody would begin appearing as himself in Chicago stage melodramas, alternating between winter flings at acting and summers guiding wealthy hunters like Dunraven and Russia's Grand Duke Alexis. (Cody of course was one of the great showmen of American history, and his career is a classic case of the merging of life and art in a single persona.)

Buffalo Bill and Texas Jack, Dunraven would recall a half-century later, impressed him as "tall, well-built, active looking men, with singularly handsome features."

Bill was dressed in a pair of corduroys tucked into his high boots, and a blue flannel shirt. He wore a broad-brimmed hat, or

Texas Jack Omohundro, from Dunraven's The Great Divide.

sombrero, and had a white handkerchief folded like a little shawl loosely fastened around his neck to keep off the fierce rays of the afternoon sun. Jack's costume was similar, with the exception that he wore moccasins, and had his lower limbs encased in a pair of comfortable greasy deerskin trousers, ornamented with a fringe along the seams. Round his waist was a belt supporting a revolver, two butcher knives, and in his hand he carried his trusty rifle, the "Widow"—now in my possession. Jack, tall and lithe, with light brown close-cropped hair, clear and laughing honest blue eyes, and a soft and winning smile, might have sat as a model for a typical modern Anglo-Saxon. . . . Bill was dark, with quick searching eyes, aquiline nose, and delicately cut features, and he wore his hair falling in long ringlets over his shoulders, in true Western style. As he cantered up with his flowing locks and broad-brimmed hat, he looked like a picture of a cavalier of olden times.

Although he would soon become an international celebrity and a man of cosmopolitan tastes, Cody had not yet been anywhere east of the Mississippi when Dunraven first met him. Both he and Texas Jack "knew scarcely more of civilization and the life of great cities than the Indians around them."

Cody for his part recalled Dunraven, who was just shy of thirty, as a "pleasant young fellow" who came with a letter of introduction from General Philip Sheridan, commander of the Army's western division. The kind of sport enjoyed by the Dunraven party is suggested by Cody's description of an elk hunt on the Nebraska plains that summer:

Six or seven of us would start at sunrise on our prairie horses, and get as close as possible to the elk, which would be feeding in the open, two or three hundred, perhaps, in a bunch. These long-legged beasts were swifter than the buffalo, and they would let us get within a half mile of them before they would give a mighty snort and dash away after their leader. Then came the test of speed and endurance. They led the horses a wild race, and it put our chargers to their mettle to overtake the game. Right in among them we would spur, and, dropping the reins, use the repeating rifle with both hands.

Only the master of the hunt or his guests did any shooting, Cody added, while the hunters and attendants occupied themselves in lassoing the young elk and bringing them back alive to camp. Dunraven, he noted, "shipped a good many of those captured in this way to his place across the water."

The young earl was the second British sport whom Cody had

the privilege of guiding. Two years earlier he had escorted Sir John Watts Garland, a hearty spirit who threw himself into his western adventure with as much zest as Sir William Drummond Stewart a generation earlier. Sir John, wrote Cody, "soon discarded the English saddle which he brought with him [being apparently of a more practical and less chauvinistic vein than Grantley Berkeley], and the truly British custom of declining to drink anything until after dinner, when the day's work had been finished."

No great time was required for him to learn that a cocktail before breakfast was considered entirely the thing on the prairie, and that anything else than a California saddle was out of place. His democratic ways made him very popular with the plainsmen. When he went out with a party, he roughed it like the rest of us, slept in the open on his blanket, took his turn at camp duty, and rode his own horse in the races which we often got up for our amusement. He discovered speedily that the English thoroughbred was by no means so well fitted for frontier use as the coarser western horse, which was more accustomed to avoiding prairie-dog holes and better understood the lay of the land.

Dunraven embraced the West with an enthusiasm equal to Garland's, and in the fall of 1872 he and Kingsley were back to hunt sheep, elk, and other game in Colorado's South Park (Ruxton's beloved Bayou Salado). Enthralled with the grandeur of the Colorado Rockies, Dunraven dreamed of purchasing the entirety of Estes Park, north of Denver, as his private game preserve. He hired an agent to buy up land for him, built a hunting lodge and a gabled cottage with an ample whiskey cellar, and stocked the land with a herd of Swiss cattle. In the spring of 1874 he was back at Estes Park to check his growing estate before heading north with Kingsley for an expedition into the fabled "Wonderland," as it was called, of the upper Yellowstone. Guided once again by Texas Jack, the two sportsmen passed a memorable season in the land of geysers, where the earl's presence is recalled today in Dunraven Pass and Mount Dunraven.

Dunraven had longed to visit Yellowstone "since the first vague accounts of the marvels to be seen upon its shores had filtered out into the world," and with his good connections he was able to procure advice on the country from Professor Hayden himself. He hoped to break a new trail into the park from the east but was prevented from doing so by Indian troubles in the Shoshone Basin. Instead, he and his party took a more roundabout route by stage, "shot like shuttles in a loom for four days and nights" between Salt Lake City and Bozeman. They stopped for a brief rest at Virginia City, Montana's boomtown territorial capital, already falling into ruin, whose fleeting glory had been built on the gold-flecked sands of Alder Gulch. "Virginia City. Good Lord! What a name for the place!" the astonished earl exclaimed as he surveyed the dust-choked streets lined with shanties, bars, and brothels.

The played-out mining town of Stirling, where they changed to buggies for the final leg of the trip, was equally uninviting; consisting of a post office, a store, and one or two houses, it seemed destined "to revert at no distant date to the wild sheep

Dunraven marveled at the "mystery" of mule packing and at the "diabolical ingenuity" of mules for slipping their packs.

and goats" looking down on it from the craggy summits of nearby mountains. Their spirits lifted as soon as they left this last, pathetic vestige of civilization behind. Singing and whooping and yelling, with Texas Jack riding beside them on a prancing mustang, they crossed the tailings-choked Madison and then the clear-running Gallatin, arriving late in the day at the cavalry outpost of Fort Ellis "in the jaws of Bozeman Pass," commanding the valleys of the Yellowstone and the Three Forks of the Missouri.

They lingered several days at the fort as guests of its officers before descending into the Yellowstone Valley for the trek into the park, sixty miles up river. Their first sight of the mighty Yellowstone, flowing through the gates of what would later be called Paradise Valley, inspired in Dunraven "the silent enthusiasm of a pilgrim who sees in the far distance St. Peter's dome or the minarets of Mecca."

The presence in this part of the valley of a Crow Indian reservation was an opportunity that the earl could not pass up. Promising to rejoin the party at Bottler's Ranch upstream, Dunraven and Kingsley spun off for a visit to Stewart's old adversaries. The Crows, he found, "were a fine race, tall, straight, clean-limbed, well-proportioned" and—among the males at least—possessed of inordinate vanity. "The beauty of long locks, with us a crown of glory to the fair sex, is, in the lodges of the Crows, appropriated entirely by the men; who take infinite pains with their hair, usually wearing it in long heavy plaits. I don't know how it is with the women, but probably they have not time or opportunity to cultivate it or keep it in order, for among Indians it is the men who spend hours in beautifying themselves and looking in the glass." Like all Indians in regular contact with whites, the Crows by now wore a mixture of native and European clothing. Dunraven was struck by the motley wardrobe of a typical brave, consisting of fringed buckskin breeches, "puritanical-looking hard felt hat" and "skimpy diminutive tail-coat" of the type worn by liveried servants. "The sublime and the ridiculous, the comic and the tragic element, are so absurdly blended in these people that at one moment you are convulsed with laughter at their ludicrous appearance, and at the next are astonished at the dignity of their gestures, the ease of their carriage, and the grand simplicity of their movements."

Having grown up on Cooper's stoic caricatures, Dunraven was surprised (as Murray had been forty years earlier) to find the typical Indian "by no means the taciturn melancholy individual he had been described to be. On the contrary, when he has enough to eat and is warm he is loquacious enough, and is a very jovial, joke-loving fellow. When we entered the room we found the chiefs and braves all seated round, leaning against the walls, smoking, laughing, talking, and carrying on great chaff with the interpreter, who was bantering them upon their love affairs, and displayed an intimate acquaintance with the domestic vicissitudes of some of the party, which was much relished by the others."

In short, like the more generous-spirited of all our British sportsmen, Dunraven liked Indians and was capable, more or less, of accepting them on their own terms. And as a sportsman and conservationist he could admire them too as "the game preservers of the country," for wherever "Red Indians are numerous, you will be sure to find herds of wapiti, bands of white-tail and black-tail deer, antelope, sheep, buffalo, and everything else." The white man, he noted by way of contrast, was the great despoiler. If one of these reservation Crows could see "how we have blackened and disfigured the face of Nature, and how we have polluted our streams and fountains, so that we drink sewage instead of water; could he but see that our rivers are turned to drains, and flow reeking with filth, and guess how by our manufactures we have poisoned our rivers, destroyed our fish, and so impregnated the very air we breathe that grass will not grow exposed to the unhealthy atmosphere; could he take all this in, and be told that such is the outcome of our civilization, he would strike his open palm upon his naked chest, and thank God that he was a savage, uneducated and untutored, but with air to breathe, and water to drink; ignorant but independent, a wild but a free man."

Following their sojourn among the Crow, the earl and the doctor hastened to rejoin their party at Bottler's Ranch. The travelers were so taken by the beauty of the mountain-flanked valley that they paused to toast it with a "wee drappie" from Kingsley's flask. To his shocked dismay, the good doctor searched his pockets in vain to discover that he was missing not only the flask but also the billfold carrying all their cash. Doubling back some five miles on the trail, they were fortunate enough to recover both. "If it had not been for our whiskey-drinking proclivities," Dunraven concluded, "the pocket-book would not have been missed until night" and surely lost for good. "We then and there poured out a libation, and determined never to join any Temperance society, except that excellent one recently started in San Francisco, where it is ruled that 'nothing stronger than wine, beer, or cider shall be drunk on the premises, unless any member be suffering from a sense of discouragement, in which case whiskey is allowed.' "

Bottler's Ranch, a pleasant halfway station between Fort Ellis and the park, was situated in as lovely a spot as Dunraven could imagine. One of the valley's many spring creeks—famous to future generations of anglers—flowed through the property. A visitor who came several years after Dunraven observed that the creek "swarmed with fat and lazy trout which are daily fed and so tame that one can catch them with the hands." The earl and his party lay at the ranch for three days, "full up to our eyes of hominy, milk, and other products of the dairy and the farm—what a refreshing wash we had and how we did enjoy our supply of fresh eggs, chicken, cream, butter, and cheese, and plenty of Japan tea."

With the wonders of Yellowstone beckoning, the party was on its way again, proceeding into a sleety rain that put all of them temporarily out of sorts. After a two days' ride they set up camp near Gardiner, at the north entrance to the park, pausing there to await the arrival of Dunraven's cousin, a man named Wynne who had lately resigned his active commission in her majesty's colonial forces. On an excursion into the surrounding mountains, Dunraven and Texas Jack shot a pair of elk whose skinned and beheaded carcasses provided some unexpected entertainment from the local grizzlies. For the next several nights they listened to the big bruins tearing up the slaughtering ground as they prepared their winter larders.

These bears behaved in a very singular manner. They scarcely ate any of the flesh, but took the greatest pains to prevent any other creature getting at it. I had hung a hind-quarter of one of the does on a branch, well out of reach, as I supposed, and had left the skin on the ground. To my great astonishment, on going to look for it in the morning, I found the meat had been thrown down by a bear, carried about 300 yards, and deposited under a tree. The brute had then returned, taken the skin, spread it carefully over the flesh, scraped up earth over the edges, patted it all down hard and smooth, and departed without eating a morsel. All the carcasses were treated in the same way, the joints being pulled asunder and buried under heaps of earth, sticks, and stones. The beasts must have worked very hard, for the ground was all torn up and trampled by them, and stank horribly of bear.

Despite such entertaining distractions, this pause in their Yellowstone odyssey was not entirely pleasant. They were well into September now and caught in the change of seasons, with the weather turning "very coarse and disagreeable" as rain, sleet, and snow turned their camp into a cold and clammy quagmire. A fortnight later the brooding sky finally broke, and under a rising sun and scudding clouds they marched into the park toward Mammoth Hot Springs, overlooking the Gardiner River.

With their calcite terraces and bubbling pools, the springs more than lived up to their reputation for otherworldly splendor. But the local accommodations—a "shanty which is dignified by the name of hotel"—were another matter. "No doubt the neighbourhood of these springs will some day become a fashionable place. At present, being the last outpost of civilization—that is, the last place where whisky is sold—it is merely resorted to by a few invalids from Helena and Virginia City." The owner of the hostel had diverted some of the hot spring water into "three rude huts answering the purpose of bathing-houses." In keeping with the custom for spas of the era, the carbonaceous water was used for both bathing and drinking.

Dunraven found more "hunters, trappers, and idlers" there than bona fide tourists. The natives represented "a curious race" who eked out a living by selling meat to tourists and shipping heads and skeletons of game animals to eastern museums. Some of them also made curios for the tourist trade by weaving basket-like ornaments and placing them in the springs to acquire a thick calcium deposit. "In the winter they

"Indians, by Jove!" from Dunraven's The Great Divide.

hibernate like bears, for there is absolutely nothing for them to do. If you ask a man in the autumn where he is going and what he is going to do, ten to one he will tell you that it is getting pretty late in the season now, and that it won't be long before we have some heavy snow, and he is going 'down the river or up the canon.' "

Despite a gulf in breeding wider than the Grand Canyon of the Yellowstone, Dunraven found much to admire—even to envy—in these wilderness dropouts. They were, he concluded, "very good fellows as a rule, honest and open-handed, obliging and civil to strangers if treated with civility by them." One afternoon, while exploring up the Gardiner River, they passed "a patriarchal camp, composed of two men with their Indian wives and several children; half a dozen powerful savage-looking dogs and about fifty horses completed the party. They had been grazing their stock, hunting and trapping, leading a nomad, vagabond, and delicious life." The squawmen had been out of touch all season and pumped the British travelers for news of the outside world, which for their purposes did not extend beyond the borders of Montana Territory. The "great question" of the day, the earl observed, was "whether Virginia City would continue to be the capital, or whether her mantle should be taken from her shoulders and transferred to the back of her more prosperous rival, Helena." (For the record, Virginia City lost out in these territorial sweepstakes two years later; it lives on today as a restored ghost town on the tourist circuit.)

For the next two weeks they wandered the fabulous plateau under a flawless Indian summer sky. Like pilgrims out of time, they marveled at the "gloomy forbidding gorge" of Hell Roaring Creek and "the basaltic columns arranged with perfect regularity" above Tower Creek. They camped for several days above Yellowstone Falls, "in a little cozy grassy bay that indented the forest shores. The sun sank in a quiet sky; the stars shone clear, bright, and steady with unwavering light; the universe rested and was at peace. The wind talked to the trees, and the pines in answer bowed their stately heads, and with a sigh of melancholy swept their gloomy branches to and fro. All through the night the mysterious music of the distant falls rose and fell upon the breeze."

We can forgive Dunraven—here and elsewhere—for his occasional lapses into pathetic fallacy, for he was merely following the romantic conventions for the nature writing of his day. Although such passages sound dated to us now, they are rescued by the author's animated style and his refusal to exaggerate the wonders that he saw. "When the Yellowstone leaves the lake of the same name," he wrote, "it flows in a calm steady current for many miles, and then, before charging through the phalanx of the mountains which oppose its passage to the north, it performs a series of gymnastics over rapids, cascades, and waterfalls, as if exercising its muscles and sinews, preparing itself and gathering strength for the mighty effort by which it tears a passage through the granite flanks of the range." As for the falls of the great river, he conceded that their volume of water "is not very great, and there is nothing stupendous or soul-searching here as there is at Niagara; neither are the Falls very remarkable for their height. But they have a savage beauty all their own, a wild loveliness peculiar to them; and what they lack in volume, power, and general grandeur is amply atoned for in the pre-eminently distinctive character of the scenery about them."

They spent several days exploring the country above the falls, following the river "with light hearts full of merriment, happy with the exhilaration of animal health, rejoicing in the sheer pleasure of being alive." In keeping with the holiday spirit, the ex-soldier Wynne "enlivened the road with humorous stories; and many a song, composed and sung by some camp-fire in the Crimea, or in some far-away bivouac of India, rang through the forest and awakened the echoes." In the upper Hayden Valley the party stopped at the Mud Pots to observe an expected geyser eruption. The geyser, alas, proved something of an Old Faithless as they "sat for hours, a ludicrous-looking group, three men and a dog gazing earnestly at a lot of mud which slowly, slowly rose, while the sun rapidly sank." To goad the spring into action, they pelted it with sticks and stones, but to no avail. "I suppose, acting on the principle that a watched pot never boils, this geyser sternly refused to do its duty. It would not get angry. Every now and then a slight spasm would shake its placid, muddy countenance, but it was rather, I think, a smile of derision than a grin of rage that crossed it."

They had better luck in the upper basin of the Fire Hole River. Crossing a gentle divide into the watershed of the Madison, they entered the lower Geyser Basin, then turned south and rode up the river to Castle Geyser. The distance, wrote Dunraven, "is about ten or twelve miles, and over more extraordinary miles I have never travelled." The seething landscape offered nothing less than a vision of Hell. The face of the country was "honeycombed and pitted with springs, ponds, and mud-pots; furrowed with boiling streams, gashed with fissures, and gaping with chasms from which issue hollow rumblings, as if great stones were rolling round and round."

Dunraven rated Old Faithful "a very fine geyser," although its fury could not be compared to neighboring Castle Geyser's. Arriving there late in the day, they found the Castle "placidly smoking" and its innards growling. Learning that it was due to erupt at eleven o'clock that night, they settled into camp to await the spectacle.

Scarcely had we got things fixed and supper under weigh, when a yell from Boteler, 'He's going to spout!' caused us to drop teapot and pannikin, and tumble out of the tent in half no time.

It was getting dark, but there was quite enough light to see that the fit was upon the imprisoned monster. We ran upon the platform, close to the crater, but were very soon driven from that position and forced to look on humbly from a distance.

Far down in his bowels a fearful commotion was going on; we could hear a great noise—a rumbling as of thousands of tons of stones rolling round and round, piling up in heaps and rattling down again, mingled with the lashing of the water against the sides as it surged up the funnel and fell again in spray. Louder and louder grew the disturbance, till with a sudden qualm he would heave out a few tons of water and obtain momentary relief. After a few premonitory heaves had warned us to remove to a little distance, the symptoms became rapidly worse; the row and the racket increased in intensity; the monster's throes became more and more violent; the earth trembled at his rage; and finally, with a mighty spasm, he hurled into the air a great column of water.

The surging fountain reached a good 250 feet in the air, while the spray and steam shot even higher. Dunraven found the noise of the eruption "indescribable," but on reflection managed to compare it to the roar of a gale at the edge of a seaside cliff.

Throughout his adventures in Wonderland, the earl showed a fine esthetic, not only for the natural beauty and marvels around him, but for the unadorned pleasures of outdoor living. "If a man wishes to be comfortable in camp, . . . let him give up the idea of being *too* comfortable." Instead, he advised, "reduce yourself to primitive simplicity; one suit, and a change of under garments. If it is cold, put on your change and extra suit; if it is very hot, go without your coat or waistcoat—or breeches, if it pleases you." As with dressing, he added, "so it also is with cooking," for in the wilderness at least there is "nothing between the high art of a *cordon bleu* . . . and a steak toasted on a stick."

The earl and his friends left the land of geysers in soaring spirits, although a shortage of game and grass on the return to Bottler's Ranch weakened both men and horses. After the usual dreary and bone-rattling stage ride across the Montana Rockies, they pulled up at Corrine, Utah, in time to catch the eastbound Union Pacific. It was good, all in all, to be back to civilization. While he loved the rugged life of the wilderness, a man as amiable and outgoing as Dunraven also thrived on the pleasures of society:

> How luxurious appeared the Pullman car, how smooth the motion, how soft the cushions, how snug the beds! With what awe did our unaccustomed eyes regard the ladies! How gorgeous they appeared, how graceful they were, how marvellous their costumes, and how stupendous their back hair! How extraordinary seemed the harmonium, and the singing thereto! How full of pictures were the periodicals, how full of lies the newspapers! How clean one felt in a 'boiled rag' and fresh suit of clothes, and how sound we all slept that night!

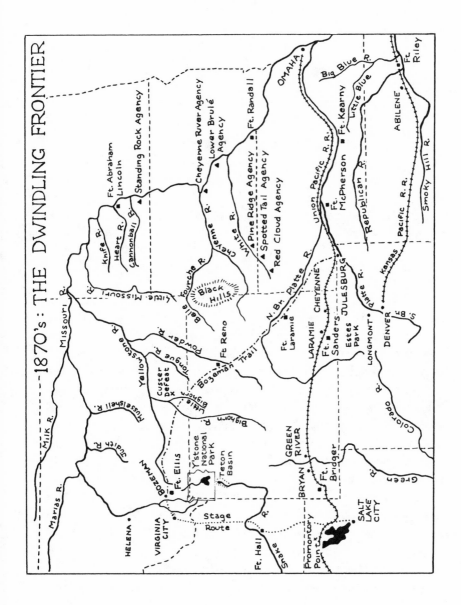

1870's: THE DWINDLING FRONTIER

Milk R.
Marias R.
Missouri R.
Helena ●
Sun R.
Teton R.
Smith R.
Musselshell R.
Yellowstone R.
VIRGINIA CITY
Ft. Ellis
BOZEMAN
Stage Route
Ft. Hall
Snake R.
Y'stone National Park
Teton Basin
Promontory Pt.
SALT LAKE CITY
Green R.
BRYAN
GREEN RIVER
Ft. Bridger
Colorado R.
Custer Defeat ✕
Bighorn R.
Little Bighorn R.
Tongue R.
Powder R.
Ft. Reno
Bozeman Trail
Belle Fourche R.
Little Missouri R.
Knife R.
Heart R.
Cannonball R.
Ft. Abraham Lincoln
Standing Rock Agency
Cheyenne R.
Cheyenne River Agency
White R.
Lower Brulé Agency
Ft. Randall
Pine Ridge Agency
Spotted Tail Agency
Red Cloud Agency
Black Hills
N. Br. Platte R.
Ft. Laramie
LARAMIE
CHEYENNE
Ft. Sanders
Estes Park
JULESBURG
LONGMONT ●
DENVER ●
Platte R.
S. Br.
Union Pacific R.R.
Ft. McPherson
Republican R.
Little Blue
Big Blue R.
Ft. Kearny
OMAHA
Kansas Pacific R.R.
ABILENE
Smoky Hill R.
Ft. Riley

175

11

The End of the Game

Seriously speaking, there is, I suppose, no country in the world on which so much has been written, based on less personal experience.
—William Adolph Baillie-Grohman,
Camps in the Rockies

As THE UNION PACIFIC rolled on under the prairie night, Dunraven dreamed of the bizarre country of boiling paint-pots and surging geysers receding behind him. Although he would not return to Yellowstone again, the following season found him back at Estes Park attending to the details of his growing estate. Over the next several years he extended his land holdings, built a fancy tourist hotel beside an artificial lake, and imported the famed landscapist Alfred Bierstadt to render for him a grandiose portrait of Long's Peak. But legal complications arising from his agent's efforts to buy up homestead claims began to undermine his visions of a Rocky Mountain empire. Denver newspapers turned against the free-spending Irish dude, attacking him when he tried to dislodge squatters from his land and running gleeful accounts of a certain "Lord Dunraven" (an imposter, it turned out) making rows in the city's fanciest brothels.

Things reached such a state that the earl took to visiting Estes Park incognito. Finally, in 1880 he made a farewell hunt and bid goodby to his beloved West for good, at first leasing and then eventually selling his entire 6,600-acre Estes Park property. The earl was in his forties now and had perhaps outgrown his boyish enthusiasm for the out-of-doors; even without the legal harassment and damage to his reputation suffered in Colorado, he may simply have been ready for other things. He actually went to work for a time, serving in the best *noblesse oblige* fashion as Queen Victoria's under-secretary for the colonies, while his avocational attentions turned to yachting; in the 1890s he would twice mount unsuccessful attempts, with his *Valkyries II* and *III*, to regain for Britain the America's Cup.

The decline and fall of Dunraven's standing in Colorado underscores the ambivalence of westerners toward the British gentry who had become so prevalent on the frontier scene. Coloradans may have prided themselves on lack of pretense and class distinction, but they were obviously fascinated by these exotic types and envious of their opulent lifestyles. Newspapers—often with considerable embellishment— followed their comings and goings closely. Pendarves Vivian, a British sportsman visiting Colorado in the 1870s, stopped with his party in Longmont, where he read with arched eyebrows about the arrival of "members of the English Parliament and other English notables" whose extensive impedimenta, the the local paper claimed, included eleven guns and sixty-two blankets. Actually, Vivian noted, their baggage consisted of just four blankets and six guns. (The paper also exaggerated the size and prestige of the party but was at least partly right on one score—Vivian was, in fact, a member of Parliament.)

Vivian dismissed this account as just one more example of the "tall writing" indigenous to frontier journalism. "But I am sure," he could not help adding, that "every excuse should be made for the fearful *ennui* of enterprising minds doomed to pass an existence in this wretched place."

With hair-trigger sensitivity, westerners were ready to take offense at the slightest hint of condescension, and they could make life miserable for anyone putting on English airs at their expense. Advice on the proper treatment of hired hands runs through the travel narratives of the era. John Mortimer Murphy, who distilled his seven years of hunting in the West into a practical manual for other would-be adventurers of his class, warned that a guide "will bear no high-handed dictation or any assumption of superiority." Anyone breaking this rule, he suggested, would find himself led "many weary miles over rugged mountains, through precipitous canyons, and over tiresome plains" devoid of game.

Murphy recalled coming across one particularly insufferable English party whose members had followed a buffalo herd for three days without a shot. He knew the guides to be good ones and was surprised at the group's empty bag until he spoke to the chief scout. "His explanation, which was made with many expletives, and in exceedingly vigorous language," was that his clients "were constantly dictating to himself and his companions what they should and should not do in the most frigid and supercilious manner; that they never spoke to them except to give some command or make an impatient inquiry; that they kept entirely to themselves both in camp and on the march, and never once offered to share the contents of their flask with them; that their English servants were even as consequential as their masters, and evidently looked upon them (the guides) as barbarians and mudsills, and would obey no order unless it came from 'mawster'; and that all, when by themselves, were overheard running down the country in every way."

If his clients kept up "their foreign style," the scout promised, they would get no nearer to any buffalo. Murphy later learned that he was as good as his word: the party saw buffalo "in immense numbers" but in two weeks killed none.

*   *   *

William Adolph Baillie-Grohman, who hunted throughout the West between 1879 and 1881 and who wrote of his exploits under the name "Stalker" in the *Field*, was one of those sportsmen who needed no such advice. Like Ruxton, Messiter and others representing the best of his breed, he could make himself as easily at home in the roughest cowtown saloons as in the poshest salons of Knightsbridge. A man utterly without pretension, he traded jokes with the boys in his outfit and could enjoy a story told at his own expense. Baillie-Grohman admired westerners for what he saw as their "three great qualities" of "self-help, self-confidence, and adaptibility"—traits, in fact, that he himself possessed in abundance.

Better perhaps than any other observer of his time, Baillie-Grohman grasped what was (and, many would say, remains) the essential character of the West and its people:

Mentally and physically, ethnographically and topographically the West is a land of experiment. Everything is tried and tested—the soil, the climate, and Nature generally, no less than man; his spirit, his endurance, his honesty, and his depravity, one and all, are experimented on with a ruthless vigour of which it is difficult to form an adequate idea. No contrivance can be too new, no idea too original. Reverence for old landmarks and time-hallowed institutions the frontiersman knows not, for there are none of these venerable finger-posts to mature civilization. Nothing on the face of the broad Earth is sacred to him. Nature presents herself as his slave. He digs and delves wherever he fancies; forests are there but to be felled, or, if that process be too slow and laborious, to be set ablaze; mountains are made to be honeycombed by his drills and sluices; rocks and hills exist but to be blasted or to be spirited away by the powerful jet from the nozzle of his hydraulic tube. Landscape itself is not secure, for eminences may be levelled, lakes laid dry, and the watercourse of rivers may be turned off, as best suits his immediate desires.

The same hands that tackle nature in such a robust though shockingly irreverent manner, show little respect for the mandates and dignity of a more orderly social condition. They build a church that in weekdays can be used as a grain elevator; and with the same unceremonious haste that a "graveyard" is started, it will, should the soil happen to prove rich in precious ores, be turned into a silver mine. The Western man makes his own laws—not a day before they are required; and he enforces them himself. He is his own judge, father confessor, and executioner; but one and all are mere experiments. The laws, the judge, and the sheriff are just as much on their trial as the culprit.

Baillie-Grohman criticized British travel writers, including sportsmen, whose accounts of the West reinforced popular stereotypes and exaggerated, in his view, the country's lawlessness and violence. "We laugh at the American tourist who at Holyrood mistakes the butler for the Lord Chamberlain, and in Westminster Abbey addresses a chorister as the Dean; but surely the mistakes our tourists make are equally startling, for they believe very harmless blusterers to be desperadoes of the worst type, and that to visit the West without a revolver in each coat-tail pocket is risking their lives in a very reckless manner."

Westerners could, to their advantage, play on the very stereotypes imposed on them by awed eastern and European observers. In a story reminiscent of Grantley Berkeley's encounter with the "bloody arm of the Rocky Mountains," Baillie-Grohman relates his meeting in a Wyoming town with one "Bearclaw Joe." The Englishman was preparing for his first American hunt and seeking a man who knew the country to serve as guide. There seemed no scarcity of local talent, for in his fortnight's stay he was approached at the hotel by more than a dozen pistol-packing characters who personified, at least in their appearance, all the romance and lore of the frontier scout. In dress and manners, the most resplendent by far was Bearclaw Joe. To hear him tell it, old Joe had spent his life fighting Indians and slaughtering game from the Saskatchewan to the Rio Grande.

Baillie-Grohman admitted that he was "green, very green" when he first crossed the Missouri, but his innocence did not completely blind him to certain doubtful details of Bearclaw Joe's outfit:

> The buckskin suit, the broad Texan hat, no less than the long hair that fell down to his shoulders, were all as greasy as became a great Indian fighter; but I remarked that his sporting accoutrement was decidedly new, and had evidently seen but little wear and tear. The ponderous cartridge belt round his waist was as brand-new from the saddler's shop as his big six-shooter and Winchester rifle from the gunmaker's. Nailed to the stock of his rifle were the front claws of a grizzly, and on my making some cautious inquiries respecting it, and the name by which he introduced himself to me—'Bearclaw Joe'—he proudly informed me, that though he had had that rifle but a short time, it had already annihilated the biggest bear in the Territory, a fierce hand-to-claw fight having preceded the monster's demise."

Having hunted extensively on the Continent, Baillie-Grohman knew "something of bears in other parts of the world"

180

and wondered about the marks on the rifle butt. They looked suspiciously like hammer marks, although his prospective guide assured him they had been made by the bruin's teeth. Later,

> Bearclaw Joe and I were walking through the streets of the town, when we happened to pass one of the five or six meat and game shops the town boasts of. On a strong iron hook attached to the outside hung the carcass of a big grizzly. Naturally I was interested in the sight, and stopped to examine the slandered one's corpse. My companion seemed in a hurry, and when finally I pointed out that the bear's forepaw had been cut off, his haste to get away increased.

Poor Bearclaw Joe! His ruse was up completely when the butcher appeared at the door, shaking his fist at the "cussed bull-whacking son-of-a-bitch" for "cutting off that er' forepaw last night." The butcher took off in pursuit, "But fortunately the next corner was put between the two in the shortest of time, while the greasy locks of the thief streaming behind him were the last I saw of noble 'Bearclaw Joe.' "

*   *   *

Baillie-Grohman found the kind of man he was looking for in a taciturn ex-Indian fighter named Port. Tall, squarely built, and with a steely gaze that immediately inspired confidence, Port incarnated the sterling character of the frontiersman at his best. Raised on the Kansas frontier, he had trapped in the Rockies as a teenager, scouted for the Army in his twenties, and had slept in a "proper bed" just two nights out of the last eleven years. Port had true grit and a courage anchored in the firmest "bottom sand." The boss admired him as well for his sense of humor—a "quiet, dry, hammer-and-tongs humour" and "sparkling bantering wit" that spared no one, including Baillie-Grohman.

Recognizing it as an essential ingredient of western character, Baillie-Grohman agreed with Abraham Lincoln that "the grim grotesqueness and extravagance of American humour" were its most striking features. Closely related was the "lingo

of the West, so rich in happily coined words" and wild trans-
mogrifications. Thus, for instance, were the mundanely descriptive names supplied by the old French trappers felicit-
ously converted by the Anglo-Americans who succeeded them:

> We find such names as *six cailloux* (the six pebbles) spoken of as
> *Siskyou*, the Indian tribe *Bois Brules* are known as *Bob Rulys*,
> the *Bois Blancs* as Bob Longs. The river known to the Spanish of
> Mexico as *Les Animas* (the souls), and to the French as the
> *Purgatoire*, is called by the western man, *Picket-wire*, remind-
> ing one rather of the frontier rendering of Wilkes Booth's words
> after shooting Lincoln, *Six semper tyrannis, i.e.* into *six serpents
> and a tarantula*.

Garbling language to this degree showed a profound—if
unconscious—ingenuity on the part of westerners, who were
forever amazing Baillie-Grohman with their novel solutions to
the practical problems they confronted. One incident left an
especially vivid impression. He had stopped by a frontier
shanty and noticed, lying against the wall in the shade, an
infant strapped to a board and sucking complacently on a
pacifier cut from a piece of pork rind. Attached to the pork were
several pieces of twine. One of these was secured to a board
overhead so the pork would not be lost if it dropped from the
baby's mouth. For reasons that escaped Baillie-Grohman, the
other string was tied to the baby's toe.

He was contemplating this arrangement when, to his chagrin, the baby started fussing. "Its face suddenly got very red,
then bluish, its eyes filled with tears, and its little arms beat
the air with frantic energy." His years of outdoor experience
had not prepared him for this, and he was on the verge of panic
when the mother at last appeared.

"That baby is choking!" he cried.

"No he ain't, and he can't," the woman replied.

Understanding dawned on the Englishman when "the infan-
tile legs" began to work—"one kick, two kicks, and there on the
bib lay the obstruction, the piece of pork, jerked from the
baby-throat by the judiciously kicking little leg."

Baillie-Grohman found himself "vastly relieved, but also
vastly impressed" by the ingenuity of the choke-proof pacifier.
Even a confirmed bachelor like himself, he allowed, might be

persuaded to endure the "blissful condition" of matrimony if it led to "rigging up such an arrangement in strings, and seeing it work in his own nursery."

Finally, in Baillie-Grohman's view, two other outstanding qualities could be attributed to the westerner: hospitality and compassion. Both arose out of the loneliness of the frontier and the proximity of death from any manner of cause—whether by violence, accident, or disease. How many times, the Englishman wondered, had he ridden "cold, hungry, and weary" up to some isolated ranch, looking for a meal and shelter for the night? Whenever he did so, without exception the "best of everything would be offered. Hay, always scarce in those regions, would be given to my horse, and the snuggest corner, the warmest blankets be forced upon me. Many times have I extended my visit for two or three days, and yet not a penny would my hosts accept on parting."

As for compassion, he cited as one of many examples the assistance provided by Port and the other men in his outfit when they came upon what must have been an all-too-familiar frontier sight:

> While crossing a range of hills we happened to pass a little settlement, consisting of four families, living in miserable, tumble-down, windowless adobe hovels. The males were all away "tie-chopping," and during their absence diptheria had swept off, in less than four-and-twenty hours, the entire infant population, consisting of five children, who were now lying dead in the huts. In my absence, and at the prayers of the distracted mothers, the two men who were with the waggon emptied some dry-goods (grocery) packing-cases, and turned them into coffins for the little ones, and, moreover, after unloading the rest of the contents, drove the wretched mothers with their dead little ones to the nearest settlement, fifteen miles off, where diptheria had caused a children's graveyard to be started.

*   *   *

The only way one could really get to know the character of westerners and the West, Baillie-Grohman maintained, was to go afield with the simplest possible outfit and to live as close to the land and its people as possible. He listed three ways from which the gentleman sportsman could choose to visit the West: as a "top shelfer" accompanied by servants and guided by professional hunters, *a la* St. George Gore or John Watts Garland; as a guest of post commanders of frontier forts, carrying letters of introduction from general officers and hunting in the company of a cavalry escort; or—"the cheapest, the freest, the most pleasant manner provided its rough sides have no terrors for you"—going with trappers and living in the mountains like the fur hunters of old.

Baillie-Grohman had tried all three and by a substantial margin preferred the third. Joining a trapper outfit assured the sportsman access to the most remote parts of the West, the only areas in fact where game could still be found in abundance, and at a moderate cost compared to the ten or fifteen pounds per day paid by a top shelfer with his extensive retinue and baggage train. In the company of trappers, he asserted, one could enjoy "the good-fellowship of thoroughly trustworthy men, and while they do their trapping or wild-poisoning, you, who are tacitly considered the 'boss' or master, and are addressed as such, can roam about at your own free will" while learning woodcraft under the tutelage of "trapper masters."

At its best, camp life on a trapping expedition offered a bucolic existence, in which troubles faded as quickly as alpenglow on a sandstone bluff. Arriving near dusk at a mountain meadow close to timberline after a bracing climb through spruce and pine forests, they unpacked their horses and began setting up. The ground was littered with gear and provisions—sacks of flour, a powder keg, pelts, steel traps, rifles, and holstered Colt revolvers—while the pack animals, shed of their burdens, rolled in the grass and cantered in circles, kicking and neighing in "wild delight." Before long a fire was burning, "pleasantly perfumed by the cedarwood which produces it," the blue smoke rising in lazy swirls and blending with the deepening sky. "How content, how pleasant and pleased, everything looks!" exalted Baillie-Grohman, who suppressed an urge to roll in the "green fragrant mountaingrass" like the horses and dogs.

His reverie over their arcadian retreat in the Wind River Mountains was made sweeter by the hardships suffered in getting there. They had been on the trail since setting off in late June from an unnamed Wyoming town. Seared by a two-year drought, the high plains were bereft of game, which by now (1880) would have been scarce even under the best conditions. It was not unusual to ride fourteen hours without a drop to drink, resting during the hottest part of the day and collapsing at night in a "dry camp" whose only water—muddy and laden with alkali—came from a shallow well dug with picks and spades by the light of sagebrush torches.

On entering the foothills they at last found water plentiful enough to slake their thirst. But game still eluded them, and with provisions nearly exhausted they subsisted as best as possible on bread and coffee. "A good hunger is a very nice thing," Baillie-Grohman ruefully observed—"nothing nicer in fact when just about to be appeased; but to have that selfsame hunger grow older, outstrip baby proportions, assume a more aggressively manly form, and finally turn into a regular grizzly older veteran hunger, getting up with you at night, bathing with you in the cool beaver pool or mountain stream, sitting on your horse through long weary rides, gnawing at your vitals, wrecking your even temper, turning your pleasure-trip into a wretched parody—this, I say, was hard to bear."

Worse, they were now beset by a biblical plague of mosquitoes—besieged and "overwhelmed by enormous clouds of these torments, the creation of the abnormal drought which had laid dry lakes and creeks." The humans in the party were partly spared after fashioning makeshift netting from flour sacks. But the animals enjoyed no such respite—several of the lighter-colored horses were blanketed by the maddening swarms and appeared at a distance to be uniformly dark. "Life," Baillie-Grohman lamented, "became an intolerable misery, men and beasts suffering alike." They dragged themselves along like "ludicrous scare-crows with swollen faces and half-closed eyes, in the despairing listlessness of men who for a week knew not what a night's rest was, and who for a fortnight had not sat down to the semblance of a square meal." The poor horses, meanwhile, staggered on, "reduced to walking skeletons by the bloodthirsty pests."

Their fortunes changed as soon as they reached high country.

185

Game was plentiful near treeline, and their bellies were soon filled to bursting with meat of mountain sheep, elk, and other fare. The alpine lakes swarmed with cutthroat trout, which they cooked in bear fat and garnished with beaver tail. Between four men and two dogs, they sometimes consumed forty pounds of fish a day. Baillie-Grohman also demonstrated an epicure's taste for the inner organs of beast and fowl, commandeering one of the outfit's frying pans on which he "fried, broiled, stewed, or boiled such odds and ends as struck my fancy."

> Beaver tail and bear liver were general favourites, not so elk brain or kidney. Cooking these little tidbits of campfire reminds me always of that most delightful occupation of the juvenile mind, making mud-pasties on the sands of the sea. Let the liver be a blotched mass of half-cooked gore, or the brain a jelly-like mass, or the kidney cinder on the outside and raw inside, yet you find it nice, and are happy. These latter delicacies the men never touched; for trappers are very fastidious in the choice of their meat, and I believe they thought me next to a barbarian for gourmandizing on kidneys, which they consider "unclean, and not fit for a dog."

During a winter encampment later in the year, Baillie-Grohman demonstrated to the men the art of making soap from various natural ingredients.

> I fancied that I remembered to have once been taught that soap was made of tallow, lye, and lime; but being neither a chemist nor a geologist, I committed the grave error of supposing that the alkaline earth of the usual bad-land formation, containing a large percentage of soda and alkali, would act as a substitute for lime. After filling the camp kettle with lye of wood ashes, concentrated by several hours boiling, I began to mix it in the gold-pan with some elk tallow and alkaline earth, using my hands for this purpose. To my surprise the result was a sticky, tar-like, greasy, black mess, of the consistency of thick glue—in fact, anything but soap; and when I finally gave up the attempt, I found to my horror that the black stuff coating my hands resisted all attempts to remove it. I tried every conceivable means to get it off, parboiling them in steaming water, rubbing them with gunpowder, salt, pitch from the trees, earth, ashes,

steeping them till I could bear it no longer in the hot lye; but everything failed to remove the infernal tarry stuff from my hands. Even half a pint of precious whiskey was wasted in my vain endeavour to subdue the "boss's soap," as of course it at once was nicknamed. The men laughed till tears coursed down their cheeks; and I threatened to try some on *them*, if they did not resist.

In desperation he turned next to baking soda as an antidote to the tenacious goo, which by now had assumed the "consistency of melted indiarubber." Immersing his hands in a pot of the stuff dissolved in hot water, he heard a distinct fizz as a "wretched chemical process" went to work. Alas, several hours of soaking failed to improve his plight, and at the end of the day he surrendered to the black mess and donned a pair of gloves "so at least to be able to eat." Eventually the muck dried out sufficiently so that most of it could be scraped off with a dull skinning knife, although it was several months before the last traces of it disappeared. "It was altogether one of the few incidents that refused to yield a bright or useful side," Baillie-Grohman concluded, "except perhaps one, that it showed how *not* to make soap."

In contrast to his ineptitude at camp chores, Baillie-Grohman displayed in the field a consummate skill at stalking and shooting big game. In his first encounter with large herds of elk he killed nine bulls and could have "easily trebled the number" had he chosen. In retrospect he admitted that even nine was much too high a number, although "the glorious sight of many hundreds of splendid stags . . . carried me away and awoke that reprehensible love of slaughter inherent in most men's natures." His men laughed at what we would call his conservation ethic, but which they derided as "English squeamishness." The western hunter, he concluded sadly, "seems to fancy the game resources of his land perfectly limitless." What was the point, Port and the others asked, of holding fire when "the rascally Redskins or a parcel of skin-hunters" would harvest the animals sooner or later anyway?

Like Moreton Frewen and other gentlemen sportsmen, Baillie-Grohman found elk an uncomfortably tame and not very challenging quarry, at least when stalked in the traditional manner. Bighorn sheep, however, were another matter entirely. The skittishness of mountain sheep, as well as their nearly impassable habitat, made them a superbly challenging quarry. He never tired of tracking them, and the harder the conditions the better he liked it. The chase was particularly bracing above treeline, with winter closing in and a north wind blowing streamers of snow off the peaks—a wind that raged so hard that standing up in it could be dangerous. Bundled in a shaggy buffalo coat and with his legs swaddled in wolf skins, he once stalked an old ram with a giant set of horns for twelve days until the weather forced him back. Later, a pair of trappers told him a tall tale of a ram with horns so big they left tracks in the snow. Baillie-Grohman listened attentively, then did them one better: The horns of *his* ram, he boasted, were so enormous they had sleigh runners attached.

"Stalking the Ram"–difficult terrain and skittishness of mountain sheep made them a favorite quarry.

Baillie-Grohman became obsessed by the majesty and sporting qualities of bighorns, studying them for hours at a time through binoculars and bagging, over the course of several years, more than seventy rams—a truly profligate figure, but one that failed to twitch his conservationist's conscience. Once, in "a piece of singularly good luck," he surprised a small herd on a highland meadow. Leaving his rifle in its scabbard, he drew his Colt revolver and took off in pursuit, six-gun blazing, toppling a fine ram as it leapt to cover amid the crags of a nearby escarpment. Although not overly large, the animal's horns became the prize in his collection for the unique manner in which he acquired them.

On another occasion, he shot an old ram at some distance with his trusty Express rifle, then climbed out onto the narrow ledge where the animal had fallen. The ram had dropped "as if struck by lightning" and seemed "as dead as a stone" when he reached it and began measuring its horns with a tape measure. But to the hunter's astonishment, his quarry came suddenly to life, leaping to its feet and "flinging me back like a feather," then bounding off along the ledge with his measuring tape waving goodby from the ram's horn. His bullet had apparently only creased the ram in the neck, sending it into temporary shock.

In his long and detailed accounts of bighorn and other animals, Baillie-Grohman reveals himself as a careful observer in the best hunter-naturalist tradition. Like John Palliser, he was fascinated by beavers, devoting an entire chapter on the natural history of North America's largest rodent. He would sometimes go to exceptional lengths in his pursuit of knowledge—squeezing, for example, into a beaver's bankside burrow to examine its lodge by candlelight. "On several occasions have I thus surprised solitary old males in their winter abodes, the frightened tenant, unable to escape, crouching in the furthest extremity of his bare and cold cavern, and eyeing me with his small and not particularly expressive eyes."

He had this to say on the long-standing question of beaver "intelligence":

There are very numerous traits in the beaver's activity that appear incompatible with the argument that only blind instinct moves the little workers. To watch two beavers at work gnawing down a big cottonwood-tree, three feet and a half in circumference—each worker keeping strictly to his side, the incision being made to bring the tree in its final plunge to the very spot they want it, athwart a creek, or, as an additional protection to their dam, a foot or two on the upper side of it, where the danger from the swift current is greatest, is a sight which will probably convince even the most unbelieving. An experiment made on several different occasions by me tells its own tale.

Coming, in the course of my rambles, upon quite fresh beaver work, say a moderately big cottonwood-tree five or six inches in diameter, standing on a slope, and partially cut through by them, I would put my shoulder to it, and, if possible, break it down, so that it fell up the slope in a direction opposite to that which the beaver evidently intended. Visiting the spot the next day, or two days afterwards, the tree was invariably lugged round, with the top downhill or athwart the little creek, the foundation work probably of a new dam.

Baillie-Grohman noted that prime beaver pelts brought two dollars a pound from furriers in New York City. Assuming this was a markup of at least 100 percent from what the trappers themselves received from jobbers to whom they sold their pelts, the beaver hunter in 1880 could expect, per pound of skins, only a fourth or less of what his counterpart earned at the height of the fur trade fifty years earlier. Yet this was still enough to attract small numbers of trappers, who like their forebears showed the same obsessive secretiveness toward aspects of their calling. Most of the trappers he met, said Baillie-Grohman, were "fanatical believers" in their particular recipe for "medicine," the aromatic mixture of castoreum (beaver musk) and other ingredients for luring the animal to the trap. One pelt hunter told him of his six-year apprenticeship with an old veteran who refused to divulge his recipe until his dying day. "Finally, mortally wounded by an Indian arrow, he revealed, while lying on the ground gasping for breath, the grand secret of his life to his faithful partner."

Baillie-Grohman was touched when several old trappers entrusted to him "in whispered confidence" the names of several ingredients of their respective concoctions, "which they begged me to send them from Chicago or New York—a sufficiently overwhelming token of confidence to make an old man of me in the conscientious endeavour to keep the secrets. I am not transgressing my trust if I mention that they were of the most varied nature, some of the commonest being oil of aniseed, of amber, of cassia, of cloves, of fennel seed, of thyme, and oil of rhodium."

*　　*　　*

On his third and final expedition, Baillie-Grohman was determined to visit the legendary haunt of trappers, the Teton Basin, an area noted for its spectacular beauty since the days of the mountain rendezvous. "There are few spots in the Western mountain lands around which there hangs so much frontier romance," he stated, while admitting to having "Teton Basin on the brain" from the stories he had heard about it over the years. With so much talk about its awesome scenery and plentiful beaver, he expected the place to be overrun by trappers but was pleasantly surprised to find the opposite. Guarded by the rugged Teton and Gros Ventre ranges and reachable by only a few Indian trails, it was also a hunting ground for the Nez Perces and Bannocks, who did not take kindly to whites invading their garden paradise. But when Baillie-Grohman reached the basin in 1880, both tribes had been recently confined to reservations following last, desperate attempts to reassert their rights to the old nomadic ways. "With two exceptions, I saw not a single white man from the end of July to the end of November, and for three months of that period saw no Indians."

Lined with cottonwoods, the Snake River emerged from Jackson Lake and cut an emerald swath through a vast green meadow. Out of this "mass of brilliant verdure" rose the Grand Teton, its tooth-like shape recalling the Matterhorn, although in Baillie-Grohman's view it easily exceeded the "Swiss master-peak" in dramatic effect. The Teton Basin, he declared, was nothing less than a "mountain-girt Eden" boasting "the most sublime scenery I have ever seen."

They spent ten days in the Teton Basin and would have passed at least another fortnight there, except that a forest fire threatened to invade the valley. Winter was approaching, too, and they had made plans to pass the ice months in another part of the mountains. By late November, Baillie-Grohman found himself ensconsed in winter quarters in a canyon at eight thousand feet, a pall of snow covering "peak and forest, lake and gulch; thermometer 35 degrees below zero Fahr.; distance to the next white man's habitation, 105 miles; date of the newest newspaper, September 2." For nearly half a year, he added, "our eyes have not feasted on a civilized female face," and the last news from the outside world was the temperature in New York: 95 degrees in the shade.

The author's abode was a dugout—one of the simplest yet, when properly constructed, coziest shelters a man could make for himself in the wilderness. (At least, if you didn't mind a little smoke.) A dugout was nothing more than a crude hollow excavated from the dry, south-facing bank of a stream, its entrance piled with stones and plastered mud and with a small opening for crawling in and out. The interior was about ten feet square and lit by a "devil," a shallow iron basin filled with elk tallow and burning a rope wick. The space was adequate for "four men, two dogs, a dozen or more saddles and pack-saddles, the stores, sundry shooting-irons, two dozen beaver traps, bales of fur, and trifles too numerous to mention, all of which have to find shelter in this Rocky Mountain Welbeck Abbey."

The author happily described himself writing these words as he sat on a powder keg—"the only chair-like article in our dwelling"—while "plying his pen in front of a novel species of camp writing-table" made of elk horns, with a piece of rawhide stretched across the middle tines to make a crude but adequate writing platform. Outside, winter raged in all its Rocky Mountain fury.

> An eight days' heavy snow hurricane is a very stern truth-teller, and makes us for the moment forget that our habitation's chief merits—warmth in winter and coolness in summer—are amply counterbalanced by its failings, its uncommonly annoying dust-producing qualities, and such minor disadvantages as the fact that it is hardly ever clear of the smoke produced by the open fire in the centre of the floor, and that, on account of its smallness, it is apt to crowd the "outfit."

If Baillie-Grohman could make living under these conditions sound like fun, it was doubtless because he genuinely enjoyed it for the simple challenges involved.

It would be idle to describe how all the outfit found room in this box-like home. It is not the first or the second time, but perhaps by the experience of a dozen trials, that you and your men succeed in getting everything into it. To store the flour sacks where no driving snow can get at them; to pile the saddles and the bales of valuable beaver, otter, and grey wolves' skins upon each other without their toppling over; to put your coffee and sugar where the ever-falling dust from your loam roof cannot find them; to hang up the wet garments and soaking saddle blankets where they are least in the way; to find room for the cooking-utensils and the water-bucket; to discover a snug corner for the dogs; and, finally, to plan out space enough for yourself and the men to move about in—this, and a lot more, can only be learnt by long experience, no easier to acquire and no less useful than the knack of making a dugout with but one spade and one pick, with the ground frozen to the consistency of lead, and a snowstorm just setting in preceded by an intensely cold wind freezing out of the shivering snow-soaked mortals almost the last vital spark.

When the weather cleared he liked to explore the snow-hushed countryside and consort with a local band of Shoshone Indians. Often five or six braves would appear at the dugout entrance for a visit. They took an immediate liking to "the man with the split body," as, for unexplained reasons, Baillie-Grohman was called, in part because he offered them *gratis* much of the meat he shot. (The arrangement was symbiotic, as it allowed him to collect trophy heads with a clear conscience.) While admiring their skill at stalking game with bow and arrow, Baillie-Grohman found his red friends "very indifferent shots" with a rifle. "I never heard so much shooting and saw so little hitting as I did in the month we were right among these perfectly wild Indians. Often I have counted fifteen shots to one poor deer; and there would be more shooting and waving of arms, and riding at full split up and down the most amazingly steep slopes, than would supply an evening's entertainment at a circus."

*   *   *

Baillie-Grohman enjoyed the Indians he encountered, who

besides Shoshone included Crow, Bannock, and Arapaho. But unlike earlier writers such as Murray and Townshend, he made no mention of their inherent playfulness or high spirits, giving us instead a more Cooperian portrait as he noted their "inbred seriousness." Perhaps by 1881 Indians simply had nothing left to laugh about. With the exception of the Apaches in far-off Arizona, every western tribe had been subdued by now and reduced to living on reservations and government handouts. Only in the most remote pockets of the West could game be found in anything like the extraordinary abundance that Stewart, and even Messiter only a decade before, had taken for granted. While enough elk, mountain sheep, antelope, and even grizzly remained to make hunting for them worthwhile, the buffalo had all but disappeared from most of its former range. Baillie-Grohman spotted not a single one in his travels, nor did Dunraven in his perambulation of the Yellowstone plateau.

By 1882 only one sizable herd of buffalo still roamed the American plains. It comprised about 75,000 bison grazing the short grass in a great triangle bordered by the Yellowstone, Missouri, and Musselshell rivers in central Montana. By the end of two bloody seasons the hide hunters had killed all but about 300. Another, smaller herd of some 10,000 survived north of the Black Hills but by the fall of 1883 had been reduced to 1,100. When Sitting Bull learned that this remnant herd had been sighted near the Standing Rock Reservation, he led a thousand of his warriors to meet it. They were the last Indians ever to run buffalo. The hunt lasted two days, and they killed every animal.

The Sioux returned to the reservation and in the spring took up their hoes again—learning, with however little enthusiasm, the white man's ways. An era had ended, with more of a whimper than a bang. The gallant Charles Messiter, who had left the West for a few years in 1878, returned several times in the eighties and nineties but felt no obligation to describe these later visits. In many cases he did not even recognize his old hunting grounds, "so much had ranches and enclosures changed the face of the country." The whole of his beloved Judith Basin, he added, was "a mass of sheep ranches" and the game and Indians gone from it for good.

End Notes

For complete bibliographical information on sources cited here, see bibliography, p. 207.

Chapter 1. Wellington's Soldier

1. "Sleep in those days. . . ." Stewart, *Edward Warren*, p. 7.

2-3. The description of the buffalo chase is adapted from various parts of *Edward Warren* and other accounts of the buffalo hunt, including pp. 37-39 of DeVoto, *Across the Wide Missouri*.

3. "that glorious race. . . ." Stewart, p. 4

5. "hung on the side. . . ." Stewart, p. 6

5. "one man in all that region. . . ." Stewart, p. 6

Stewart's outfit. Stewart, p. 64. Stewart writes of his Manton gun without distinguishing which Manton brother, Joseph or John, made it. The author assumes it was Joseph, who was better known for sporting rifles.

6. Numbers of buffalo. Dary, *The Buffalo Book*, p. 29.

Indians and horses. Haines, *The Plains Indians*, pp. 58-69.

6. "the hiccoughing jargon. . . ." Townsend, *Narrative of a Journey*, p. 83.

7. "the mountain man's Christmas. . . ." DeVoto, p. 226.

7. Stewart's rendezvous outfit. Porter and Davenport, *Scotsman in Buckskin*, p. 48. A similar account appears in Stanley Vestal's *Jim Bridger*. The author is unable to trace this story to its original source, but it rings true so he has included it.

8. Rabid wolf story. DeVoto, pp. 106-07.

8. "light brown hair. . . ." Stewart, p. 378.

9. Baptiste Charbonneau. DeVoto, pp. 115-16.

Grizzly encounter. DeVoto, p. 14.

10. "The cry . . . was no sooner off. . . ." Stewart, p. 202.

11. Incident with Crows. DeVoto, pp. 25-31; Porter and Davenport, p. 72.

13-14. Markhead. Stewart, p. 289.

14. "I go as Paul. . . ." DeVoto, p. 179.

14. "a total stranger. . . ." DeVoto, p. 208.

Animals in entourage. DeVoto, p. 204.

15. "The service. . . ." Wyeth Journal, entry for July 15, 1834.

15. "A most excellent. . . ." Stewart, p. 260.

15. "In the mountains. . . ." DeVoto, p. 230.

Chapter 2. Kilts and Buckskins

17. Introductory quotation is from Catlin, *North American Indians*, Vol. II, p. 25. Murray's background. Maxwell, *The Honourable Sir Charles Murray*, p. vi.

"sigh and soften. . . ." Maxwell, p. 80.

Smashing fist through door. Maxwell, p. 93

19. "Who can wonder. . . ." Murray, *Travels in North America*, Vol. I, p. 239.

Murray's outfit. Murray, p. 248.

19. Murray's appearance. Murray, p. 382.
20. "a weak, and daily decreasing. . . ." Murray, p. 252.

July 4 celebration. Murray, p. 254.

20. "a strange and wild. . . ." Murray, p. 258.
20. "carefully grouped. . . ." Murray, p. 260.

Carolina paroquet. Murray, p. 261

"Ribs, head. . . ." Murray, p. 262.

21. "tearing the meat. . . ." Murray, p. 256.
21. "as tender. . . ." Murray, p. 394.

Pawnee eating contest. Murray, p. 348.

Pawnee diet. Murray, p. 266.

21. Pawnees as hunters. Murray, p. 67.
22. Shooting antelope. Murray, p. 367.

"Frequently my brother. . . ." Murray, p. 375.

22. "He said he would like. . . ." Murray, p. 411.
24. "The feeling of the responsibility. . . ." Murray, p. 473.
25. "I regret very much. . . ." Murray, Vol. II, p. 50.
25. Smallpox. Haines, *The Plains Indians*, p. 47.

The remainder of Murray's life is worthy of note. After leaving court he entered the British diplomatic corps, serving with distinction in Naples, Cairo, Berne, Teheran, Dresden, Copenhagen and Lisbon. As consul general in Egypt he earned the monicker of "Hippopotamus Murray" for bringing back alive England's first hippo, which resided for years in London's Hyde Park Zoo. The animal would greet Murray with great grunts whenever he visited, and Murray would reply by hailing the hippo in Arabic.

Murray married twice. His first wife was Elise Wadsworth, an American whose father lived on an estate neighboring James Fenimore Cooper's in Geneseo County, New York. Elise became the model for the "Prairie Bird," the Indian princess in Murray's romantic novel of the same name.

Murray was knighted in 1866 at age sixty. He died, at age eighty-eight, in 1895.

Chapter 3. 'H'ar of the Grissly'

26. The introductory quotation of Eliza Spalding comes from Drury, *Marcus and Narcissa Whitman and the Opening of Old Oregon*, Vol. I, p. 189.

Stewart's first three years in West. DeVoto, *Across the Wide Missouri*, p. 235.

Stewart's sign. Tyler, *Alfred Jacob Miller*, p. 22.

27. Stewart's outfit. Porter and Davenport, *Scotsman in Buckskin*, p. 111.
27. "He was about. . . ." DeVoto, p. 20.

28. "three servants. . . ." Gray, *A History of Oregon*, p. 116.

28. "they being the first. . . ." Russell, *Journal of a Trapper*, p. 116.

"is supposed to have once said. . . ." DeVoto, p. 247.

Stewart's longing for domesticity. DeVoto, p. 253.

30. "wild child. . . ." DeVoto, pp. 307-09.

30. "Lies tumbled. . . ." Ruxton, *Life in the Far West*, p. 7.

"a corpus. . . ." DeVoto, p. 11.

"At other times. . . ." DeVoto, p. 313.

30. "I would be glad. . . ." DeVoto, p. 313.

"the management of unruly spirits. . . ." DeVoto, p. 313.

"In five minutes. . . ." DeVoto, p. 314.

32. "The ruling passion. . . ." DeVoto, p. 314.

Antoine and the buffalo. Tyler, p. 6.

32. "wild sons of the West. . . ." Tyler, "Artist on the Oregon Trail," p. 48.

White Plume. Porter and Davenport, p. 35.

33. "flair for conveying. . . ." Tyler, *Alfred Jacob Miller*, p. 5.

33-34. Meek at rendezvous. Stewart, *Edward Warren*, p. 287.

34. Walker's alleged cannibalism. Tyler, *Alfred Jacob Miller*, plate 80.
Walker's biographer, Bil Gilbert, does not give this story much credence.

Gift of moccasins. DeVoto, p. 323, and Porter and Davenport, p. 155.

35. Stewart fishing. DeVoto, p. 334.

Lake paintings. Tyler, *Alfred Jacob Miller*, p. 52.

Stewart's vow. Porter and Davenport, p. 62.

Chapter 4. Goodbye to All That

36. "for the Indian country. . . ." Field, *Prairie and Mountain Sketches*, p. xxi. The quotation is from the St. Louis *Missouri Republican*.

37. "of the Armey. . . ." Field, p. xxx.

37-38. Stewart at Murthly. Porter and Davenport, *Scotsman in Buckskin*, p. 201.

"I want for nothing. . . ." Field, p. xxvii.

Page Audubon. Field, p. xxiv.

40. Wreck of the *Weston*. Porter and Davenport, p. 222.

"I am receiving every courtesy. . . ." Field, p. xxvii.

40. Great Migration. Lamar, *The Reader's Encyclopedia of the American West*, p. 885.

41. Stewart's outfit. Porter and Davenport, p. 21.

41. *Romeo and Juliet*. Porter and Davenport, p. 24, and Field, p. xxvii.

Prairie flora. Costello, *The Prairie World*. Kennerly in old age recalled the country beyond Westport as flat and arid, but he was probably remembering the high plains farther west.

42. Travelers' outfits. Kennerly, *Persimmon Hill*, p. 144. Kennerly dictated his remembrances of youth while in his eighties. It makes interesting reading, but his memory was foggy, and much of his account of the Stewart expedition fails to jibe with contemporary accounts.

42. Osage horse thieves. Field, p. 146.

Stewart faces down Osages. Porter and Davenport, p. 28.

42. "dull, gloomy, weary. . . ." Field, p. xxv.

"some of the company. . . ." Field, p. xxvi.

43. "Every soul of us. . . ." Field, p. 86, and Porter and Davenport, p. 147.

44. "together with tongue and hump. . . ." Kennerly, p. 147.

"averted only by exerting. . . ." Kennerly, p. 147.

"and it was only after many apologies. . . ." Kennerly, p. 149.

45. Plumb pudding. Porter and Davenport, p. 234.

46. Visit of Sioux chiefs. Porter and Davenport, p. 237.

47. Lake Stewart. Field, p. xxxiii.

Reciting Walter Scott and Shakespeare. Kennerly, p. 155, and Porter and Davenport, p. 239.

47. Mini-rendezvous. Porter and Davenport, p. 239.

Kennerly's buckskins. Kennerly, p. 156.

"the moment of farewell. . . ." Porter and Davenport, p. 241.

48. "We have spent. . . ." Field, p. 159.

48. "glad of the move. . . ." Field, p. xxxiv. The party appears to have returned by the same route that it came. Kennerly, in his memoirs dictated in old age to his daughter, claims that the caravan proceeded home "by a more northerly route" and camped within the boundaries of what is now Yellowstone National Park. His accounts of hot springs and geysers are detailed and colorful, but his memory was playing tricks on him—he made subsequent trips west and may have visited Yellowstone on one of these. Matt Field's contemporary account makes no mention of any such geothermal wonders, and even a casual study of the itinerary shows that, given the leisurely pace of the journey and the long stay at Lake Stewart, it is extremely unlikely that they went as far as the Yellowstone plateau—a journey that, round-trip, would have taken them several hundred miles out of their way.

"*His omnipotence*. . . ." Field, p. xxxvi.

48. Baltimore doctor. Porter and Davenport, p. 182.

49. "The Bull roared. . . ." Field, p. 182.

49. "Sir William. . . ." Kennerly, p. 167.

Chapter 5. Ruxton of the Rockies

51. The opening quotation is from Lewis H. Garrard's *Wah-to-yah and the Taos Trail*, p. 250. Garrard is mistaken about Ruxton having traveled in India.

52. "that one meets. . . ." Ruxton, *Ruxton of the Rockies*, p. 307. (All subsequent Ruxton citations are from this book.)

"Seated Indian fashion." Ruxton, p. 231.

53. "The gun had ever. . . ." Ruxton, p. 37.

"as primitively as in the days. . . ." Ruxton, p. 46.

54. Ruxton's mission. Ruxton, p. 106.

54. "The senora. . . ." Ruxton, p. 110.

"decidedly low. . . ." Ruxton, p. 31.

55. Cantina incident. Ruxton, p. 114.

56. Thief tortured. Ruxton, p. 142.

56. "The infuriated Mexicans. . . ." Ruxton, p. 149.

57. "I thought then. . . ." Webb, *Adventures in the Santa Fe Trade*, p. 239.

Ruxton the naturalist. Ruxton, p. 150.

58. Apache attacks. Ruxton, p. 161.

Auxiliares. Ruxton, p. 162.

American trading caravan. Ruxton, p. 167.

58. American bivouac. Ruxton, p. 169.

Kearney's troops, Ruxton, p. 179.

59. *Yanqui* invaders. Ruxton, p. 179.

59. Rattlesnake oil. Ruxton, p. 194.

59-60. Rio Colorado, Ruxton, p. 198.

60. Laforet. Ruxton, p. 197. Ruxton spells the trapper's name phonetically as "Laforey."

60. "Not a hole or corner. . . ." Ruxton, p. 228. The Gila runs through what is now Arizona.

61. "I had now. . . ." Ruxton, p. 199.

62. Antelope. Ruxton, p. 200.

62. "If a deer. . . ." Ruxton, p. 214.

Bighorn sheep. Ruxton, p. 257.

63. Buffalo. Ruxton, pp. 251-52.

65. "As might be inferred. . . ." Ruxton, p. 281.

65. "I once saw two Canadians. . . ." Ruxton, p. 250.

66. Markhead. Ruxton, p. 220.

Manitou Springs. Ruxton, p. 41.

66. "I never recall. . . ." Ruxton, p. 262. The name Bayou Salado derives from the Salt Springs in this region.

66. St. Louis. Ruxton, p. 297.

66. "I found chairs. . . ." Ruxton, p. 297.

67. "As you say. . . ." Ruxton, p. 308.

Chapter 6. The Solitary Rambler

71. Indians and buffalo robe trade. Haines, *The Plains Indians*, p. 170, and Ruxton, *Ruxton of the Rockies*, p. 252.

71. "with the boundary of. . . ." Ruxton, p. 249.

71. Movement of Sioux west of Missouri. Haines, p. 147.

Palliser's background. Spry, *The Palliser Expedition*, introduction.

Palliser's Canadian expedition. *Dictionary of National Biography*, Vol. 15, pp. 116-17.

72. "inhabited by America's. . . ." Palliser, *The Solitary rambler*, p. 2.

William Fairholm. Palliser, p. xviii.

"all the eagerness. . . ." Palliser, p. 5.

Tom Thumb. Palliser, p. 5.

73. Stage travel. Palliser, p. 14.

New Orleans visit. One Palliser chronicler notes that he possessed "a good baritone voice" and while in New Orleans sung "both the bass and tenor parts" at a charity performance of the oratorio David when a professional soloist failed to appear. (Spry, introduction)

73. James Kipp. Palliser, p. 82.

Kipp's background. Hafen, *The Mountain Men and the Fur Trade of the Far West*, Vol. II, pp. 201-05.

74. Mormons, Lamar, *Reader's Encyclopedia of the American West*, p. 772.

"an indefatigable set. . . ." Palliser, p. 84.

74. "the grass growing. . . ." Palliser, pp. 87-88.

75. "as only travellers. . . ." Palliser, p. 85.

75. Yankton Sioux camp. Palliser, p. 97.

76. "the atmosphere in these regions. . . ." Palliser, p. 105.

76. Shooting buffalo. Palliser, p. 113.

77. Dangers of river ice. Palliser, p. 153.

78. Incident with Ishmah. Palliser, p. 158.

Fort McKenzie. The fort, near present-day Loma, Montana, was named for Kenneth McKenzie, the celebrated factor for the American Fur Company, whose name is spelled in some accounts as Mackenzie.

78. Beaver. Palliser, p. 225.

"Fortunately for these little people. . . ." Palliser, p. 226.

80. "A strange anomaly. . . ." Palliser, p. 261. "Minetaree" was the name applied to these Indians by the neighboring Mandans, who lived along the Missouri just to the south. They called themselves Hidatsa and were also known in the trade as Gros Ventres or Big Bellies—a verbal rendering of the gesture for them in sign language. (The same name was also applied to the unrelated Atsina, who lived farther up the Missouri.) The Minetarees were closely related to the Crows. Like the Mandans, they were mainly agricultural and lived in earthen lodges. The smallpox scourge of 1837 took a great toll of Minetarees, forcing a consolidation of several settlements along the Missouri into the single village at Fort Berthold. (Swainton, pp. 275-76)

Etienne Provost. Hafen, Vol. VI, p. 385.

Provost as soul of the mountain trapper. Lamar, p. 981.

82. "I drew my shot. . . ." Palliser, p. 275.

82. Minetaree chief. Palliser, p. 285.

83. "Far away along. . . ." Palliser, p. 286.

83. Steamboat *Martha*. Palliser, p. 287.

"who preferred silently. . . ." Palliser, p. 288. Palliser returned home via New Orleans. As noted in the text, he was back in North America in 1857 as head of an expedition to detemine the Canadian-United States boundary line from Lake Superior to the Pacific. He spent three seasons in the field—1857, 1858, and 1860—and for his pioneering survey work was elected to the Royal Geographical Society. He died at Comragh, County Waterford, Ireland, in 1887 at age eighty. (*Dictionary of National Biography*, Vol. 15, pp. 116-17)

Chapter 7. Wretched Excesses

85. Poore's background. The details of Poore's life are drawn from *Paul Kane's Frontier*, edited by J. Russell Harper, whose research indicates that Poore hunted "buffalo, elk, deer, antelope, grouse, racoons, turkeys, bears, and wolves" on his first western adventure. Harper believes this hunt did not last longer than a month.

87. Poore hires Kane. Harper, p. 30.

88. Whitman massacre. Harper, pp. 20-24.

89. "met and passed. . . ." Harper, p. 32.

89. Dissatisfaction with Kane. Harper, p. 333.

91. Pemmican. DeVoto, *Across the Wide Missouri*, p. 164; Dary, *The Buffalo Book*, pp. 72-75; Harper, p. 17.

91. Poore at Fort Garry. Harper, p. 333.

91. "We shall have to pass through. . . ." Harper, p. 334.

92. Shooting death. Harper, p. 335.

"truly a free young man. . . ." Harper, p. 31.

93. Poore's later years. Harper, p. 32.

93. Gore's hunt. Clark C. Spence, "A Celtic Nimrod in the Old West," p. 56. This is the most thorough (and only documented) secondary account of Gore's safari. Spence deflates the more fanciful popularizations of the expedition. He is the author's chief source for this chapter along with Forbes Parkhill, *Wildest of the West*, pp. 129-40.

93. Gore's background. Spence, p. 60; Heldt, "Sir George Gore's Expedition," p. 146. Dundreary whiskers, named after a character in the 1858 stage comedy *Our American Cousin* (the play Lincoln was watching when he was assassinated), were bushy sideburns covering the side of the face but not the chin.

94. Mongrel descendants of Gore's dogs. Parkhill, p. 139.

94. Fitzwilliams's telescope. Parkhill, p. 130.

95. "would come all the way. . . ." Cody, "Famous Hunting Parties of the Plains"; Dary, p. 84.

95. "brave and true-hearted. . . ." Parkman, *The Oregon Trail*, p. xiii.

95. *The Oregon Trail*. Lamar, pp. 191, 894. The "celebrated hunter" Henry Chatillon was lauded by another British adventurer, Henry J. Coke, who crossed the plains in 1850. Coke met Chatillon in St. Louis at the start of his journey and later engaged Henry's older brother, Joseph, as a guide at Fort Laramie.

96. Fort Laramie Treaty. Haines, *The Plains Indians*, p. 160.

Gore's hunt in North and Middle parks. North Park lies along the upper reaches of the North Platte in Jackson County, Colorado. Middle Park is along the upper Colorado in the region of Hot Sulphur Springs. South Park—Ruxton's "Bayou Salado"—is on the headwaters of the South Platte in Park County, Colorado.

96. Gore shoots standing up. Parkhill, p. 132.

96. Gore Pass. Parkhill, p. 153. Today, Gore Pass is traversed by State Highway 134.

97. Bridger's background. Neider, *The Great West*, p. 148; Lamar, pp. 121-22; Alter, *Jim Bridger*.

97. "Sir George's habit. . . ." Alter, pp. 263-64.

98. "You can just go yer pile. . . ." Alter, p. 64. Bridger's reference, of course, is to Andrew Jackson and the Battle of New Orleans.

99. Death of Uno. Spence, p. 62.

99. Blackfeet attack. The first raiding party was made up of Bloods, one of three subgroups of the greater Blackfeet nation. The second group of raiders were Piegans, cousins to the Bloods. According to DeVoto (p. 138), the Piegans were the easiest going of this capricious and most martial of tribes, while the Bloods "were the most Teutonic of all . . . the first to take offense, the first to break a truce, the first to murder."

99. Culbertson's background. Dary, p. 75.

100. Criticism of Gore. Spence, pp. 64-65.

100. Gore threatens Sioux. Spence, p. 65.

101. Gore to Fort Berthold. Heldt, p. 146.

Gore's return home. Heldt, pp. 46-47.

101. "he contributed little...." Spence, p. 66. A lifelong bachelor, Gore died without heirs at Inverness on December 31, 1879 at age sixty-eight.

102. Berkeley's background. *Dictionary of National Biography*, Vol. II, p. 357.

105. New York City. Berkeley, *The English Sportsman in the Western Prairies*, p. 428.

Attitude toward democracy. Berkeley, pp. 30, 45

Spitting. Berkeley, p. 34.

"bloody arm...." Berkeley, p. 150.

105. Underrates costs. Berkeley, p. 114.

Western saddle. Berkeley, p. 116.

106. "soon began to see...." Berkeley, p. 118.

Excessive drinking. Berkeley, p. 220.

106-07. View of Negroes. Berkeley, pp. 87, 350.

"objectional conversation...." Berkeley, p. 188.

107. Bison hunt. Berkeley, p. 290.

110. Pawnee grooming. Berkeley, p. 423.

Chapter 8. Envoys from the Great White Mother

111. Campion's attitude toward British sportsmen. Campion, *On the Frontier*, p. 76. "Battue" refers to beating the bushes to scare up game.

"English tourist-sportsman...." Campion, p. 70.

113. British sportsmen as easy marks. Campion, p. 71.

113. Campion's background. Campion, p. 1.

First buffalo hunt. Campion, p. 33.

114. Skinning buffalo. Campion, pp. 52-55.

114. Return to Fort Riley. Campion, p. 66.

115. "Not many days...." Campion, p. 111.

"There they lay...." Campion, p. 112.

116. "pass the word...." Campion, p. 113.

Santee uprising. Lamar, *Reader's Encyclopedia of the American West*, p. 750.

117. St. Paul. Lamar, p. 1202.

118. Englishmen in St. Paul. Messiter, *Sport and Adventures Among the North-American Indians*, p. 4.

118. Massacred settlers. Messiter, p. 5.

Red River. Messiter, p. 6.

119. "In the excitement...." Messiter, p. 20.

120. Chased by Little Fox. Messiter, pp. 88-96.

121. "It is not bad...." Messiter, p. 96.

"Specious men...." Messiter, p. 105.

124. Sioux retreat. Messiter, p. 121.

124. "I do not think...." Messiter, p. 133.

125. Fox. Messiter, p. 163.

125. Butcher. Messiter, p. 26.

Washita massacre. Taylor, *The Warriors of the Plains*, p. 94.

126. Pawnee renaissance. DeVoto, *Across the Wide Missouri*, p. 35. The

North brothers, Frank and Luther, both led Pawnee battalions. They had come of age on the Nebraska frontier in the 1850s and had made friends with Pawnees living near their family homestead. By this time the Pawnees were settled on a reservation along the Loup River, a tributary to the Platte, and riding with Nebraska militia against their traditional enemy, the Sioux. (George Bird Grinnell, *Two Great Scouts and Their Pawnee Battalion*, p. 57)

127. Indian atrocities. Townshend, *Ten Thousand Miles of Travel, Sport, and Adventure*, pp. 105, 107.

127. Pawnee auxiliaries. Townshend, p. 114.

127. Breaking horses. Townshend, p. 115.

128. New York pick-pockets. Townshend, p. 130.

128. Irish soldiers. Townshend, p. 114.

Soldiers on frontier duty. Townshend, p. 141.

128. Sand Creek massacre. Townshend, p. 142.

130. Massacred soldiers. Townshend, p. 151.

Chapter 9. Hell on Wheels

133. "since the war...." Messiter, *Sport and Adventures Among the North-American Indians*, p. 185.

133. Vigilante justice. Messiter, p. 194.

Breaking horses. Messiter, pp. 195-96.

134. Black cowboys. Taylor and Maar, *The American Cowboy*, p. 20.

134. "I could easily...." Messiter, p. 206.

135. Tonkawas. Messiter, p. 211.

135. Asahabe. Messiter, p. 213. .

136. Messiter's armory. Messiter, p. 214.

"filling buckets...." Messiter, p. 217.

137. Scalping. Messiter, pp. 218-19.

137. "Yelling their war-whoop...." Messiter, p. 219.

139. Julesburg. Messiter, p. 241.

139. Hell on wheels. Clark, *Frontier America*, p. 680.

140. Street fight. Messiter, p. 239.

140. "The first night...." Messiter, p. 240.

Professional gamblers. Messiter, p. 241.

141. "Almost every night...." Messiter, p. 242.

142. Mrs. Hughes. Messiter, p. 263.

143. "It would occupy a volume...." Townshend, *Ten Thousand miles of Travel, Sport, and Adventure*, pp. 148-50.

Col. John Gibbon would figure prominently in the campaign against the Sioux and Cheyenne leading up to the Battle of the Little Bighorn.

144. "many a glass...." Townshend, p. 175.

Beaver. Townshend, pp. 174-75.

Benton, Wyoming, was adjacent to Fort Fred Steele—"a wretched outpost," according to Townshend—which can still be found on the maps of Wyoming. Benton itself, however, has disappeared.

Stagecoach ride. Townshend's route followed the approximate course of present-day US 80.

145. "crowded together...." Townshend, pp. 183-84.

145. Mired in mud. Townshend, pp. 184-85.

Fort Bridger. Townshend, p. 185.

146. "The absence of gambling saloons. . . .." Townshend, p. 194.

147. "In a town where. . . ." Townshend, p. 198.

147. Yankee view of Mormons. Townshend, p. 193.

Brigham Young. Townshend, p. 195. Townshend's comments were echoed by another English traveler, George Alfred Lawrence, who passed through the City of the Saints after the Civil War. Lawrence noted that Young possessed a "remarkable face, assuredly, and far from attractive; but a certain square firmness of outline saves it from ignoble sensuality. . . ." Young's "deep-set eyes," he added, were "rather calculating than cruel." Like most gentile observers at the time, Lawrence and Townshend allowed their moral indignation over Mormon polygamy to color their descriptions. (Lawrence, *Silverland*, p. 52)

148. "very rough fellows. . . ." Messiter, p. 270.

English cowboy. Messiter, p. 275.

148. "One day. . . ." Messiter, p. 291.

149. Judith Basin. Messiter, p. 301.

150. Pharoah's serpents. Messiter, p. 306.

150. "The game consisted. . . ." Messiter, p. 317.

151. Indian agent's thievery. Messiter, p. 295.

Red Cloud. Taylor, *The Warriors of the Plains*, p. 103.

Chapter 10. Wonderland

152. The quote from Cornelius Hedges comes from Chittenden, *Yellowstone National Park*, p. 60.

Easier access to West. Pomeroy, *In Search of the Golden West*, p. 76.

153. Squaw "effluvium." Gillmore, *A Hunter's Adventures in the Great West*, p. 67.

153. Indian character. Leveson, *Sport in Many Lands*, p. 238.

154. "this romantic valley. . . ." Leveson, p. 257.

British ranchers in Wyoming. *Time*, October 22, 1984, p. 47.

Mrs. Randolph Churchill. Pomeroy, p. 77.

Home Ranch. Lott, "Diary of Major Wise," p. 90.

"Proper" game. Frewen, *Melton Mowbray and Other Stories*, p. 205.

154. Trout Creek. Frewen, p. 205.

155. "If the stockman. . . ." Pomeroy, p. 79. (Quoting William Baillie-Grohman in the *Fortnightly Review* of September 1880.)

155. Meeting with Sitting Bull. Frewen, pp. 131-32.

156. Black Hills gold. Utley and Washburn, *The American Heritage History of the Indian Wars*, p. 244.

"gold at the roots. . . ." Lamar, *Reader's Encyclopedia of the American West*, p. 282.

157. "Gold, the great civilizing agent. . . ." Price, *The Two Americas*, p. 308.

157. Red Cloud. Brown, *Bury My Heart at Wounded Knee*, p. 182.

158. "The older Indians. . . ." Price, p. 305.

Meeting Custer. Price, p. 354.

Riding a cow-catcher. Price, p. 245. William Baillie-Grohman in *Camps in the Rockies* (p. 31) makes reference to a certain "Scottish Duke" who "rode on the cow-catcher of a locomotive" during a trip west. "Although it was not just a thing a Western man would do—at least, if he did not get paid for such a purposeless job—it yet evinced such a pleasing aberration from the usual stiffly-starched, brilliantly white cloak of British superiority, that the Western people as a man rose, and hailed him with acclamation."

159. Grant in Laramie. Price, p. 309.

160. Bridger at Yellowstone. Merritt, "William Henry Jackson," p. 23.

160. Yellowstone legislation. Lamar, p. 1298.

160. Dunraven background. Dunraven, *The Great Divide*, p. 26.

161. Palliser. Dunraven, *Past Times and Pastimes*, p. 206.

"my boyish brain-cells. . . ." Dunraven, *Past Times*, p. 65, and Sprague, *A Gallery of Dudes*, p. 48.

162. Buffalo Bill. Dunraven, *Past Times*, p. 74.

163. "Six or seven of us. . . ." Cody, "Famous Hunting Parties of the Plains." p. 136.

164. "No great time. . . ." Cody, p. 133.

164. Dunraven place names. Sprague, p. 165.

165. Virginia City. Dunraven, *The Great Divide*, pp. 37, 43.

166. Fort Ellis. Dunraven, *The Great Divide*, pp. 43-55.

"the silent enthusiasm. . . ." Dunraven, *The Great Divide*, p. 60.

166. Crow vanity. Dunraven, *The Great Divide*, p. 62.

166. "The sublime and the ridiculous. . . ." Dunraven, *The Great Divide*, p. 84.

"By no means the taciturn. . . ." Dunraven, *The Great Divide*, p. 86.

167. Indians as conservationists. Dunraven, *The Great Divide*, p. 91. Wapiti, of course, is the correct name for elk, a term that in England, as Dunraven noted, is reserved for the animal that Americans call a moose.

"how we have blackened. . . ." Dunraven, *The Great Divide*, p. 111.

167. Losing flask. Dunraven, *The Great Divide*, p. 135.

168. Bottler's Ranch. Doane, *Battle Drums and Geysers*, pp. 463, 229. Dunraven spells the rancher's name as "Boteler."

168. "These bears. . . ." Dunraven, *The Great Divide*, p. 154.

169. Arrival at Mammoth Hot Springs. Dunraven, *The Great Divide*, p. 164.

"three rude huts. . . ." and "very good fellows. . . ." Dunraven, *The Great Divide*, p. 208.

"a patriarchal camp." Dunraven, *The Great Divide*, p. 211.

171. Helena vs. Virginia City. Dunraven, *The Great Divide*, p. 211.

171. "gloomy forbidding gorge" Dunraven, *The Great Divide*, p. 213.

"in a cozy little grassy bay. . . ." Dunraven, *The Great Divide*, p. 217.

171. Yellowstone Falls. Dunraven, *The Great Divide*, p. 221.

"with light hearts. . . ." Dunraven, *The Great Divide*, p. 228.

"enlivened the road. . . ." Dunraven, *The Great Divide*, p. 229.

172. Mud Pots. Dunraven, *The Great Divide*, p. 237.

172. Fire Hole Basin. Dunraven, *The Great Divide*, p. 262.

Castle Geyser. Dunraven, *The Great Divide*, p. 271.

173. "scarcely had we got. . . ." Dunraven, *The Great Divide*, p. 266. "Boteler" is Fred Bottler of Bottler's Ranch.

173. Camp comforts. Dunraven, *The Great Divide*, pp. 15-16.

174. "How luxurious. . . ." Dunraven, *The Great Divide*, p. 377.

Chapter 11. The End of the Game

176. Dunraven's later career. Sprague, *A Gallery of Dudes*, pp. 170-79.

177. Frontier newspapers. Vivian, *Wanderings in the Western Land*, p. 134.

178. Insufferable English party. Murphy, *Sporting Adventures in the Far West*, pp. 19-21.

178. "three great qualities." Baillie-Grohman, *Camps in the Rockies*, p. 68. "mentally and physically. . . ." Baillie-Grohman, pp. 20-22.

179. "We laugh at. . . ." Baillie-Grohman, p. 25.

180. Bearclaw Joe. Baillie-Grohman, pp. 13-14.

181. Port. Baillie-Grohman, pp. 16-17.

182. "We find such names. . . ." Baillie-Grohman, pp. 368, 372.

182. Choke-proof pacifier. Baillie-Grohman, pp. 367-68.

183. Western hospitality. Baillie-Grohman, p. 364.

183. "While crossing. . . ." Baillie-Grohman, pp. 40-41.

184. "the cheapest, the freest. . . ." Baillie-Grohman, p. 9. "the good-fellowship. . . ." Baillie-Grohman, p. 11.

184. "How content. . . ." Baillie-Grohman, p. 55.

185. Dry camp. Baillie-Grohman, p. 36.

185. "A good hunger. . . ." Baillie-Grohman, p. 48.

185. Mosquito attack. Baillie-Grohman, p. 49.

186. "Beaver tail. . . ." Baillie-Grohman, p. 60.

186. Making soap. Baillie-Grohman, pp. 199-201.

187. Elk hunting. Baillie-Grohman, pp. 150-51.

188. Bighorn sheep. Baillie-Grohman, pp. 165-66.

189. Resurrected bighorn. Baillie-Grohman, pp. 174-75.

189. "There are very numerous. . . ." Baillie-Grohman, p. 242.

190. Beaver "medicine." Baillie-Grohman, p. 251.

191. Teton Basin. Baillie-Grohman, pp. 205-08.

192. Dugout living. Baillie-Grohman, p. 263. "It would be idle. . . ." Baillie-Grohman, pp. 263-64. Indians as marksmen. Baillie-Grohman, p. 267.

194. Decline of buffalo. Branch, *The Hunting of the Buffalo*, pp. 210-19.

194. "a mass of sheep ranches." Messiter, *Adventures Among the North-American Indians*, p. 365.

Bibliography

Adams, James T. *Atlas of American History*. New York: Charles Scribner's Sons, 1943.

Alter, J. Cecil. *Jim Bridger*. Norman: University of Oklahoma Press, 1982.

Athearn, Robert G. *Westward the Briton*. Lincoln: University of Nebraska Press, 1962.

Baillie-Grohman, Willam Adolph. *Camps in the Rockies*. New York: Charles Scribner's Sons, 1898.

Bartram, William. *Travels*. Salt Lake City: Peregrine Smith, Inc., 1980. Introduction by Robert McC. Peck.

Berkeley, Grantley F. *The English Sportsman in the Western Prairies*. London, 1861.

Bradley, James H. "Sir George Gore's Expedition." *Contributions to the Historical Society of Montana*, 1923, Vol. IX, pp. 245-51.

Branch, E. Douglas. *The Hunting of the Buffalo*. Lincoln: University of Nebraska Press, 1962.

Brown, Dee. *Bury My Heart at Wounded Knee*. New York: Bantam Books, 1972.

Campion, J. S. *On the Frontier*. London: Chapman & Hall, 1878.

Clark, Thomas D. *Frontier America*. New York: Charles Scribner's Sons, 1959.

Catlin, George. *Letters and Notes on the Manners, Customs, and Conditions of North American Indians*. (2 vols.) New York: Dover Publications, 1973.

Chittenden, Hiram M. *Yellowstone National Park*. Stanford: Stanford University Press, 1940.

Cody, William F. "Famous Hunting Parties of the Plains." *Cosmopolitan*, June 1894. Vol. XVII, No. 2.

Coke, Henry J. *A Ride Over the Rocky Mountains to Oregon and California*. London: Richard Bentley, 1852.

Costello, David F. *The Prairie World*. New York: Thomas Y. Crowell Co., 1975.

Dary, David. *The Buffalo Book*. Chicago: The Swallow Press, 1974.

Dictionary of National Biography. Oxford: Oxford University Press, 1959.

DeVoto, Bernard. *Across the Wide Missouri*. Boston: Houghton Mifflin, 1947.

Doane, Gustavus C. *Battle Drums and Geysers*. Chicago: Sage Books, 1970. Ed. by Orren H. and Lorraine Bonney.

Drury, Clifford M. *Marcus and Narcissa Whitman and the Opening of Old Oregon*. Glendale: The Arthur H. Clark Co., 1973.

Dunraven, the Earl of. *The Great Divide*. Lincoln: University of Nebraska Press, 1967. Introduction by Marshall Sprague.

Field, Matthew C. *Prairie and Mountain Sketches*. Norman: University of Oklahoma Press, 1957. Ed. by Kate L. Gregg and John F. McDermott.

Frazer, Robert W. *Forts of the West*. Norman: University of Oklahoma Press, 1965.

Frewen, Moreton. *Melton Mowbray and Other Memories*. London: Herbert Jenkins Ltd., 1924.

Garrard, Lewis H. *Wah-to-yah and the Taos Trail*. Norman: University of Oklahoma Press, 1955.

Gilbert, Bil. *Westering Man: The Life of Joseph Walker*. New York: Atheneum, 1983.

Gillmore, Parker ("Ubique"). *A Hunter's Adventures in the Great West*. London, 1871.

Gray, W. H. *A History of Oregon*. Portland, 1870.

Grinnell, George Bird. *Beyond the Old Frontier*. New York: Charles Scribner's Sons, 1913.

Grinnell, George Bird. *Two Great Scouts and Their Pawnee Battalion*. Lincoln: University of Nebraska Press, 1973.

Hafen, LeRoy R. *The Mountain Men and the Fur Trade of the Far West*. Glendale: The Arthur H. Clark Co., 1965.

Haines, Francis. *The Plains Indians*. New York: Thomas Y. Crowell Co., 1976.

Harper, J. Russell. *Paul Kane's Frontier*. Austin: University of Texas Press, 1971.

Heldt, F. George. "Sir George Gore's Expedition. " *Contributions to the Historical Society of Montana*, 1876. Vol. I, pp. 128-31.

Kennerly, William Clark. *Persimmon Hill*. Norman: University of Oklahoma Press, 1958.

Kingsley, George H. *Notes on Sport and Travel*. London: MacMillan and Co., Ltd., 1900.

Lamar, Howard R., ed. *The Reader's Encyclopedia of the American West*. New York: Thomas Y. Crowell Co., 1977.

Lawrence, George Alfred. *Silverland*. London: Chapman and Hall, 1873.

Leveson, Henry Astbury. *Sport in Many Lands*. London, 1890.

Lott, Howard B., ed. "Diary of Major Wise, an Englishman." (Details of a hunting trip in Powder River Country, 1880.) *Annals of Wyoming*, April 1940.

Maxwell, Sir Herbert. *The Honourable Sir Charles Murray, K. C. B., A Memoir*. Edinburgh, 1898.

McDonald, John. *The Origins of Angling*. Garden City: Doubleday and Co., Inc., 1963.

Merritt, John I. "William Henry Jackson." *The American West*, September 1980.

Messiter, Charles A. *Sport and Adventures Among the North-American Indians*. London, 1890.

Mullen, W. ("Oliver North"). *Rambles After Sport*. London, 1874.

Murphy, John Mortimer. *Sporting Adventures in the Far West*. New York, 1880.

Murphy, John Mortimer. *Rambles in North Western America*. London, 1879.

Murray, Charles Augustus. *Travels in North America*. London, 1839.

Neal, W. Keith and Black, D. H. L. *The Mantons: Gunmakers*. New York: Walker, 1966.

Neider, Charles. *The Great West*. New York: Coward-McCann,1958.

Palliser, John. *Solitary Rambles*. Rutland: Charles E. Tuttle Co., 1969.

Parkman, Francis. *The Oregon Trail*. Boston: Little, Brown and Co., 1902.

Pomeroy, Earl. *In Search of the Golden West*. New York: Alfred A. Knopf, 1957.

Porter, Mae Reed and Davenport, Odessa. *Scotsman in Buckskin*. New York: Hastings House, 1963.

Price, Sir Rose Lambart. *The Two Americas: An Account of Sport and Travel*. London: Sampson Low, Marston, Searle, and Rivington, 1877.

Ross, Martin C. *The West of Alfred Jacob Miller*. Norman: University of Oklahoma Press, 1951.

Russell, Osborne, *Journal of a Trapper*. Lincoln: University of Nebraska Press, 1965. Ed. by Aubrey L. Haines.

Ruxton, George Frederick. *Life in the Far West*. Norman: University of Oklahoma Press, 1951. Ed. by LeRoy R. Hafen.

Ruxton, George Frederick. *Ruxton of the Rockies*. Norman: University of Oklahoma Press, 1950. Collected by Clyde and Mae Reed Porter. Ed. by LeRoy R. Hafen.

Sprague, Marshall. *A Gallery of Dudes*. Lincoln: University of Nebraska Press, 1979.

Spry, Irene M. *The Palliser Expedition*. Toronto, 1963.

Stewart, William Drummond. *Edward Warren*. London, 1854.

Swanton, John R. *The Indian Tribes of North America*. Washington: Smithsonian Institution Press, 1952.

Taylor, Colin. *The Warriors of the Plains*. New York: Arco Publishing Co., 1975.

Taylor, Lonn and Maar, Ingrid. *The American Cowboy*. Washington: American Folklife Center, Library of Congress, 1983.

Townshend, Frederick Trench. *Ten Thousand Miles of Travel, Sport, and Adventure*. London: Hurst & Blackett, 1869.

Tyler, Ron. *Alfred Jacob Miller, Artist on the Oregon Trail*. Fort Worth: Amon Carter Museum, 1982.

Tyler, Ron. "Artist on the Oregon Trail." *American West*, August 1981.

Utley, Robert M. and Washburn, Wilcomb E. *The American Heritage History of the Indian Wars*. New York: American Heritage, 1977.

Vestal, Stanley. *Jim Bridger, Mountain Man*. Lincoln: University of Nebraska Press, 1970.

Vivian, A. Pendarves. *Wanderings in the Western Land*. London: Sampson Low, Marston, Searle & Rivington, 1879.

Webb, James J. *Adventures in the Santa Fe Trade*. Ed. by Ralph P. Bieber. Glendale: The Arthur H. Clark Co., 1931.

Index

211

214

Vivian, Pendarves, 177

Waiilatpu Mission, 88
Walla Walla Valley, 229
Walla Walla, Washington, 88
Walker, Joseph R., 7, 33-34, 47, 197
Wapiti. *See* Elk
Wasatch Mountains, 146
Washburn Expedition, 152
Washington, D.C., 157
Washita Massacre, 126
Waterford, Ireland, 72
Waterloo, Battle of, 4, 98
Weapons: Colt revolver, 52, 189;
    Express rifle, 189; Hawkins rifle,
    34; Manton rifles, *vi*, 6, 10, 94,
    109; Purdy, *vi*, 19, 24, 94; Metford
    shells, 137; Tranter revolver, 120;

Whestley Richards rifle, 94
Westport, Missouri, 40
Westworth, Fitzwilliam, 94
Whitman, Rev. Marcus and
    Narcissa, 15, 26-29, 40, 88
Wichita River, 147
Willamette Valley, 15
Wind River and W. R. mountains, 9,
    29, 35, 47, 93, 95, 141, 184
Wolves, 62, 142, 200
Wyeth, Nathaniel, 7-8, 14-15

Yellowstone Falls, 171-72
Yellowstone River and country, 26,
    35, 79-80, 158, 160, 164-74, 194,
    198
Yosemite Valley, 34, 159
Young, Brigham, 74, 97, 147, 204